SHAYKH MURTAḌA MUṬAHHARĪ

Reformation and Renewal of Islamic Thought

Ordering Information:
Quantity sales. Special discounts are available on quantity purchases by corporations, associations, and others. For details, contact the distributor at the address below.

Shia Books Australia
www.shiabooks.com.au
info@shiabooks.com.au

ISBN 978-1-907905-11-7

Second Edition 2021

SHAYKH MURTAḌA MUṬAHHARĪ

Reformation and Renewal of Islamic Thought

Dr. Khanjar Hamiyyah

Translated by

Muḥammad Zamin & Zainab Alayan

British Library Cataloguing-in-Publication Data
A catalogue record for this book is available from the British Library.

ISBN: 978-1-907905-10-0 (hbk)

ISBN: 978-1-907905-11-7 (pbk)

This English edition first published in 2013

This book is the translation of the original book titled, "*Al-Shaykh Murtaḍa Muṭahharī: al-Ishkāliyyah al-Iṣlāḥiyyah wa Tajdīd al-Fikr al-Islāmī*", which was published in Arabic language by the Center of Civilization for the Development of Islamic Thought, in 2009, Beirut, Lebanon.

MIU Press
133, High Road, Willesden
London NW10 2SW

CONTENTS

	Preface	VII
	Transliteration	IX
	Introduction	1
1	**An Introduction to the Prevailing Times: Political and Intellectual Conditions in Modern and Contemporary Iran**	**5**
	Preface	7
	1. Indications and Precursors: Politics and Culture in Iran during the First Half of the 20th Century	10
	2.The Peak of Struggle and the Formation of the Ideology of Reform Within Political Islam (The Era of Muṭahharī)	27
	3. Consequences of the Experiences of Struggle and Reform, and the Crystallisation of the Theory of Islamic Government by Imām Khomeinī (R)	43
2	**Murṭaḍa Muṭahharī: Biography, Experience and Intellectual Paths**	**55**
	1. Biography	57
	2. Intellectual and Political Struggle	61
	3. The Aspects of His Scientific Personality	65
	4. The Intellectual Methods Portrayed in His Writings	69
3	**Reformation and Renewal of Islamic Thought**	**85**
	Preface	87
	1. Revival and Renewal: The Meaning and the Justifications	90
	2. Revival and Renewal: Methods and Tools	96

4 **Domains of "Intellectual Confrontation" in the Renaissance Project of Muṭahharī** **187**

Introduction 189

1. An Islamic Analysis of Society and a Historical Critique of Materialism 193

2. Emphasis on the Moral Dimension of the Human Being, and a Criticism of Materialistic Tendencies and Nihilism 221

3. The Issue of Ethics 233

5 **Conclusion** **249**

Muṭahharī, for History and Experience 251

6 **Brief Bibliography** **257**

Introduction 259

List of Sources and References 275

Index 287

بِسۡمِ ٱللَّهِ ٱلرَّحۡمَٰنِ ٱلرَّحِيمِ

PREFACE

We are pleased to provide our valued readers with this latest tour de force as part of the series on leading figures in intellectual thought and reformation in the Islamic world. The philosophy of this series focuses on shedding light on the ideas of various authors and thinkers who have played a part in exercising a lasting impact on our awareness as individuals in the modern era, and continue to do so. We shall not reiterate the objectives envisaged by this project, but it will instead suffice to state that we are not addressing any one particular thinker within the scope of this series. Rather, the aim is to shed more light on the biography and intellectual development of selected scholars in order to unveil the most significant issues that preoccupied them, and which in all probability continue to be relevant to us.

Every individual we have documented has a story and underlying motivation which inspired us to research more about him and his intellectual journey. As for Shaykh Martyr Murtaḍa Muṭahharī, our primary aim in addressing this personality is the range of unique factors that distinguish him and which invite us to take interest in his thought, the most prominent features of which are as follows:

Firstly, the originality and contemporary relevance of his approach, both of which encourage us to take a greater interest in him and his thought. When one surveys the issues covered by Muṭahharī, it is as if one is reviewing today's contemporary problems rather than those of the past century. He wrote on topics such as divine justice, social justice, Islamic social movements and the *ḥijāb* (Islamic veil) amongst others, all of which continue to be pertinent issues that engage the minds of both the young and old.

And secondly, the most notable features of Muṭahharī are his openness to contemporary issues and his willingness to plunge into the depths of the serious challenges confronting religious thought during his time. This may cause some wonder, but what really distinguishes Muṭahharī from other advocates in this area is that he is simultaneously a reformer, for his defensive role neither drove him towards a closed and introverted outlook, nor did his goal of reform lead him to lapse into forsaking core principles.

We hopes that this series will be a valuable contribution to Islamic thought that is of value to the general reader and the researcher alike. We similarly hope that this series forms a link showing the way for those who seek advancement.

Centre of Civilisation for the Development of Islamic Thought &
Al Mustafa International Research Institute (M.I.R.I.)

TRANSLITERATION

Arabic characters	Roman Equivalent
ء	’
ب	b
ت	t
ث	th
ج	j
ح	ḥ
خ	kh
د	d
ذ	dh
ر	r
ز	z
س	s
ش	sh
ص	s
ض	ḍ
ط	ṭ
ظ	ẓ
ع	‘
غ	gh
ف	f
ق	q
ك	k
ل	l
م	m
ن	n
ه	h
و	w

Arabic characters	Roman Equivalent
ى	y
	(construct state)

Long Vowels

ىٰ ; آ	ā
ـُو	ū
ـِي	ī

Short Vowels

ـَ	a
ـُ	u
ـِ	i

Diphthongs

ـَو	aw
ـَي	ai ; ay

Persian letters added to the Arabic alphabet

پ	p
چ	ch
ژ	j
گ	g

INTRODUCTION

Presented here is a general and concise review of the main intellectual, philosophical and religious elements in the reformation project of Martyr Murtaḍa Muṭahharī, as well as the foundations upon which he based his call for the revival of Islamic religious thought.

Since the writings of Muṭahharī are broadly comprehensive and universal on the one hand, whilst replete with digressions and a lack of clear order, obtaining an understanding of his works through study and research thus entails a great deal of difficulty. This is because the material primarily consists of extracts of lectures, seminars and discussions. This being so, we have tried to confine our efforts to certain aspects of his overall thought that we will review in terms of a general application and comprehensiveness incorporating the ruling ideas and fundamental principles, in addition to the application of his methodology. We have attempted to shed light on these areas in order to bring to light the particular logic expressed within such a huge literary output spanning a wide range of issues.

Although this approach may deprive readers from discerning Muṭahharī's viewpoints on some particular issues he addressed, our main aim is to help them clarify the analytical approach and general methodology of his research. Furthermore, it will also introduce readers to the fundamentals upon which his intellectual outlook was based.

In his quest to address quickly the pertinent issues of education, culture and sociology, Muṭahharī gave little attention to fully describing the foundations of his methodological approach or identifying particular instances that illustrate his conclusions and the inferences drawn therefrom. Therefore, we are left on our own to come to a conclusion about all these facets. We have to gather various scattered pieces to discern the elements in the depths of his literary output. This is a necessary task to undertake in spite of the obvious difficulties. Moreover, the interpretations provided by some of our predecessors may interfere with the task either in the shape of omissions which may serve to suggest a particular understanding, or conversely, as a result of widening the boundaries of the definition of his thought, lead to liberal musings which infer meanings and connotations that do not actually exist in Muṭahharī's writings. There are many factors which illustrate this.

For example, Muṭahharī's theoretical and epistemological dimensions are understandable once they are placed in a standardised context, something with which some earlier thinkers were not concerned. He was preoccupied with epistemology within the context of the historical experiment in which he found himself, amidst certain necessary facts and events. As a man struggling for ideals, Muṭahharī was not interested in formulating theories in isolation from the practical context of the circumstances of his time.

Furthermore, Muṭahharī developed his ideas over a period of more than twenty-five years, during which they evolved in light of different events and experiences. Such an extended span of time makes it necessary for us to trace the elements of his thought with a view to their development, growth and final maturity in terms of their general characteristics. What is therefore required from us is first of all to analyse and piece together his thought before interpreting and expounding upon his outlook in light of the prevailing historical circumstances and the intellectual and political milieus. On this basis, this present study is an interpretative overview of Muṭahharī's work. His writings are examined in order to form a general yet comprehensive view of his methodology and discover a logical common foundation governing his thought that connects the extremes of his epistemology. In essence, this remains to be one particular interpretation for which no claim is made for complete accuracy, nor to its being exhaustive. Neither do we claim that its intellectual point of departure is flawless. In short, we do not consider this study beyond further strict critical evaluation.

The present study is divided into six chapters. The first focuses on Muṭahharī's era since it seems impossible to comprehend the dimensions of his thought except in light of two factors. Firstly, the epistemological challenges faced by Muṭahharī at the turn of the last century, which defined a headlong lunge of the Islamic world into direct contact with the intellectual heritage of Western thought, the socio-political challenges that overshadowed the second half of the last century. These two factors were deeply interrelated and outlined the context within which Muṭahharī found himself as a man of thought and endeavour.

In Chapter 2, I have sought to briefly identify general elements of Muṭahharī's personal characteristics and biography. Chapter 3 constitutes our main theme, and concentrates on addressing the issue of a revival in Muṭahharī's thought in terms of its inception, elemental content, methodology and meaning, as well as obstacles to its path, and is a summary of various elements of Muṭahharī's intellectual feats in general. The aspiration of revival was the principal motivation upon which the stages of Muṭahharī's intellectual journey and activities were based.

In Chapter 4, I have tried to trace the perspective taken by Muṭahharī towards those Western intellectual schools which generally affected the core of awareness of the intelligentsia of his time, whether in Iran or elsewhere in the Islamic world. It attracted a younger generation with the temptation of its logical, coherent approach and the attractiveness of its content. In this respect, Muṭahharī examined three approaches: one relating to society and the movement of history; the second concerns the challenges of materialism, atheism and nihilism; and the third involves values and ethics. These are all issues which have deeply influenced Western civilisation, which has in turn inescapably resonated upon and influenced Islamic societies.

Chapter 5 is an attempt to concisely sketch Muṭahharī's work and philosophical contribution, and to assess the undertakings for which he strove. In other words, to determine his legacy in the present context, having taken into account the nature of the contentions that generated it, the challenges of his time in terms of their magnitude, complexity and diversity. We do not aim to evaluate the efficacy that this thought still possesses at the present time, for intellectual thought can only be evaluated in light of the realities that generate it. From my own perspective, it would be incorrect to isolate and decontextualise his thought in order to demonstrate its feasibility or worth outside the limits of its original framework, but in light of the lessons, methodology and values that it can establish.

Chapter 6 is devoted to a brief glossary of Muṭahharī's writings in Persian and works translated into Arabic which in any event must remain incomplete, particularly since it is known that most of Muṭahharī's legacy is contained in the form of seminars and lectures that have not been fully transcribed from original recorded tapes up until the present time. In addition, there is still a large amount that is unpublished or unedited. In this regard, I have relied on authoritative resources dedicated to documenting, re-evaluating and systematising his legacy.

Finally, I do not claim that the content presented herein is either faultless or comprehensive. In essence, it is a humble endeavour to unveil the intellectual and epistemological dimensions of this exceptional personality, especially those concerning reformation and renewal. It is my sincere hope that I have been successful in presenting something useful and beneficial, otherwise I apologise for this modest effort; and only Almighty Allah guides to success.

Khanjar Hamiyyah

CHAPTER 1

AN INTRODUCTION TO THE PREVAILING TIMES: POLITICAL AND INTELLECTUAL CONDITIONS IN CONTEMPORARY IRAN

PREFACE

One cannot obtain a clear picture of Muṭahharī's era and its political, intellectual and ideological currents of thought without comprehensively returning to the first half of the 20th century. More specifically, to the phase that immediately followed Muḥammad Rezā Shāh Pahlavī's accession to the throne and Iran's subsequent rush to embrace Western values in various fields. This tendency transparently appeared in various aspects of political, administrative, social and intellectual life. It was evident in legislation as well as encouraged in the values and norms of social interaction. Its mark was apparent in financial and economic institutions, in educational curricula, as well as well-established in military and security dealings, to name but a few. In addition, this strong sense of alignment with the West was also evident in the attempt to completely sever the nation from various aspects of its Islamic heritage. Amongst its manifest expressions was the deliberate distortion of established concepts, laws and norms that were deeply rooted in society and consolidated by Iran's Islamic history.

This predominantly Western predisposition, accompanied by a reign of despotic authoritarianism and bigoted repression, generated an opposition of political movements and resistance groups whose efforts were crowned by the overthrow of the regime and the formation of a national government presided over by Musaddiq. The new national government instigated a set of political reforms with a discernible liberal tendency. Within no time, however, the project ended because of disputes between its various members. These internal conflicts facilitated the return of the Shāh under the aegis of direct American influence. The return of the Shāh signalled the end of a project for change and progress. The dreams of liberty, justice and democracy inspired by the National Front, for which the public campaigned, were all crushed in one blow.

Nevertheless, despite disappointments and failures, this period bore the hallmarks of political, intellectual and cultural dynamism. This background was further supplemented by the existence of various ideologies that swept through the world at the time, and different ideas and directions took shape. Amongst these was an extreme form of Marxism as well as a moderate socialism, each confirming its validity by expressing slogans with a clear reference to Islam. There was also a liberal-nationalist movement, and a democratic movement adopting a Western political pattern and citizenship rights as its ideals. Islamic reform movements, with various backgrounds and aims, were another sign of the cultural dynamism of this period. Despite their diversity, these groups united in a common cause which transcended their differences and affiliations, a cause revolving around the necessity of bringing about a change in Iranian political life that would carry the nation towards new horizons.

The aspiration was to establish Iran as a landmark on the global stage, and rid its people of the painful experience of long years of failure and degeneration which had drained the talents and energy of the people. The diverse factions unanimously agreed on the need for a definitive transition from an era that had generated nothing but a sense of impotence and unparalleled submission to a despotic and repressive authority – an authority characterised by plunder and exploitation, and demanded the absolute subordination of its own citizens, whom it despised and deprived of the most basic rights. It had fettered them with abject poverty and underdevelopment, deprived them of education, and took away the will to express themselves.

All these factors shaped the background for the emerging ideologies of reform in the latter half of the 20th century. They gained experience from both their successes and failures in direct political action, and profited from the general climate of discussion within academia, books, newspapers and other mass media. This swing also affected the republican parties – or quasi-parties – which promoted the same objectives, attracted supporters, and established their own maxims. By this time the social experiment had matured, and could declare its presence. It was defined by a firm structure and a clear vision of the kind of ideological reform that had sparked its inception.

At the outset, these movements were characterised by a motivation of the collective aspiration of the community towards reform and progress. Firmly refusing to succumb to the status quo, they yearned for freedom, justice and human rights. The movements then transformed into parties with integrated programmes of thought and action, well-defined ideological and epistemological foundations and an organised structure. They offered a distinct vision of the individual person, society, the world and existence in general. They were also aware of the particular requirements of the time, through a clear historical understanding and the mechanisms and conditions for progress. Furthermore, their perspective included the fundamental nature of civilisation, and the conditions which brought about growth and decline, and factors which would overcome the latter.

None of these factions were isolated from other contemporary problems that affected every Muslim society, and they were not immune from the challenges that stood in their path. Furthermore, there was a clear connection with other reformation experiments and developments taking place in various other parts of the Islamic world. Radical change had weakened the overall structure of the Islamic world and its people, leaving them in the shadow of events that threatened to impose upon many of their traditional values.

Some benefit and inspiration may be drawn from these experiences with a logic that surpasses the more superficial considerations, avoids a blind imitation, and instead seeks a constructive way forward. This is applied especially in the context of a very complicated environment such as that of Iranian society, which is distinguished by unique experiences and traditions. Moreover, the political and intellectual movements, whose signs became evident during that part of the century – based on earlier, more limited experiments, such as the 1920 Revolution, the Tobacco Movement, the Nationalisation of Oil and the Constitutional Revolution – would gradually increase in prominence in the light of complex and sensitive transitions. Their significance would grow, along with their basic characteristics, methods, structures and objectives. These in turn formed the groundwork for the 1979 Iranian Revolution as a comprehensive ideology for reformation and revival, which definitively changed the Iranian scene. It subsequently ushered in a new era in the life of contemporary Iran, whose repercussions have left an indelible mark on the world picture in more than one respect.

1

INDICATIONS AND PRECURSORS: POLITICS AND CULTURE IN IRAN DURING THE FIRST HALF OF THE 20TH CENTURY

The events that swept through Europe at the beginning of the century had an eradicable impact around the world. Traditions were shaken, ideas and perceptions transformed, regimes toppled and empires overthrown. This new wave unleashed calls for the rebuilding of states on new foundations. Moreover, it also gave rise to competing ideologies which sought to affirm their authority, and secure their respective interests regarding various trans-territorial conflicts spanning the globe. In order to mollify these conflicts, two wars centred in Europe were required, killing millions, and resulting in indescribable destruction that erased the identity of various nations and ethnic groups. Repercussions were felt throughout the world, and the momentum thereof contributed to an organised plunder of wealth and resources, and the operational exploitation of the physical and mental resources of people wearied by long years of submission, mistakes, increasing cultural deterioration and underdevelopment. The two World Wars provided the parties that emerged victorious with the basic materials to assert their prominence in an era of industry, technology and business. They were able to rebuild what was destroyed during the years of conflict, and reconstruct the weakened economic and financial infrastructure of civilisation.

The historical development of modern Europe is based on concepts that sprung from the Age of Enlightenment, which brought about a radical proscription of traditional perceptions concerning man, his place in existence, where he comes from, and his final end. These ideas altered the direction of society and humanity as a whole. They made man the focal point of an anthropocentric outlook, where he became the prime mover of his own destiny and the shaper of history. Henceforth the human being was seen as the architect of his own future, who could realise his own interests as dictated by his direct needs and what was of benefit to him. As a result, the argument that gave birth to the two World Wars had not come to an end.

In actuality, the conflict concealed beneath the tumult of death and destruction still continues, and today is manifested in the form of a struggle to secure dominion over boundaries and resources. This ongoing struggle over interests and fortunes follows a logic of power, hegemony and exclusivity. The state of affairs is maintained by a system of international relationships which generally guarantees a balance, and is furthermore complemented by a system of institutions that has a great interest in protecting its mechanisms. As a result, the subordination of those who have had no effective role in this historical process is further entrenched, and they pay a heavy price by submitting to its diktats and conditions by being forced to circulate in its orbit and surrender to its destructive effects, meanwhile failing to attain even a small share of its achievements and power.

This historical development in modern Europe had a twofold impact on the sidelined nations. On the one hand, it generated a desire for freedom and self-determination, giving rise to aspirations of a future outside the boundaries of a powerful framework of enslavement. In addition, it developed a longing for the reformation of identity, and the ability to invest vigour into their own resources in order to redefine their present situation. On the other hand, there was a sense of usefulness in all this, and an inclination to imitate, which generated an admiration of and a sense of pride in material progress and the kind of framework that made it possible. It prompted an interest in better living standards and a race for renewal, development and the exploration of ideas of freedom, justice and progress. It also revitalised an interest in the arts and human values, all of which were visions that delighted the minds of those who contemplated the consequences of long years of impotence and despair.

Despite a principle that dictates that the vanquished should submit to the ways of the victor in order to be reborn, the sidelined nations found themselves unavoidably acquiescing to two direct influences. The first had been generated by the historical development of modern Europe in terms of administration and urbanisation; and the second was the proliferation of ideas concerning human values, existence, religion, history and epistemology. All these issues had a profound influence and provoked many questions. As a result, people were overwhelmed. They were trapped between their own identity and sense of belonging, deeply rooted in history through language, tradition and beliefs, and the challenge of opening up to other philosophical, political and social standards which presented themselves as attractive and intellectually stimulating.

The Islamic nations were a true reflection of this situation. It began with a characteristic hesitation, but grew with a dynamism whose main features have yet to appear distinctly. This dynamism was initially generated during the period known as the Renaissance. Many scholars of that time were occupied with ideas concerning tradition, modernism, science and progress, and various conclusions were reached, with conflicting principles and aims. In general, there were no distinct features, and at the time the various energies did not produce a project with clear objectives. However, what is evident is that the subsequent development of the modern West has had a great impact in many domains, such as sociology, economics and politics, as well as influencing ideas about tradition, religion and life as a whole.

Iran was not isolated from the wider context. The contemporary world cast its shadow over Iran, which similarly experienced the hesitation symptomatic of the Islamic world as a whole, but it left an impression on values, tradition and thought. We can clearly discern movements such as nationalism, liberalism, socialism and Marxism, in addition to philosophical trends that include positivism, existentialism and secularism. Furthermore, the intellectual élite was deeply affected by ideas that were predominant in the Western intellectual milieu during the last century, and began to express views which were essentially of European origin in a compounded form, by amalgamating them with traditional perspectives. We can observe the general presence of this trend in the intellectual, political and social context of contemporary Iran.

The reign of Rezā Khān saw the most distinct attempt to configure modern Iran according to the ideas and experiences of the West. This period witnessed an experiment with economic liberalism, and entrenched a secular character within the state, and various manifestations of Western civilisation in the educational curricula.

Rezā Khān was a staunch secularist with an opinionated disposition. He gave free rein to his nationalistic ambitions and proceeded to firmly suppress religious expression. During his reign his general ambition was to revive Persian nationalism on racial grounds, inspired by contemporaneous European nationalist experiments that saw the rise of Nazism and fascism.[1] He enacted a range of laws covering education that excluded the religious scholars,[2] and later limited the authority of the Religious Courts to the sphere of personal affairs.[3]

In 1934, he instigated a series of modern laws regarding religious endowments (*awqāf*). He was especially strict on the matter of holding commemoration gatherings to mourn the martyrdom of Imām Ḥossein (al-Majālis al-Ḥosseiniyah).He afterwards proceeded to ban the veil (*ḥijāb*) and replaced the Hijrī calendar with the solar calendar. The cultural élite, as well as some religious scholars, strongly supported his actions.

The move towards Westernisation in Qajarite Iran, upon which Rezā Khān relied to launch his reforms, was coming to an end. A group of the so-called Enlighteners, including Talebof, Malkom Khān, Yūsuf Khān (the State Advisor in 1895), and Khān al-Kirmānī amongst others, called for the application of modern Western techniques in the realms of science, technology and law. Generally, they tended to clothe such calls in an Islamic facade, which deceived many people, including notable clergymen. As a result, their ideas managed to find fertile ground and have a wide influence,[4] since they focused on themes such as freedom, justice, common law legislation and the fragmentation of authority. These models struck a chord with the deep desire for liberation amongst the masses, following a long and arduous period of submission to a fierce monarchical regime.

Rezā Khān acceded to the throne in kind of coup d'état. He managed to extend his authority throughout Iran with relative ease, and with it began a new era of political change and mobilisation. During this period, he exercised various forms of oppression against those who opposed his policies. Suppression was directed towards both the Islamic opposition, personified by Hasan Mudarris, as well as the newly formed socialist movements, whose demands focused on the themes of justice, equality and social development, which at the outset, however, was strongly connected with the idea of global socialism.

Rezā Shāh helped weaken the force of these movements, which suffered from internal schisms and lack of organisation. Nonetheless, this period carried the early seeds of experiences whose positive impact will be examined later. The parliament led the first trial of developing legislation based on the *shari'ah* (Islamic law), and installed a parliament that was open to the political diversity of opposing political alliances. Parties who sought to establish their presence through organised media activities were also present.[5] Nonetheless, these parties were fostered by a direct Western presence in Iran, whose diverse activities included establishing modern schools, hospitals and media outlets. Furthermore, the process was aided by the virtual abstention of leading religious authorities from any involvement, as a result of differences between prominent figures in both Najaf and Qom in the aftermath of the failure of the 1920 Revolution and the removal of its founding group.[6]

During this stage of political upheaval, armed opposition groups, such as Mirzā Kochek Khān's Movement in northern Iran, made up of clergy, traders and intelligentsia, or Muḥammad Khaiabani's Democratic Radical Movement in Azerbaijan, were barely more successful.[7] They ended without having had much impact on the political life in Iran of the first half of the 20th century. The fall of Rezā Shāh, following the entry of the Allied Forces into Iran after the latter's victory in the Second World War, and the transfer of power to his son, Muḥammad Rezā, with direct foreign support, marked the beginning of a new era in contemporary Iran.

The most significant expression of this new phase was a conspicuous foreign intervention in Iran's domestic affairs. The effects were to bolster the dictatorship, suppress any public opposition that demanded change, and systemically plunder wealth and resources. In addition, it stimulated the transformation into a secular state akin to modern Turkey, by attempts to purge Iranian culture of its Islamic legacy and severing intellectual and cultural links with the Arab world. These stormy events were hard to remove from the collective memory of Iranian society, and their impact would ignite the already latent desire for change.

These transformations were all one way or another associated with the fall of the 1920 Revolution in Iraq, the upheaval (*nikba*) of the Palestinian nation and the establishment of the Zionist entity, the devastating consequences of the Second World War on the peoples of the region, and repercussions of the downfall of the Ottoman Empire. These changes marked the beginning of a political and intellectual dynamism that was not unconnected with the calls for reform made by the Constitutional Movement, with its central themes of freedom, independence, national security and a comprehensive economic development programme. This dynamism provided a glimmer of hope for the latent desire for change, especially within the circles of the emerging movement that had its roots in the political experiment of Sayyid Hasan Mudarris. This fervour was personified in the nationalist orientation under the leadership of Musaddiq, with whom Mudarris was partnered in opposition to the regime of Rezā Shāh. He gained considerable parliamentary experience, participating in Iranian political life after the fall of the Qajar Dynasty. He had witnessed its transformations and tensions, and experienced Navvāb Safavi's traditional revivalist Islamic movement, which sought to establish an Islamic government and to offer a comprehensive ideology for life based thereon.[8]

The various political movements appearing during this period desired real change across the board in politics and social values. They sought to rid themselves of political oppression. Seldom have dilemmas swept through the Arab world like those stemming from the Renaissance and resulting with modernism, and generated such strong feelings. The leaders of these movements were acutely aware of all this.

It will become clear that the reform movements that began to form during this period generally relied on the experiences of other revolutionary and reform movements across the world as the basis of their ideologies. Undoubtedly, one of the most significant of these was Marxism, whether in a universal context or particular regional circumstances, such as the nationalist liberation movements in Cuba, South-East Asia and Latin America, or Maoist China. What made Marxism attractive was the revolutionary character of its concepts of freedom, justice and equality. As far as it was seen as a factor that restored a belief in the effectiveness of human action, and gave hope to those who had experienced the devastating effects of tyranny and oppression, it was seen, at least in form, as consonant with the legacy of Islam.

Despite arbitrariness in some areas, if we wished to classify this dynamism into movements, we could outline four trends: the Marxist in various guises, the National Democratic, the radical Islamic, and the reformative, revivalist approach. These various forms will be described later, but it was on the basis of these movements that the move towards reform was to crystallise during the second half of the 20th century.

1. The Marxist Approach

The Tudeh Party, as an ideological remnant of global communism, was the first Iranian Communist party to effectively appear on the political scene during the reign of Muḥammad Rezā Shāh Pahlavī. It cemented its position following the fall of the Shāh's regime and the formation of Musaddiq's government. The party opposed the new government, accusing it of being an American puppet, and tried to overthrow it. The Tudeh Party subsequently claimed that it was unable to bring about such a change, despite having played a part in getting the Musaddiq government to power.

As soon as Musaddiq's government was overthrown, the party's activities were significantly constrained, and its influence virtually came to an end. It had no presence on the political scene; its party structure was disassembled and it was unable to reorganise. As scholars have observed, the main reason for the party's deterioration was its opposition towards Musaddiq's government. Additionally, the party's overt confrontation with the rising Islamic reformist movements led to the loss of much of its popular support. After his return to power under the aegis of America's Central Intelligence Agency (CIA), the Shāh launched a brutal onslaught against the party, which culminated with the systematic execution of the party's military cadres, thus forcing those remaining to flee the country.[9]

Regarding the background of its ideological outlook and organisational structure, the Tudeh Party was, it seems, based on a manifest tendency of exclusion. As an illustration, it caused class tension, the inevitability of a revolutionary change, with economics taking priority over politics, and society at large over individuality, with other prominent Marxist views. This not only resulted in clashes with other political groups, but also generated conflict within the party and breakaway movements. This is what happened with the renowned leftist theorist, Jalāl Āl-e-Ahmad, who separated from the Tudeh Party and revised his outlook.

Jalāl Āl-e-Ahmad was one of the most prominent Iranian thinkers of the 1960s.[10] He joined the Iranian Communist Party (Tudeh) and left three years later, following the coup d'état against Musaddiq. After that he abstained from political activity, and during this period, he went through a process of re-evaluation. He criticised the Iranian intelligentsia in general, and left notable works, the most important of which was his book Gharbzadegi, or "Westoxification," which was published in 1962 and upheld his critique of the intelligentsia.

His analysis principally addressed the phenomenon of Westernisation and the emphasis on the national economy at the expense of spirituality. He thought that Western influence was an aberration affecting the life and civilisation of Iran, for it had no relation to the history and traditions of the Iranian people. Nevertheless, he saw no harm in consciously utilising and benefitting from the West, as long as it did not turn into a blind imitation of Western cultural standards. He believed that Westernisation had become entrenched because of the transfer of modern technology to Iran. More specifically, the adoption of modern technology had led to its diffusion and popularity, and it was impossible to espouse the benefits of Western industrial progress in isolation from Western culture.[11]

In order to avoid the misconception that Westernisation is characterised by a self-ascendancy that allows it to inevitably proliferate, Jalāl Āl-e-Ahmad, on the contrary, regarded Westernisation not as a dominating phenomenon, but as a social ailment of external origin. According to him, the domestic educational system contributed to its dissemination. Therefore, it was a malady with two dimensional – internal and external – which threatened to undermine the basis of cultural, political and economic integrity.[12]

Āl-e-Ahmad was particularly aggressive towards the Iranian intelligentsia, and considered them the main cause of the weakness within Iranian society. He resorted to a pungent critique in order to stimulate an awareness of the risk of a devastating impact from Westernisation.

It is worth pointing out that Āl-e-Ahmad regarded the development of the modern West as defined primarily in terms of its technologies, which divided the world into "producers" and "consumers," and led to the spread of unemployment. Therefore, his criticism was concentrated on the negative effects of technology – its unmanaged utilisation, and the blind release and exploitation of its overwhelming capabilities.[13] This reminds us of the position of certain Marxists who flourished in the Frankfurt School, such as Markus, Max Horkheimer and Jürgen Habermas, or Heidegger's view of the devastating impact of technology on society. However, we cannot ascertain whether or not Āl-e-Ahmad was influenced by these.

2. The Nationalist Movement and the Inclination towards Democracy

Throughout the last century, Iran witnessed various nationalist movements, some of which called for the revival of the historical Persian heritage and disseminated a sense of the greatness of the legacy of the ancient civilisation. The state was the principal advocate for such movements. It spent large sums of money promoting propaganda campaigns and publishing books to this effect. Moreover, this aspiration became stamped within the educational curricula, and drew cultural and artistic support from many writers and thinkers.

This kind of revival had a tendency to draw inspiration from extreme racial, nationalistic trends, as happened in the West with Nazism, or with the changes implemented by Ataturk. The nationalistic trend was also accompanied by a rapid drift towards Westernisation in many spheres. Furthermore, the drive to adopt Western values dovetailed with a growing hostility towards religious expression. All this fitted in with the state's ambitions at the time, and was more of an instrument of the state than a force with an independent identity. Because of this, it has not been treated alongside other movements of this particular time, irrespective of its power and influence. At the same time, we find a moderate nationalistic tendency defined by citizenship, which was underpinned by a desire to secure the welfare of the nation amidst the turbulence of global interests.

Represented in this movement were those Muslims who perceived the problems within their society, the changes occurring around them, and the dangers posed by foreign supremacy. Most of them followed the example of Muhammad Musaddiq and Ayatullāh Kāshāni in their social and political views. Recognising justice and democracy as gateways to reform, this trend was made up of various nationalist movements with different objectives. However, the factor that brought them together was a common goal of finding a way to guarantee the peoples' interests and identity, as well as an awareness of the danger posed by the reckless adoption of Western ideals.

All these objectives were watchwords that needed to be translated into practical programmes, but no sooner had the experiment of Musaddiq begun, it collapsed. Many of those involved broke away at the first crossroads. For example, Tāleqāni criticised Musaddiq's government for going beyond the remit of institutions by exploiting the widespread popularity it enjoyed, by continually catering to public interest at the expense of parliament, thus exhibiting an excessive nationalistic indulgence. Similarly, the People's Party, having had a considerable role in the formation of Musaddiq's government, later abandoned it, calling for its overthrow and acting to this effect.[14]

With the fall of Musaddiq's government, the National Front, which had flourished on his personality and principles, degenerated and collapsed, and could not thereafter make an effective comeback in Iranian political life. An observer will find but a weak presence of its perspective in subsequent political reform. In principle, the National Front began as a mixture of political and intellectual figures with differing fundamental viewpoints. However, patriotism and the opposition to imperialism were the factors that united them within a broad political framework. After the overthrow of Musaddiq's government, nothing remained of these sentiments other than a persistent desire in the national consciousness, but there was no clear programme for confronting the challenges they faced.

Later on, a considerable number of former followers of this movement went on to join other groups, whether revivalist, radical, Islamist or leftist. By guidance and evaluation, these figures effectively reinforced the experiment of reformation in the second half of the 20th century, as we shall see later.

3. The Radical Islamic Movement and its Trends

The failure of the reform movements in Iran and Iraq towards the end of the 19th century and at the beginning of the 20th century had an adverse impact that reached the heart of the religious establishment, casting a gloomy shadow between it and society as a whole, particularly the various groups involved in the developments of the time. As a result, for a considerable time the religious infrastructure abstained from any involvement, and prohibited its main figures from taking any part in reform.[15]

However, an Islamic reform movement began to emerge clearly during the 1940s within the religious institutions, at certain points involving some of the leading figures. In general, the motivation was the dilemmas of internal reform as well as a desire to bring about change in the social and political status quo. Moreover, there was an urgent need to put an end to the problems that had swept through the ummah (the Muslim community), and face its challenges. The Islamic movement came to the fore as a result of events that shook the Islamic community, uprooting its structure and exposing it to the consequences of the Second World War.

Initially, this movement was exemplified by the efforts of Ayatullāh Kāshāni. Having participated in the 1920 revolution in Iraq, he was subsequently sentenced to death, but he managed to escape and return to Iran where he began to take part in political life. Towards the end of the Qajarite reign and the transfer of power to Rezā Shāh, he became a member of parliament.

Ayatullāh Kāshāni was an exceptional politician who raised the call for change. He firmly believed in the necessity of engaging Islam in social and political reform, and in confronting foreign intervention in the Islamic world. To this end, he was involved in various internal battles, such as the fight for the nationalisation of oil, which in turn strengthened his presence as one of the most prominent personalities in the movement. He also defended fundamental questions pertaining to the future of the Islamic world, such as the Palestinian issue and Islamic unity. He shared the concerns of other Islamic states, and closely followed the activities of various reform movements.[16]

Despite deep-rooted nationalistic inclinations and an unswerving hostility towards dictatorship, Kāshāni nevertheless resisted the idea of establishing a republican regime in Iran. His belief was that republicanism would act as a bridge that would allow foreign forces to exert their influence over Iranian politics, and thereby buttress Western hegemony. For this reason he clashed with Musaddiq, who was accused of promoting favourable conditions for republicanism, despite his repeated denials.[17]

Kāshāni's movement falls within the context of another one, namely, the Fadā'iyān-e-Islam Movement, founded by the religious scholar Navvāb Safavi, who resided in Najaf for a brief period, before returning to Iran in 1949 and involving himself in politics. He engaged in militant action against the symbols of the state, as well as secular writers who defended it. He assassinated one of the secular writers, Kasravi, for his opinions on Islam, and fled to Mashhad, then later to Najaf. As a result, his reputation spread, and the popularity of his movement grew amongst young people and the wider public.[18]

Subsequent to these events, the Fadā'iyān-e-Islam Movement effectively became the executive wing of the Movement for the Nationalisation of

Oil, and some figures in the royal court who sought to silence the demands for nationalisation were killed. This series of killings forced the parliament to approve nationalisation out of fear for those of its members who opposed it, and thus avoid more bloodshed.

Navvāb Safavi participated in the National Front, which brought about Musaddiq's government. However, he later opposed him and split away – as happened with Kāshāni – because he realised that the government, which had assumed power on the promise of reform, was inclining towards violations of the *shari'ah* and instating a republican regime. Safavi fiercely rejected this proposition, and steadfastly adhered to his call for governance based on the *shari'ah*, and the establishment of an Islamic state. His perspective is apparent in the message he sent to Musaddiq after splitting from his ranks, in which Safavi warned Musaddiq of the consequences of the latter's path, and expressed his readiness to cooperate on condition that Musaddiq changed course and returned to the principles of the *shari'ah*.[19]

The religious establishment, which continued abstaining from political life after the fragmentation of the National Front and the withdrawal of Kāshāni, did not approve of such a move. The highest religious authority, Ayatullāh Borūjerdī, expressed his dissatisfaction with the methodology of the Fadā'iyān-e-Islam Movement vis-à-vis its political activity. However, it would seem that they felt they did not require a *fatwā* (legal ruling) from a religious authority in order to legitimise their revolutionary agenda. Moreover, they did not consider the religious authority capable of playing such a role after a lengthy period of isolation. Consequently, they generated for themselves a distinct perception of Islam, as well as a modus operandi that utilised Islamic concepts. In this regard, they were heavily influenced by revivalism in the Arab world, and the prominent personalities who were particularly engaged in establishing a new hermeneutic of concepts such as struggle, or *jihad*. The leaning towards a revised interpretation was motivated by the need for it to serve the present reality, and cope with the requirements of what they perceived as threats to cultural and religious identity. The personalities in question included, for example, Rashīd Riḍa,[20] Ḥasan al-Bannā and Sayyid Quṭb. There were also others, whose work Navvāb Safavi could access directly, or whom he could meet in person at different events, such as the Islamic Conference held in al-Quds (Jerusalem) in 1953.

It is evident from the ideology of the Fadā'iyān-e-Islam Movement that it was deeply influenced by the Muslim Brotherhood,[21] and the two groups closely liaised with each other across several Arab countries. They regarded themselves as the ones really capable of bringing about reformation within Islamic society, and delivering it from a vicious cycle of acquiescence and decline.[22] This movement would be a powerful inspiration later on, and as we shall see later, its strategy would be imitated by other groups with differing aims and systems.

Regardless of the ultimate achievements of the Fadā'iyān-e-Islam Movement, it disintegrated under continuous attack from the state, and its leaders were cruelly terminated. This was concurrent with the deteriorating success of the National Front, following the setbacks that afflicted the Musaddiq – Kāshāni Movement. This situation dramatically affected the rejectionist approach of radical Islam, forcing it to withdraw from the political arena and retreat to its traditional domain (namely, the religious seminary or *ḥawzah*), creating fissures in its organisation, and resulting in a considerable loss of fortune. As a result, there was a surge in the demand for the separation of religion and the state, and the exclusion of the clergy from party activities. Amongst the voices involved, the most significant was that of Ayatullāh Borūjerdī, a central figure of the religious establishment, who warned against the involvement of the clergy in politics. Ayatullāh Borūjerdī spoke out during the climax of the events surrounding the coup d'état led by Zahedī against Musaddiq, and the return of the Shāh to the seat of authority.[23]

However, the stance taken by Borūjerdī did not express his real convictions. Despite his reservations about the methods adopted by many of the reform movements, he believed in the union of religion and politics within Islam. He believed it was necessary to organise the affairs of society in accord with the *shari'ah*, and he considered the guarantee for the realisation thereof was the responsibility of the *faqih* (jurisprudent). His convictions are evidenced by his practical concern for the problems that affected the Islamic world and his diligent effort to unite Muslims, as shown by his grand project to bring the various schools of thought closer together.[24]

His attitude was probably underpinned by the necessity of excluding the *ḥawzah* from the political enterprises that undermined its structure and diminished its standing in the hearts of the people. It was therefore a provisional viewpoint that was dictated by existing realities, which were on the whole neither reliable nor successful, and left a resounding impact on the structure and function of the religious establishment.

Nevertheless, the stance of political abstention generated a closed religious milieu that was encouraged by the political authorities, who exploited the situation in order to marginalise any influence from the clergy in the political arena, and the potential dangers posed by their authority. This background formed an incubator for Salafi ideas, based on concepts such as intercession (*shafāʿah*), dissimulation (*taqiyyah*) and awaiting (*intiẓār*).

These ideas were later incorporated within the outlook of regressive trends such as the Anjoman-e Hojjatiyeh, whose popularity grew with overt backing from the authorities. Their following increased in size due to its confrontational position towards Baha'ism, amongst its other initiatives. In addition, they expressly appealed for a restriction of the role of the clergy to the sphere of education, underlining the necessary separation of religion and politics based on a principle which claimed that religious scholars were not responsible for the establishment of an Islamic government before the appearance of al-Mahdī. Also appearing within this milieu was the rise of revivalist Salafī movements that began their activities during the 1940s, and which established their groundwork and gained some significance with concepts similar to those known to Arab world at the beginning of the Renaissance. However, what was generally noticeable in the structure of these movements, despite their call for a return to the Qur'an and the *Salaf al-Ṣāliḥ* (the Pious Predecessors), was their superficial interest in a renewal of the Islamic sciences. Such movements failed to develop as soon as they encountered others that opposed their position.[25]

4. The Approach of Renewal and the Appearance of Revivalist and Reform Ideology

Revival movements in Iran during the first half of the 20th century were not confined to extreme nationalist trends supported by the regime, those against which Muṭahharī's wrote in his book The Reciprocal Services between Islam and Iran, as we shall see later. Nor were they restricted to revolutionary Marxist movements that called for social justice through the elimination of class distinctions. The general trend, having a radical and practical appearance, became distinctly effective in its appeal to the social category of workers and peasants. In addition, we find other movements that were deeply influenced by Western modernisation and technology. One was the secular belief that scientific knowledge presented the only solution for the problems besetting contemporary Iranian society, and was the golden key to progress and the fulfilment of all human needs.[26] Thus motivated, some rushed to brazenly confront the traditional concepts of religion and man, which were seen as a backward and ill-informed, the inevitable result of fear and superstition in the face of natural phenomena and the universe.[27]

Another example is that of nihilism, which, from the beginning of Rezā Shāh's reign up until the time of Musaddiq and the National Front, expressed the psychological deterioration of those familiar with Western intellectualism. According to this group, the project of reformation was expressed in the form of an irony mixed with sadness and contempt for the petit bourgeois and the bazaar merchants. Their efforts were dominated by a sense of despondency which underscored the meaninglessness of life. In general, it was a manifest example of Western nihilism, and was characterised by a radical literary and artistic output.[28]

During this era in particular, there were early indications of comprehensive Islamic reform movements, whose ambitions were focused on a complete ideological restructure in the light of contemporary challenges, a vision of Islam crystallised in a position that primarily addressed the social, political and economic dilemmas regarding the Western epistemological position.

At its outset, this trend focused on the relationship between religion and science, and prompted fierce debates that culminated twenty years later with a conference in Tehran. Various Islamic groups representing a cross-section of academia, including educators, doctors, engineers and students, participated in the conference. At its conclusion, some significant recommendations were revealed, some of which were as follows:

> Islam represents the most excellent path for the reformation of society, and contains the best laws and methodology for the nourishment and prosperity of humanity.
>
> Belief alone is not enough, and should be expressed in active and sincere service.

> Society should correct the mistakes of the past, and also keep up with the latest ideas and scientific advances. In addition, society must be equipped with effective tools provided by modern civilisation in order to be rid of the enduring retrograde cycle that had affected the spheres of thought, ethics, politics and economics, and which, if left uncorrected, would lead to its downfall.[29]
>
> Greater cooperation between Islamic states in the fight for liberation is necessary and strongly recommended.[30] As the religious establishment was abstaining from any such discussion or involvement, and instead concentrated on its traditional tasks, the advocates, including eminent clergy such as Muṭahharī and Ṭabāṭabā'ī, proclaimed the necessity of reform within the religious establishment, making changes that would gradually lead to a development of its structure so as to cope with the contemporary needs of society and the dilemmas presented by a rapidly changing world.[31]

This initiative gave rise to strategies that were jointly published in a book by influential reformers including Beheshti, Mahmūd Taleqāni, Musawi Zanjāni, and Mahdī Bāzargān, and which concentrated essentially on the necessity of developing the religious institutions so that they would thereby play an effective role in serving both Islam and society.[32] This was to be achieved through various means, such as ensuring the financial independence of the religious institutions; the formation of a supreme council for *iftā'* that would be comprised of prominent Shi'ite figures; the Islamisation of all aspects of social life; reducing the focus on *fiqh* (jurisprudence) in the religious seminaries, instead of developing the teaching of other sciences such as ethics, philosophy and theology; expanding the tools of *ijtihād* as a means to discover Islamic precepts pertaining to various contemporary aspects of life; reviving the principle of enjoining virtue and forbidding vice; and encouraging the Mujtāhidin to seek specialisation and develop a sound epistemology to overcome individual negative traits.[33] At the time, this book was considered the most significant publication on the subject of the *ḥawzah* in Iran during the second half of the 20th century, and echoes of it have reverberated within the circles of the reform-minded Iranian intelligentsia up to the present time.[34] In spite of disapproval of the ideas contained in it from parts of the religious establishment, the book nevertheless gained an unparalleled popularity. It was well-received by young people and the intelligentsia, and formed a practical framework that later would be an indispensable inspiration, with ideas that would be expressed in different ways by an entire generation of reform-oriented intellectuals and clergy.

At the time there were also other groups that enjoyed a limited popularity, such as the leftist Islamists founded by Jalāl al-Dīn Ashtiyānī, a well-known clergyman renowned for his interest in philosophy and theology. The group was defined as socialist, and mainly concentrated on social justice and democracy as concepts consonant with and stemming from the principles of monotheism. There was also a militant revivalist group founded by Muḥammad-Taqi Sharī'atī (the father of 'Alī Sharī'atī), who challenged the theory of historical materialism and its influence. He sought to present an image of Islam that was, in his view, compatible with the contemporary era. In addition, there was a non-militant reform movement whose most prominent figures included Atā'-Allah Shehāb and Mahmūd Shehābī, who founded the institution of Tablīgh-e Islamī. Their activities revolved around the publication of books, and they later launched a magazine as the official mouthpiece for their organisation. Their efforts were mainly centred on the exploration of the function (*maqasid*) of the *shari'ah*, and gained prominence amongst well-known revivalist thinkers in the Arab world, such as Tahir bin 'Āshūr, whose ideas were translated and spread throughout Iranian society.[35]

The relative freedom that prevailed in Iran between 1958 and 1959 allowed for the formation of a number of small parties within the Parliament. These later formed the basis for the so-called Second National Front. From this setting, a new group emerged that included personalities such as Mahdī Bāzargān, Mahmūd Taleqāni and Dr. Sahābī, who formed what came to be known as the Liberation Movement of Iran during the second half of the 20th century.[36]

In the midst of these developments, the signposts to a new phase in an intellectual and political renaissance would be formed, within which can be found the foundations for the upheaval of 1979 and the Iranian Islamic Revolution. How then did the main elements of this phase appear, and who were its most significant figures? We will discover the answers to these questions later on.[37]

2

THE PEAK OF STRUGGLE AND THE FORMATION OF THE IDEOLOGY OF REFORM WITHIN POLITICAL ISLAM (THE ERA OF MUṬAHHARĪ)

This stage of intellectual and political endeavour was characterised by the harmonisation of political Islam as an ideology of reform that reconciled the competing movements. One example appears in the person of ʿAlī Sharīʿatī with the reconciliation of the most pertinent issues in the field of sociology and leftist philosophy within the Arab world with Islamic principles. Meanwhile, with Bāzargān it entailed the bringing together of science and religion. In the case of Imām Khomeinī, Muṭahharī and Ṭabāṭabāʾī, the overriding task involved resolving the heritage of traditional philosophy and scholastic theology with a compatible intellectual outlook for correctly understanding the intellectual developments that had culminated in the modern world. Despite these multi-faceted approaches, they shared a collective aspiration of re-crystallising Islamic ideology, and thus enable it to respond to the challenges of modernity, such as the relationship between science and religion, tradition and modernity, and faith and reason. They were inspired by a desire to construct a unique and independent position regarding topics such as freedom, ethics, social justice, democracy and economic development. These several approaches were expressed in the works of scholars and activists who, each in their own way, contributed to steering this ideology of reformation towards its peak in 1979 with the Iranian Revolution.

The intellectual and political efforts exerted by this cross-section were accompanied by a movement of militant activism that began in secrecy, but later intensified and came out into the open. It was centred around the experiences of the first half of the 20th century, and took advantage of the positive aspects thereof, whilst taking its failures into account.[38] Muṭahharī was engaged at both these levels. He came to the fore as an activist and theorist on issues regarding Islam and society, as well as a guide for militant movements during the most sensitive and confusing phases.

1. Movements of Armed Activities: From Reform Ideologies to Revolution

Armed struggle evolved in the shadow of the reform movements. The political groups adopted more active measures and held demonstrations. There were organised seminars overseen by scholars and others calling for reform, such as Muṭahharī, Sharī'atī and Bāzargān. However, the brutal suppression of these groups by the authorities turned them into armed movements which subsequently rose up against the state and its supporters. Sharī'atī summarised this awakening by stating:

> "Islam was transformed from a culture into an ideology; and self-awareness replaced inherited traditions."[39]

This development took shape in four organised bodies: the Islamic Coalition Authorities, the Islamic Peoples' Party, the People's Mujahedin of Iran, and the People's Combatants.

A. The Islamic Coalition

During the exile of Imām Khomeinī, several groups coalesced to form a centralised body, which acted as a link between political opposition groups and religious people of the merchant class. At first, their activities concentrated on education, but later developed into organised political action and armed struggle led by notable activists, including Mahdī Iraqi and Sadiq Amāni. Muṭahharī's book Man and Destiny was the outcome of his lectures addressed to such activists.

Their first armed operation was the assassination of Mansour Qader, the Shāh's Prime Minister, following his approval of the granting of judicial immunity to Americans. In the aftermath of the attack, SAVAK (the Iranian National Intelligence and Security Organisation) arrested the leaders, many of whom were sentenced to death, while others were imprisoned, resulting in the movement's collapse.[40]

B. The Islamic People's Party

This party was formed as a militant opposition movement by a young man called Muḥammad Kāzem Bojnourdi, whose father was a well-known man of tradition in Najaf. Amongst his aims, he aspired to overthrow the regime and establish an Islamic government. He put forward a comprehensive framework and integrated strategy comprising sixty-five provisions. He formulated practical steps on the basis of three main phases:

Distribution of information and the recruitment of followers.

Preparation for armed struggle.

Appearance on the political scene.

In 1964, after a brief period of covert action, the activities of this party were exposed, and its leading members were arrested and gaoled until the advent of the Islamic Revolution.

C. The People's Mujahedin of Iran

This movement emerged from the aforementioned Liberation Movement of Iran, of which Bāzargān was one of the leaders. Plans for its armed activity began in the aftermath the events of 1963. In most cases, this planning took place in prisons, and later proliferated in secrecy in the countryside. It subsequently announced itself publically in 1970. After the arrest of a faction from the Fadā'iyān-e-Islam Movement in northern Iran, the group realised that it was useless to work in the countryside, and so it moved its activities to the cities. Finally, it was exposed by a double agent, as a result of which its leaders were imprisoned in 1971, and those who survived the crackdown fled abroad.

In early 1975, the People's Mujahedin of Iran experienced an internal schism which affected Muṭahharī directly, due to his close contact with its activities. Some of the followers of this group left Islam and became Communists, which was a tremendous shock to Islamic intellectuals, and prompted them to reconsider much of their strategy. The People's Mujahedin of Iran originally had a nationalistic outlook, and its followers considered themselves the inheritors of the Constitutional Revolution, Mirzā Koochak Khān's Movement as well as the Movement for the Nationalisation of Oil. They were inspired by the armed struggle of liberation movements in Algeria, Vietnam, Cuba and Palestine.[41]

Based on an interpretation of Weber, they assumed that Islam could act as a worldly ideology, by which one could discover an ideological framework for a collective struggle of the masses for freedom and democracy. In addition, this would serve to form a monotheistic system, a viewpoint clearly inspired by the ideas of Sharī'atī, Tāleqāni and Bāzargān.

After the schism, they changed their convictions. At first, they attempted to adopt a form of Marxism based on the Qur'an, but this led them to the belief that differences within the Qur'an inevitably led to disunity. As a result, a unified ideology could not be based thereon, and they dropped the idea.[42]

The new tendency within the People's Mujahedin of Iran signalled Muṭahharī's point of separation from the group, and he devoted much of his work to exposing the flaws in their ideology, and the dangers this represented for the entire reform movement. As a result, he was put under a lot of pressure, and faced harsh reactions that continued until the beginning of the Revolution.

D. The People's Fadā'iyān and Nascent Communism

This movement came to the fore in 1971 as an armed militia, whose outlook was based on various Leninist-Marxist and Maoist precepts. However, the followers of this group claimed their independence from World Communism and declared their opposition to the Stalinist model. Its activities were uncovered at the outset, and its leaders and supporters were subsequently imprisoned.

2. Reformation and Renewal Ideology, and the Evolution of Reconciliatory Trends

The appearance of this line of thinking paralleled the rise of liberation movements in the Third World. The authorities responded to this trend in the worst possible way, with brutal and systematic suppression. Nevertheless, this did not stop them from undertaking a programme of education and mobilisation, and thereby forming an intellectual framework. Generally, centres for this movement were in mosques, Ḥosseiniyeh, private gatherings and universities. It gradually expanded into the cities, and intensified its activities with speeches and publications, and was unflinching in the face of the inevitable obstacles that loomed.

Several progressive thinkers and prominent leaders oversaw the affairs of this trend, of whom the most notable were Ayatullāh Tāleqāni, Mahdī Bāzargān, and 'Alī Sharī'atī. Also sharing their vision in certain aspects were others such as 'Allamah Ṭabāṭabā'i and Nasr, who largely worked towards establishing a theoretical framework based on a reappraisal of the unification of tradition and modernity.

A. Tāleqāni and Reformation Ideology

Tāleqāni is considered one of the most significant figures of this delicate phase in the political history of Iran. Amongst his efforts, he attempted to present a revolutionary and dynamic social interpretation of the Qur'an and Nahj al-Balāghah. He was motivated by a quest to uncover factors that had caused weakness and decline within Muslim society.

His interest in the Qur'an stemmed from a firm conviction that this was not just a book of theories, but also of dynamism and reformation. He regarded the Qur'an as a document from which one could derive inspiration that could be applied in all spheres of human life. Furthermore, this was not restricted to the individual, but encompassed all of society throughout time, with issues that included freedom, slavery, justice, wealth and poverty. Tāleqāni made a valuable contribution, whose mark was left clearly in the minds of an entire generation of struggling thinkers, especially 'Alī Sharī'atī.[43]

B. Bāzargān and the Renewal of Islamic Thought

Mahdī Bāzargān[44] is regarded as one of the most prominent reformation thinkers in Iran at the time, and as the first to highlight the necessity of social and political reform. Bāzargān began his political activity in 1940, and was imprisoned in 1960 for his views and activities. As a testament to his work, he left behind no less than fifty publications, all of which were focused on the expounding of Islamic concepts and his vision of reform.

Bāzargān was the first to describe a system known as "Islamic Ideology," whose premise was the conviction that religion in its essence is a comprehensive system for managing and developing the affairs of life. Indeed, he believed that the divine Prophets were chiefly sent to realise this goal.

In this regard, the most important of his books is Prophetic Mission and Ideology, in which he summarised his convictions as follows:

The necessity and centrality of the state.

That power emanates from the people.

The necessity of an ideology as a comprehensive system for guidance.

The affirmation of basic truths pertaining to the natural world and humanity.

The necessity of leadership and organisation.

In this book, Bāzargān espoused Islamic ideological concepts relating to freedom, justice and the rule of law, the necessity of an Islamic government, the definition of the relationship between the individual and society, modes of consultation (*shurā*) and election, and much else. He affirmed that there was no inconsistency between Islamic government and democracy, since the former is based on rationality, freedom of choice, allegiance (*bay'ah*) and consultation, or *shurā*. He also upheld the notion that positing Islam as a ideology for reform does not imply the renunciation of the *shari'ah*, but rather, the divine law serves to regulate and rationalise reformation in accordance with universal parameters. As a result, this would expand the scope of freedom in the application of religious precepts.

Considering that, in the reformatory outlook of Bāzargān, all this is the proper domain of man's will and activity, it was therefore natural for him to reject any form of religious aristocracy. Consequently, according to him, the jurist (*faqih*) is a guide and counsellor, and not a ruler; a legislating jurisprudent and not an administrating politician. As a result, *fiqh* takes a secondary role to ethics, values and the natural rights of humanity.

For Bāzargān, religion supersedes politics, and no one enjoys a monopoly of its understanding and interpretation. Religion is the language of the primordial nature embodied in man and the world, and articulated by revelation in the form of speech. In its transcendence, religion reveals the divine Will in the universe. Based on such an understanding, Bāzargān views the parameters of monotheism and polytheism through a sociological lens, and not a theological one. That is to say, monotheism and polytheism are not restricted to the domain of theory, but are reflected on the social plane. Therefore, to put religion at the service of politics would be a most evident manifestation of polytheism.

From Bāzargān's perspective, what is expected of religion is not the abandonment of the human will, freedom of choice and rational organisation, but for it to set the groundwork for them. Religion ought not to educate us about what our minds can already realise and grasp, but instead direct and guide our powers and capabilities. Religion, according to him, is not expected to offer direct solutions to our crises, but rather enlighten us about causes and effects. It is the role of religion to outline the general procedure by which one can arrive at a solution, thereby allowing our rational powers to seek it out. Nevertheless, religion is deemed the best means of realising human aspirations, because religion, in this view, is in complete harmony with natural law, the process of history and social dynamics. Furthermore, he locates the roots of faith in the human mind, wherein the law functions with harmony and precision. Therefore, reflecting upon nature and the world, the order of its relationships, its design and mysteries, cause man to draw closer to religious truths.

As for religious faith in a deeper sense, it signifies an affirmation of freedom through which the individual chooses to surrender to Almighty Allah as the Guide and the Guarantor of perfection in all spheres of human life. If man is free in proportion to his belief in Allah, then he is free to regulate his choices in light of the divine Law, from which originate both modes of guidance, generative and legislative, and are consonant with the natural system upon which the world was created, as affirmed by Revelation.[45] It however seems that in his final days Bāzargān abandoned the Islamic ideology he had theorised upon throughout his life. He postulated that it was not the task of prophets or religion to establish a political system, and any preoccupation of theirs in this regard stemmed from their human nature. In addition, he asserted that the affairs of politics and economics have been entrusted to one's will, and the understanding of one's best interests based on human interaction.[46]

C. 'Alī Sharī'atī: Islam as an Ideology of Social Struggle

Sharī'atī began his political life within the structure of the National Front led by Musaddiq. Later, he got involved in secret activities with the National Resistance Movement, and this lasted for roughly five years until 1959 with his imprisonment and the exposure of the movement.

He then moved to Europe and stayed there until 1964. Following his return to Iran, he experienced the turbulent times between 1964 and 1969, during which he was hindered by university activity, imprisonment and unemployment. Between 1969 and 1974, he became involved in the activities of the Ḥosseiniyeh Ershād[47] Foundation alongside other figures, the most prominent of whom was Muṭahharī.

From 1974 to 1979, Sharī'atī endured five years of harsh conditions, the most conspicuous of which were constant surveillance and imprisonment. Eventually, SAVAK executed him.

His period of study in Europe constituted the formative phase of his intellectual life. There he met Arab and African revolutionary thinkers such as Hasan Hanafi, Frantz Fanon, and others who were involved in their own causes. He witnessed the crises in various parts of the Arab world, and all these factors contributed to shaping his concerns.

At the beginning, Sharī'atī was not amongst those who believed in armed activity for the sake of reform, since he did not believe that such means stood much chance of success. According to him, any revolution that begins before the maturity of popular awareness inevitably leads to a massacre. As a result, his efforts during this period of active struggle were largely focused on guidance and instruction. Ḥosseiniyeh Ershād was the centre for his intellectual activity, and the pulpit from which he steered the youth and planted in them the seeds of awakening and determination.

Islam was the essential structure upon which Sharī'atī's ideas of reform were based. He believed that Islam transcended the boundaries of a faith of personal commitment and the rituals of worship. According to him, Islam was exalted far beyond a meagre identity for Muslims which defined their sense of belonging. Rather, in his eyes, Islam was a comprehensive outlook with a universal ideology that could be applied to the revival and development of civilisation.

Since his view of religion was so comprehensive, he criticised the established clergy for its narrow and negative understanding of Islam, which placed religion at the service of power and reduced it in a crucible of conflicting interests, whereby it was forced into isolation, detached from the issues of everyday life.[48]

According to Sharī'atī, this unconstructive position was the result of circumstances and historical accumulations, as well as a partial and fragmented understanding of religion, which consistently failed to realise the comprehensiveness of its worldview and the universality of its concepts and laws. Sharī'atī believed that in order to confront this tendency and transform it into something positive, one would need to revitalise the common understanding of Islam so as to inspire action and social change. At another level, this would entail an attempt to purify religion from the accumulations of history by adhering to the Qur'an and the Sunnah, and rise above the conditions that might push religion towards conservatism and stagnation. Religion would then represent a source of awakening that activated a return to pristine Islamic culture as a consequence of its transformation into a comprehensive ideology for revival, a framework for social practice and a revised perspective on history. Consequently, religion should not remain a phenomenon that subsists for its own sake, as this strips it of the most vital reason for its existence, and ultimately reduces it to a skeletal reality, detached from the flow of life. Rather, a historical awareness should stem from the essence of religion and the spirit of its content. Thus, there is no cognitive dimension or purpose to religion except in light of the problems that afflict humanity in all spheres, and with a view to the development of awareness and the progression of history.[49] Moreover, religion is to be understood and measured by its influence and effectiveness in transforming the behaviour of its followers, in their awareness, their relationships and their worldview.[50]

For Sharīʿatī, such a conception of religion necessarily requires the rejection of any understanding derived from narrow, stagnant texts, or any writings in isolation from the context in which they appeared, for a barren understanding that is devoid of vitality invariably leads to dullness and monotony, and generates a sense of futility and inactivity. He instead called for an understanding of the conditions of life and the character of religion, the transformations of increase and decline, life and death, as well as how religion has influenced other structures and outlooks and, conversely, been itself subject to influence. This means understanding religion as a living phenomenon that is in flux, but at the same time rooted in human consciousness and history.[51]

From the perspective of Sharīʿatī, the revelation of Islam was given for man's provision, not to enslave him or dispossess him of his will. It is for this reason that the individual is accountable for his decisions and the results of his actions. Moreover, the trust in deliverance given by the Messenger of Almighty Allah to mankind is in line with this outlook, for he is the vicegerent of Allah on Earth who participates in the mission of creating and structuring the universe. Man is accountable for his destiny[52] and is defined by his submission to Allah, and not according to the claims of the individual or society.[53]

Based on these premises, a return to the values and principles of a pure Islam in light of the Revelation is not an intellectual luxury, but rather a foremost necessity for correct behaviour. It is neither a glorification of the past or a repetition of earlier myths, for Islam prohibited such practices. On the contrary, it would be the revival of the essence of human values, which should lead to a resuscitation of the cultural assets of the *ummah*. A return to pure Islam would confirm the fundamental concepts regarding existence and the pattern of history.[54]

ʿAlī Sharīʿatī's understanding of monotheism and polytheism was similar to that of Bāzargān. He therefore emphasised a social and political responsibility, as he viewed both realities from a sociological rather than a theological or philosophical vantage point. Therefore, monotheism for him is neither an abstract belief nor a theory, but a vision of the world and the whole of existence, since both monotheism and polytheism involve consciousness, the will, good example and given objectives, and are judged by one homogenous system. On the other hand, monotheism, according to the traditional outlook, sees the universe as an empire, and regards polytheism as servitude. Consequently, Sharīʿatī does not believe in a static unity of existence or its resuscitation, but he does believe in its evolution. There is neither a duality nor a conflict between history and sociology, the human being and nature, the seen and the unseen, but rather a unity (or integration) of the world of the seen and the beyond. There exists a unity of man and nature, history and meta-history, the individual and society, and ultimately between Allah, man and the universe. This unity is a homogenous system that is alive and knowable.

Hence monotheism assumes a methodology that sees the universe as a unity.[55] Accordingly, belief becomes a type of conflict between nature and metaphysical reality, this world and the next, reason and revelation, science and religion, working for the sake of Allah and working for society. This is also seen in the relationship between politics and religion according to the view of polytheism, rather than that of monotheism.[56] To firmly establish a sense of awareness within society requires, according to Sharīʿatī, presenting it with a renewed Islamic mindset, the obligation for which is largely borne by the religious scholars who are responsible for the propagation of its message.

According to Sharīʿatī, the intellectual is not just a scholar, scientist or artist. The intellectual is one who is aware of the requirements of the age,[57] coupled with a deep sense of social responsibility.[58] It is not the role of the intellectual to assume political leadership; that rests with the masses who constitute the basis of change. They are the prime movers of history and the decisive factor in transformation.[59] The mission of the intellectual is to instil an awareness in the public consciousness of ideas for the future,[60] and to combat false notions.[61]

Thus for Sharīʿatī, social ills originate from ignorance, fear and convenience, three factors which manifest as follows:

> False notions that nullify man's will and take away his freedom; old and new forms of fascination portrayed as sciences; and polytheism in various forms, both ancient and contemporary.
>
> Loss of identity and originality; submission to cultural imperialism; and reverence of the Western intellectual and cultural heritage.
>
> Isolation from the world, which transforms the individual into a machine, so that profit becomes the objective.
>
> Any faith that transforms into a form of Sufism based on self-worship or the worship of holy personalities and places.

Additionally, the veneration of literature and science – which are manifestations of contemporary Westernisation – whereby one bestows a certain absoluteness on a theory to which one entirely surrenders.

Allowing wealth to become the focal point of human endeavour, leading to violence and control.

Displacing the natural balance with a materialistic civilisation that makes man the captive of consumption and narrow affiliations, including racism.

D. Hossein Nasr and the Complete Rejection of Modernity and Technology

Hossein Nasr is renowned throughout the world for his interest in the revival of traditional knowledge and his studies on religion, mysticism and Islamic issues.He was the Agha Khān Professor of Islamic Studies at the American University in Beirut from 1961 to 1965, and for a time he chaired the Iranian community for philosophy at the Imperial Iranian Academy of Philosophy during the reign of Muḥammad Rezā Shāh. After the Revolution, he moved to America and took up the position of Professor of Islamic Studies at the George Washington University, where he remains to the present date.

The scientific activity of Hossein Nasr is summarised by a project to crystallise Islam based upon the spiritual dimension that it encompasses. This entails the emphasis on an understanding of mind and reason that transcends Cartesian rationalism, and includes intuition, contemplative vision, illumination and theosophy. Moreover, this outlook asserts that the path to knowledge is through wisdom, which is of divine origin.[62]

Hossein Nasr delved into the study of Greek philosophy through the works of Avicenna, Suhrawardi and Mullā Sadrā Shīrāzī, and became thoroughly acquainted with the mystical legacy of Sufism. He considers himself one of the inheritors of eternal wisdom (*jāwidān kherad*), which is never extinguished by the passage of time and is passed on from generation to generation as an endless light that never fades.

As a result of the influence of spirituality in the formation of his personality and his inclination towards the metaphysical, Nasr rejects the notion of the superiority of rationality and the material body over soul and emotion. Furthermore, he warns against the dangers of extricating the divine essence from nature, for this leads to depression, decadence, the demise of human virtue, the separation of Allah from man, and the severance of the mind from the light that guides it.[63]

Islam, according to Nasr, is both the confirmation of former religions and the revealing of their quintessence. It is divine guidance towards monotheism and an attempt to restore man to a former state of glory that has been neglected. Islam thus reminds humanity of the divine beauty that it was blessed with prior to its enslavement to the material world of the senses. Prophets throughout history have affirmed the truths contained within the nature of things, and fulfilled the function of guidance and remembrance.[64]

From Nasr's perspective, there is nothing unholy in this world according to Islam. The entire world is sacred, with no duality of holy and unholy, or of the transcendent and the manifest. Christianity historically rooted this duality in its teachings, and it has now become entrenched due to the experiences of the modern world. In Islam, Allah is the origin and essence of the world and the source of its sanctity. He is all-encompassing, omnipresent and manifest in existence. Everything in the world bears in its essence something of the divine presence.[65]

Hossein Nasr believes that the differences between Eastern and Western philosophy arose during the time of the Renaissance with the spread of humanism, a departure from classical ethics, and the separation of science, religion and philosophy. As a result, the legacy of the modern West is founded on a destructive science and technology, and Islamic society should therefore confront it with the following steps:

> A revival the Islamic intellectual heritage in the areas of philosophy and mysticism (*'irfān*).
>
> Caution against the philosophies, sciences and technologies of modern Western origin and the hazards they generate.
>
> Opening up to Eastern civilisations in order to counterbalance the West.
>
> Outlining a methodology to safeguard the originality of Islamic culture.[66]

The most prominent effect of the Western cultural heritage is secularism, which is an ideology that entrenches a fault line between Allah and man. In fact, secularism in the modern world has taken on the role of a belief that is tantamount to a religion. A systematic degradation of religious traditions has led many to believe that Allah does not exist at all.[67]

According to Nasr, this poses a serious danger to culture and society, because many proponents of modernism have been influenced by secularism, though it may at times have been cloaked in religious garb. Secularism poses a brazen challenge to the principle of monotheism in every sphere by spreading polytheism and atheism.[68] But taking it for granted that secularism is an idea competing with religion is merely an illusion in souls that have been exposed to it through heedlessness and ignorance, since nothing other than esoteric knowledge can awaken people and lead them towards the truth.[69]

The shari'ah, for Hossein Nasr, is the law of the divine Will, and therefore an absolute and eternal truth. It loses nothing by people failing to act in accordance with its precepts. It is, in fact, man who loses himself, because he fails to be in harmony with the divine Will, of which the *shari'ah* is the highest manifestation.[70] Therefore, any call to change with the times and adjust the *shari'ah* in the light of developments should be completely rejected. Those who advocate such a thing have in fact lost sight of the Truth which transcends time. Such people are trapped in illusion, having been overcome by the predominant themes of modern European philosophical thought. They are barely able to recognise Truth in a pure form, since it does not harmonise with the apparent reality of the immediate context. However, Islam is based on the principle that the Truth is beyond time and transcends history, and the *shari'ah* is the criterion for judging man and his actions.[71]

With this in mind, to adjust the *shari'ah* in order to meet the requirements of the contemporary age would amount to spiritual suicide; a misunderstanding of the spirit of Islam and the submission of man to his materialistic whims and fancies.[72] Such a notion is a misleading and deadly sophistry.

Perhaps the majority of the voices raised by Westernised thinkers for a compromise between Islam and modernity, stem from the inability of that kind of thinking to appreciate the true meaning of the *shari'ah*. This is due to an affiliation with the Christian legacy, which lost the divine Law and replaced it with Roman law. At another level, these calls spring from psychological factors generated by centuries of Western pressure.

Throughout the course of time, the situation has turned into a feeling of inferiority and alienation.[73]

According to Hossein Nasr, there is a sweeping tendency in some parts of the Islamic world to borrow from the Western intellectual system, which is then masqueraded under an Islamic façade with labels such as Islamic democracy, Islamic socialism and Islamic rationalism. The purpose is to confer some sense of legitimacy to Islam in the modern age and grant it acceptability. This is something that Nasr feels is a cause of regret, since it is merely a change of appearance and a weak justification that cannot convince the discerning thinker. Moreover, it makes Islam appear either as a second-tier Western intellectual system when compared to the original, or Western thinking in search of an Islamic equivalent.[74]

It is noteworthy that Nasr thinks that this proclivity seeks a consonance between Islam and the modern world in a way that reduces the former simply to a ceremonial reality, and thereby erases fourteen centuries of civilisation and philosophy. Its supporters do not realise the inadequacy of trying to deal with the issues presented by the modern world simply by means of a rational presentation of Islam, as with any other rational method. On the contrary, it can only be done through the metaphysical insight that can be found in the treasures of traditional wisdom nourished throughout the ages by Islam, particularly within the Sufi tradition. This wisdom, according to Nasr, is not rational thinking according to the Aristotelian notion, but rather a rational wisdom which envelops insight, reflection and contemplation in line with Qur'anic concepts. In light of this, Nasr criticises Cartesian rationalism, which limits human knowledge to the level of individual thought:

> "I think, therefore I am."

In essence, this form of rationalism draws a barrier between man and Allah which amounts to a revolt against Heaven.[75]

Hossein Nasr's stance does not imply that Muslims ought to turn away and isolate themselves from the developing world, which is neither desirable nor possible, even though in certain circumstances it is difficult for Muslims to apply the *shari'ah*, which nonetheless should not be neglected because of other obligations. Having other obligations does not imply that the *shari'ah* is defective, but rather as the outcome of the shortcomings of circumstances with respect to fixed principles. Eventually, the *shari'ah* will prevail and all extraneous considerations will disappear.[76]

Consequently, if there is any notable change to occur, then it should only take place in line with the shari'ah and not otherwise, unless a reformation is simply to be a hasty decision that paves the way for corruption. Therefore, the shari'ah is not to be judged according to its consonance with the modern world, since that would amount to putting the cart before the horse, by putting human considerations in the place of divine ones. This sort of stance is totally unrelated to the Islamic perspective, and quite possibly falls under the definition of polytheism.[77]

This briefly summarises Hossein Nasr's outlook concerning tradition and modernity, religion and science, the *shari'ah* and the prerequisites of change, and so forth. His perspective is reiterated by many other figures, and echoes of it are felt in the ideas of Muṭahharī. Despite not being known for his association with politics or active movements, or even the dilemmas generated by conditions within Iran, nevertheless Hossein Nasr is a revivalist thinker of high stature. He is a theorist with strong convictions on the subject of recovery within Islam. He affirms the universality of its precepts despite the transformations of time and history. He holds his own principled position regarding Western modernity and its achievements, the impact of technology, and humanist philosophies which have severed ties with the unseen and the metaphysical. His position continues to illuminate our intellectual challenges and has influenced our thinkers at more than one level.

3

CONSEQUENCES OF THE EXPERIENCES OF STRUGGLE AND REFORM, AND THE CRYSTALLISATION OF THE THEORY OF ISLAMIC GOVERNMENT BY IMĀM KHOMEINĪ (R)

Since early in the last century, an awareness of the cultural dilemmas facing the Islamic world stirred the religious and cultural élites within Iran, urging them towards the idea of reform. Internal flaws and the bloodiest forms of political despotism were rife. There was also the influence of materialism on a restive global system. Having expanded throughout the world and monopolised the sources of wealth, it promised luxury and prosperity to one-fifth of the planet's population at the cost of others who were burdened with poverty and illiteracy, and suffered conflict and schism.[78]

It was this awareness that stirred within Islamic society at the beginning of the Renaissance and shortly thereafter. There was, of course, a realisation of what the West had achieved in terms of progress in the field of science, technology and modernisation, and the benefits brought about by bringing improved welfare and development to certain nations were acknowledged. But at the same time, it could also be seen that these achievements served a culturally materialistic project that deepened the divide between peoples, establishing a world order that guaranteed hegemony for the powerful, and gave a free rein to systematic plunder and domination. In addition, it generated conflicts in the contexts of race, gender, language and religion, and secured the interests of the strong at the price of truth and justice.

The culturally aware realised that maintaining the status quo throughout the world was an extremely complex issue. However, what could be easily grasped was that the conditions of Western civilisation were the outcome of a self-interested materialism that emphasised competition to secure prosperity for the strong. There was also the notion of the centrality of the West, which naturally excluded others who were classified as lower on a hierarchical scale, and did not have the capacity to compete in an era of conflicting interests. Included within this category, one could find "inferior" and "underdeveloped" ethnicities, excluded from the value system of human rights generated by the thinkers of the Enlightenment, and regarded as a Western monopoly.

As for conditions pertaining to the Islamic world, they primarily entailed a systematic draining away of Islamic principles, which, moreover, intensified a kind of denial of the actual conditions of Islamic civilisation at its peak. According to the reformers, a project to restore more even-handed relationships throughout the world, could only succeed through the development of Islamic ideology in all its dimensions. That is to say, that Islamic ideology should constitute, above all, a cultural project that would re-establish the internal balance of the human being and foster both solidarity and freedom amongst the members of society. On a wider scale, it would restore to peoples and nations their rights and identities.

This mission was undertaken by one man, and would spread within the ummah and captivate the minds and souls of the people. As a consequence, they plunged into a struggle that was neither a covetous desire to dominate key interests, nor based on an outlook where decisions are imposed from the top down. There was no rationale of being a guardian of state affairs, but rather a struggle underpinned by education and reform, a quest for excellence through guidance and instruction, and not authoritarian leadership.[79]

All this was exemplified in the intellectual thought of Imām Khomeinī, which encompassed the transformations witnessed in Iran and the rest of the Islamic world over the past century. Imām Khomeinī summarised the essence of his vision and defined its fundamental precepts and goals when he stated:

> "The project of Islam is founded on the application of divine laws based on the criteria of equity and justice, confronting injustice and tyranny, spreading individual and social justice, and forbidding corruption, abomination and various forms of deviation for the sake of freedom, independence and self-sufficiency. In addition, it calls for combating colonialism, slavery and exploitation, as well as deploring all conflict over material gain in the realm of international relations, and (instead) strives for the equality of all peoples."[80]

Furthermore, this vision also entailed confronting the existing relationships based on power and threat between nations, a situation which had generated instability and contained within it the seeds of its own collapse.[81]

Imām Khomeinī's awareness of the cultural dilemmas facing the Islamic world in challenging both itself and the world at large was not merely a sudden emotional reaction. On the contrary, it sprung from reflection on the one hand, and a sense of initiative on the other. Both these factors necessitated the formulation of a comprehensive vision in order to find solutions. Furthermore, it underscored the importance of an integrated understanding of things as they are, with future aspirations, and with a deep insight of history and its workings. To this end, he developed a three-dimensional project. Firstly, to challenge the Western outlook on civilisation, regarding it from the point of view of both domination and arrogance; secondly, to confront and overcome the reality of stagnation; and thirdly, to form a clear theoretical vision that would remain vital and harmonious while consider social problems. Furthermore, he emphasised the need to equip this vision with a flexible mechanism for its application, which would continue to cope with changing developments.

A. The First Dimension: Confronting Arrogance

Imām Khomeinī replaced the term "colonialism" with "arrogance," a word that describes a psychological attitude which reveals an underlying epistemology. It is also used in the Qur'an in a way that correlates perfectly with the culture of the West.

The relationship of the West to the rest of the world is not merely one of material hegemony and control in matters of security and the military, but also a cultural inclination of conceit that impacts upon both its proponents and its victims. Since arrogance translates into dominion, deprivation and the ruin of cultures and traditions, in order to confront it, one must combat its influence and the key implementers, the leaders as well as those who have become enslaved by its values.[82] This cannot be remedied without first having cultural independence and restoring self-identity and a spirit of freedom and vitality. This should be based on the unique comprehensiveness and immutability of the Islamic law, and an aspiration to return to its principles in all spheres of life, particularly those of social affairs and politics.[83]

B. The Second Dimension: Combating Stagnation

From Imām Khomeinī's viewpoint, an important cause of stagnation within society is a feeling of weakness and defeatism when confronted with the material progress of arrogant powers.[84] Moreover, it is to be found in the inferiority to Westernised academics felt by a defeatist cultural élite and static, traditionalist scholars. It may nonetheless be a driving force towards awakening.

For this reason, Imām Khomeinī began his struggle internally at two levels. First of all, he wanted to mobilise the public and sever their relationship with the intelligentsia that presided over the educational institutions, and consequently bring about a reform within education to secure its independence and prevent the penetration of Western values into the minds of the people.[85] Moreover, he sought to propagate a spirit of self-awareness, free from feelings of weakness and defeatism.[86] And secondly, he wanted to rescue the religious establishment from its comatose condition by emphasising its crucial role in the revival of culture, by keeping up with social developments and dealing with the complex problems involved.[87] The religious establishment was to be transformed into a pivotal force in the movement for reform, progress and awakening, by addressing contemporary problems and instilling vitality into Islamic concepts, values and legislation. In short, the religious establishment was to be pulled out of isolation and reconnected with the movements of history and society.[88]

Imām Khomeinī was extremely harsh in this respect, due to his keen awareness of both the existing condition of the clergy as well as the normative role it ought to fulfil.[89] The religious establishment had become a den of authoritarianism that served to distort the minds of the youth. It isolated them from the concerns of their society, made them lethargic, disseminated misleading ideas and separated them from their culture and civilisation, whereas it should have been leading the struggle and raising the call for progress and change, the principal ingredient of reform. Instead of that, it had recoiled into itself and sluggishly repeated a lifeless knowledge characterised by an immobile reactionary mindset. It glorified exoteric appearances and ceremonial rites[90] at the expense of essential content. As a result, its guardians ensured retrogression whether or not they realised it.[91] It generated a class of social opportunists and profiteers who exploited religion in their own interests, distorting its teachings to safeguard their positions and serve their patrons, who were the true guardians of these policies.[92] This was an institution that was expected to spread Islam, promote its teachings in day-to-day life, and revive its values in order to guide society and inspire it with solutions that would ensure its integrity, the justness of its laws, and the success of its institutions, and therefore be the harbinger of progress and the prosperity of society.

C. The Third Dimension: Clarity and Flexibility of Theory

Imām Khomeinī realised that the absence of a clear theory in various contemporary Islamic projects was one of the most significant dilemmas that had plagued liberation movements across the Muslim world, and a major reason for failure and defeat.

This was a general shortcoming, in spite of widespread criticism of the way things were. There had also been a correct diagnosis of errors, as was the case with the 1920 Revolution, the Constitutional Movement, the projects of Jamāl al-Dīn al-Afghānī and Muḥammad ʻAbduh, ʻAbd al-Qādir al-Jazāirī's Movement, Ibn-Badīs and al-Mahdī in Sudan, and even the Muslim Brotherhood and its extensions. It was for this reason that the Imam proposed a cultural alternative through a system of governance with clear features grounded in a coherently organised theoretical framework. He augmented the theoretical framework so that the pertinent issues and complexities of life could be understood in order to deal with rapidly changing developments. Imām Khomeinī's theoretical framework was based on two constants: Islamic political fiqh, and a formal definition of governance.

At first, the Imam set out his integrated vision for comprehensive political change, since he considered a partial constitutional change, or merely replacing the head of state with another, as insufficient, and would not lead to a fundamental transformation. Therefore, the objective was to reform the system entirely, both within and in regard to foreign policy, basing it on Islamic values. Furthermore, the principle of monotheism would guarantee its righteousness and integrity, and synthesise religion and politics so that belief and action would exist in a seamless harmony without contradiction. To this end, Imām Khomeinī presented detailed historical research in which he revealed the superiority of Islamic legislation, and an examination of the nature of its system of rule. He stressed its necessary application through a perceptive executive administration that was organised and transparent, thus forming reliable apparatus that would guarantee the happiness of the people.[93]

Since Islam not only necessitates an executive framework to ensure the application of its legislation that is not separate from the lives and needs of the people, the Imam sought a way to crystallise the practicalities. For this he presented his theory of the Guardianship of the Jurisprudent (*wilāyat al-faqīh*), wherein he defined the principles and mechanisms for ensuring sound practice and proper application.

It is noteworthy that the Imam did not submit his theory because of the rapid developments in the wake of the overthrow of the regime that led up to the Revolution. Rather, it was a viewpoint that he strongly believed in, and for which he struggled with a deep-rooted conviction. It was a philosophical schema he had elucidated many years before the downfall of the ShāhanShāh regime, that is, the Pahlavī dynasty. The details had come together whilst he was immersed in the study of how to revive Islamic values in light of contemporary developments, taking into account the many difficulties encountered in the past, and the project was completed during his years of exile in Iraq.[94]

In order to ensure a sound application and continuity amidst the flux of events, the practical framework was compared by the Imam to a release of the powers of *ijtihād* (the process of interpreting Islamic law by a jurist), which both safeguards the legal principles and allows for their specific application to particular circumstances. *Ijtihād* is a basic Islamic principle, for if Islam transcends time and place, then there has to be a flexibility for responding to all eventualities. In this regard, the worthiness of the jurisprudent becomes apparent in his ability to discern immutable principles and adapt them to contemporary developments. This skill comes to the fore with an understanding of the world and given contexts, and an insight into the mechanisms of change.[95]

In his assertion of the important role of *ijtihād* as a systematic framework outlining his theory, the Imam realised that the commonly accepted definition of *ijtihād* was not sufficient for achieving his goals. Therefore, it was important to expand its meaning in order to render it suitable for current circumstances. It was not enough to merely open the doors of *ijtihād* and identify the principles upon which the process of application was based. It was imperative to have, in addition, a holistic understanding of social affairs and politics. These were necessary prerequisites for sound planning that would safeguard the interests of Muslims and guarantee their future.[96]

Based on these two key pillars – a clear and perspicacious theory, coupled with sound practice – the Imam was presenting a project for a cultural renaissance that was confined to neither liberation from foreign domination, nor the boundaries of a political and social reformation. Rather, it was to transcend such matters by encompassing a comprehensive renaissance in all spheres.

Notes

1. Talal Majzoub, *Iran: From Constitutional Revolution to Islamic Revolution*, (*Iran min al-Thawrah al-Dustūrīyyah illā al-Thawrah al-Islamīyyah*), Beirut, Dār Ibn-Rushd, 1980, pp. 297-298.

2. Khalīl Haydar, Turban and Mace: *Shi'ite Reference in Iran and Iraq* (*al-Ammamāh wal Sawlajan, al-Marja'iyyah al-Shi'iyyah fi Iran wa al-Irāq*), Kuwait, Dār Qirtās, 1997, p. 232.

3. Riḍwān al-Sayyid, *Politics of Contemporary Islam* (*Sīyāsāt al-Islam al-Mu'asir*), Beirut, Dār al-Kitāb al-Arabī, 1997, p. 139, and Amal al-Subky, *Iran's Islamic History between Two Revolutions* (*Tarīkh Iran al-Islami Bayna Thawratain*), 'Alam al-Ma'rifah, 1999, pp. 99-125.

4. 'Abd al-Hādī al-Ḥā'irī, *Shi'ism and Consitutionalism in Iran Tashayyu' wa Mashrutiyyat Dar Iran*), Tehran, 1985, pp. 26, 27, 31 and 37.

5. Talal Majzoub, op. cit., pp. 168-192, Riḍwān al-Sayyid, op. cit., p 119, and Amal al-Subky, *'Alam al-Ma'rifah*, 250, pp. 21-38.

6. 'Alī al-Wardī, *Social Glimpses from Iraq's Modern History* (*Lamahat Ijtima'iyyah min Tarikh al-Iraq al-Hadith*), Qom, Dār al-Amīr, 1991, p. 284, and Ishaq Naqash, *Iraqi Shi'ites* (*Shi'at al-Iraq*), Damascus, 1987, p. 104.

7. Faḍel Rassul, *'Alī Sharī'atī Talked in this Way* (*Hakadha Takalama 'Alī Sharī'atī*), Dār al-Kalimah, 1987, pp. 18-19. See "Problematic Review that Missed Objectivity for this Era," in Fardain Quraishi, *Renewal of Religious Thinking in Iran* (*Tajdid al-Fikr al-Dini fi Iran*), translated by *'Alī al-Mūsawī*, Beirut, Center of Civilization, 2008, p. 197 and afterwards.

8. Muhammad Rezā Wasfy, *Contemporary Islamic Thinking in Iran* (*Al-Fikr al-Islami al-Mu'asir fi Iran*), Beirut, Dār al-Jadīd, 2000, pp. 97-98.

9. Faḍel Rassul, op. cit, p. 20.

10. Jalāl Āl-e-Ahmed was born in Tehran in 1923. His father was a prominent clergyman. He travelled to Najaf to train in the religious sciences in fulfillment of his father's wish, but did not stay for more than three months before returning to Tehran. He joined the High Institute and was awarded a Masters degree. Later, he withdrew from the university for unknown reasons before completing his PhD thesis. He abandoned his religious commitments and joined the Tudeh Party, gaining a high-ranking position. Three years later, following the coup against Musaddiq, he left the party, withdrew from political activity, and completely devoted himself to writing and education. In 1970, he was assassinated by the SAVAK (The National Intelligence and Security Organization) in obscure circumstances. He was buried in a grave bearing no mark other than his own signature, in accordance with his will.

11. Jalāl Āl-e-Ahmad, *Weststruckness* (*Gharbzadegī*), Tehran, 1964, p 21. Compare with the Arabic translation by Haydar Najaf, Beirut, Dār al-Hādī, 2000, Āl-e-Ahmad, *Enlighteners* (*Roshanfekran* which is translated into Arabic as (*al-Mustanīrūn*), translated by Haydar Najaf, Beirut, Dār al-Hādī, 2000, and Āl-e-Ahmad, *Khasi dar Miqat* translated into Arabic as (*Qashah Fi al-Miqat*), Beirut, Dār al-Hādī, 2003.

12. *Islamic Contemporary Thinking*, p 100.

13. *Weststruckness*, p. 25, compare with Dorothea Kravolski, *Arabs and Iran* (*Al-'Arab wa Iran*), Beirut, Dār al-Muntakhab al-'Arabī, 1993, pp 269-270.

14. *Islamic Contemporary Thinking*, op. cit., p. 105.

15. Participation by some clergymen was from outside the institutions, such as Sayyid Hasan Mudarris, who engaged in parliamentary action and political opposition within the provisions of law.

16. Fouad Ibrahim, *The Jurisprudent and the State* (*Al-Faqīh wa al-Dawlah*), Beirut, Dār al-Kitāb al-Arabī, 1998, p. 169.

17. *Contemporary Islamic Thought*, op. cit., p. 109.

18. Khalil Haydar, *Turban and Mace*, op. cit, p. 237.

19. Hadi KhosroShāhi, *Islam Commandos, History of Action and* Thinking (*Fadā'iyān-e Islam, Tarikh 'Amalkerd wa Andisheh*), Tehran, Ittilā'āt, 1995, p. 197.

20. It will be reviewed against verses 33–36 of:

﴿إِنَّمَا جَزَاءُ الَّذِينَ يُحَارِبُونَ اللَّهَ وَرَسُولَهُ وَيَسْعَوْنَ فِي الأَرْضِ فَسَادًا أَن يُقَتَّلُواْ أَوْ يُصَلَّبُواْ أَوْ تُقَطَّعَ أَيْدِيهِمْ
وَأَرْجُلُهُم مِّنْ خِلافٍ أَوْ يُنفَوْاْ مِنَ الأَرْضِ ... * إِلاَّ الَّذِينَ تَابُواْ..﴾

Indeed the requital of those who wage war against Allah and His Apostle, and try to cause corruption on the earth, is that they shall be slain or crucified, or have their hands and feet cut off from opposite sides or be banished from the land ... excepting those who repent,

Rashīd Riḍa, al-Manar Interpretation, *Tafsīr al-Manār*, Cairo, Part 5, pp. 366-367, and Sayyid Quṭb, *In the Light of Quran* (*Fī Ẓilāl al-Qur'an*), Cairo, Dār al-Shurūq Publication, 1986, Part 2, pp. 877-880, on interpreting these verses.

21. Riḍwān al-Sayyid "*Politics of Contemporary Islam* (*Siyassat al-Islam al-Mu'asir*), p. 141, and Abbās Khāmah-Yār, *Iran and the Muslim Brotherhood* (*Iran wa al-Ikhwan al-Muslemon*), translated by 'Abd al-Amīr al-Sā'idī, Beirut, Strategic Studies Center, 1997, p. 226, and Hamid Enāyat, *Islamic Contemporary Political Thought* (*Al-Fikr al-Siyasi al-Islami al-Mu'asir*), translated by Ibrahim Desouqi Shatta, Cairo, Madbuli, 1988.

22. KhosroShāhi, *Islam Commandos*, p. 110.

23. Fouad Ibrahim, *The Jurisprudent and the State*, p. 371.

24. Mohsen Kadivar, *The Theories of State in Shi'ite Jurisprudence* (in Farsi: *Nazariyye-hāye Dowlat Dar feqh-e Shī'i*), Tehran, Ney Publication, 1998, p. 21, and Thomas W. Lippman, *Islam, Politics and Religion in the Muslim World*, Arabic translation with title of *Jama'āt al-Islam al-Siyāsī*, translated by Rif'at al-Sayyid Ahmad, Yafa for Studies and Publishing, Cairo, 1989, pp. 17-18.

25. *Contemporary Islamic Thought*, op. cit., pp. 119-122 and p. 123.

26. Ibid., op. cit, p. 125.

27. Op. cit., pp. 123-124.

28. Op. cit., pp. 126.

29. *Contemporary Islamic Thought*, op. cit., pp. 128-129.

30. Op. cit.

31. Op. cit.

32. Op. cit.

33. Al-Faḍl Shalaq, *Ijtihād Magazine,* V. 5, 1989, p. 231.

34. The response of Soroush to Muṭahharī's article in the book *The Turban for the Crown*, p. 250, should be taken into consideration.

35. *Contemporary Islamic Thought*, op. cit., pp. 134-135.

36. Op. cit.

37. Op. cit.

38. *Contemporary Islamic Thought*, op. cit., pp. 134-137.

39. 'Alī Sharī'atī, *A Set of Relics* (*Majmou 'al-Athār*), Tehran, Ilham, 1988, pp. 23 and 250.

40. Group of Researchers, *A Close Look at Martyr Muṭahharī's Life* (*Jawlatun Fi Hayat al-Shahid Muṭahharī*), Beirut, Dār al-Hādī, 1997, pp. 127-128.

41. *Contemporary Islamic Thought*, op. cit., p. 148.

42. Op. cit., p. 149.

43. *Contemporary Islamic Thinking*, pp. 150-151.

44. Op. cit., pp. 152-153.

45. See the following consecutively: Bāzargān, *Madhhab dar Oroupa*, (*Religion in Europe*), Tehran, Islamic Culture Publication, p. 115; *Kār dar Islam*, (*Work in Islam*), Tehran, Islamic Culture Publication, p. 3; *The Mission and Ideology*, Mashhad, Dar Tolu', pp. 95-96; *Behind Inference*, Tehran, Inteshar, p. 36; *Āfāq-e Tawhid* (*Horizons of Monotheism*), Tehran, Islamic Culture Publication, p. 57; *Marz-e Miyān-e Din va Siyāsat*, (*The Board between Religion and Politics*), Tehran, Inteshar, pp. 45-46, pp. 7-9 and pp. 53-36; *Entezār az Din* (*Expectations from Religion*), Tehran, Inteshar, pp. 353-355.

46. *Expectations from Religion*, op. cit., pp. 332-339.

47. Hosseiniyeh Ershād.

48. 'Alī Sharī'atī, *Mi'ad Ba Ibrahim*, p. 384.

49. _____, *Islamic Studies* (*Islam Shenasi*), Tehran, Hosseiniyeh Ershad, pp. 18-29.

50. _____, *'Alī Sharī'atī Talked in this Way* (*Hakadha Takallama 'Alī Sharī'atī*), pp. 200-201.

51. Op. cit.

52. 'Alī Sharī'atī, *What We Should do?* (*Cheh Bayad Kard*), p. 207,

53. _____, *'Alī Sharī'atī Talked in this Way*, (*Hakadha Takallama 'Alī Sharī'atī*), pp. 35 and 38-39.

54. Op. cit., p. 175.

55. 'Alī Sharī'atī, *Islamic Studies*, p. 184 and pp. 167-169.

56. Op. cit., pp. 181-184.

57. 'Alī Sharī'atī, *'Alī Sharī'atī Talked in this Way* (*Hakadha Takalama 'Alī Sharī'atī*), p. 105.

58. _____, *Dialogue Alone* (*Goft wa Gohāye Tanhayee*), Vol. 2, pp. 1266-1278.

59. *Islamic Studies*, pp. 159-160 and 170.

60. 'Alī Sharī'atī, *Cheh Bayad Kard*, pp. 373-385.

61. Op. cit.

62. *Criticism and Perspective Magazine*, Qom, Iran, Vols. 3 and 4, 1998.

63. Mehrzād Brojerdy, *Roshanfakran Irani wa Gharb*, translated by Jamshid Shirazi, Tehran, Farzan, 1998, p. 191.

64. Hossein Nasr, *Islamic Studies*, Beirut, United Dar, 1975, p. 20.

65. Op. cit.

66. Roshanfekran, *Irani wa Gharb*, op. cit., p. 193.

67. *Islamic Studies*, op. cit., p. 21.

68. Ibid., p. 28.

69. Op. cit., p. 38.

70. Op. cit., pp. 31-32.

71. Op. cit., p 32.

72. *Islamic Studies*, p. 33.

73. Op. cit., p. 34.

74. Sayyed Hossein Nasr, *Mysticism Between Yesterday and Today* (*Al-Sufeyah Bayena al-Ams Wa al-Youm*), Beirut, United Dar, 1975, pp. 64-65.

75. Ibid., op. cit., p. 67.

76. *Islamic Studies*, p. 35.

77. Op. cit.

78. Roget Garoudy, *Islam* (*Al-Islam*), p. 15.

79. 'Alī Sharī'atī, *Nation and Leadership*, (*Al-Ummah wa al-Imāmah*), p. 38.

80. Imām Khomeinī, *Revolution Journal*, Tehran, Ministry of Culture and Islamic Guidance, pp. 19 and 44.

81. Imām Khomeinī, *Uprightness and Stability*, p. 339; *Analects*, Vol. 1, p. 103 and p. 55; *Revolution Journal*, pp. 25 and 13-14.

82. Kamel Hashim, *Manifestations of Political Policy in Imām Khomeinī's Thought* (*Ishrāqāt al-Falsafa al-Seyāsiya fe Fikr al-Imām Khomeinī*), Islamic Contemporary Issues, Vol. 1, Centre of Religion Philosophy Studies in Baghdad, p. 55.

83. Imām Khomeinī, *Islamic Government* (*Al-Hukumat al-Islamiyah*), 1st ed., Tehran, Foundation of the Imam's Legacy Publication and Organization, 1996, p. 216.

84. Op. cit., p 35.

85. Al-Hāshimi, op. cit., and Khomeini, *Islamic Government*, p. 35, *Revolution Journal*, pp. 37-38.

86. Al-Hāshimi, op. cit., p. 67.

87. *Islamic Government*, op. cit., p. 198.

88. Op. cit., p. 186.

89. Op. cit., pp. 127-166. Compare with p. 23.

90. *Islamic Government*, op. cit., pp. 207-209.

91. Op. cit., pp. 198-199.

92. Op. cit., pp. 199-220.

93. *Islamic Government*, op. cit., pp. 47-48, 53-65, 65-68 and 91-182.

94. Op. cit., pp. 91-182.

95. Imām Khomeinī, *Message to Constitution Maintenance Council*, 12/12/1988, and *Statement to Scientific Seminaries and References*, Ragab 1404 AH/1989 AD.

96. Ibrahim al-Abbady, *Ijtihād and Renewal* (*Al-Ijtihād wa al-Tajdid*), Contemporary Islamic Issues, 3, pp. 43-49.

CHAPTER 2

MURTAḌA MUṬAHHARĪ: BIOGRAPHY, EXPERIENCE AND INTELLECTUAL PATHS

1

BIOGRAPHY

Murtaḍa Muṭahharī was born in 1338 AH in Farīmān, a village in Khurāsān, in the midst of the events which have been discussed. His father, Shaykh Muḥammad Ḥossein Muṭahharī, was a pious and righteousness man of belief. Muṭahharī was raised by his father, whose ascetic way of life and consciousness of Allah greatly inspired him. This early stage of his life left an indelible mark on his spiritual and moral development, and was to shape his outlook throughout his life.

Muṭahharī began his education at one of the schools in his village, where he learnt how to read and write and memorise the Qur'an. He also studied the grammar, literature, rhetoric and morphology of the Arabic language.

In the year 1350 AH, at the age of twelve, Muṭahharī moved to Mashhad and enrolled in its *ḥawzah*. Over the next five years he was occupied with the study of logic, philosophy, the fundamentals of *sharī'ah* and Arabic literature, and completed the necessary preliminaries in the sciences that form the basis for specialisation in *sharī'ah* and philosophy. During this time, as he himself acknowledged, he exhibited an inclination towards the rational sciences.

However, while he was still twelve years old, he decided to move to the city of Qom. He was driven by a passionate desire to join its *ḥawzah* so that he could attend lessons with its eminent scholars. This dominated his thoughts, despite the decline of the religious establishment and the challenges of the systemic repression during the reign of Rezā Khān. This was in effect a leap into the unknown, with unclear prospects.[1]

Following his arrival in Qom, Muṭahharī attended the classes of three of its renowned scholars: Sayyid Ṣadr al-Dīn al-Ṣadr, Sayyid Muḥammad Muhaqqiq and Sayyid Hossein Hujjat. Between 1361 and 1373 AH he attended the classes of Imām Khomeinī on philosophy and mysticism, which were given each week on Thursdays and Fridays. This period of study was without doubt the most fruitful. It shaped his personality, gave structure to his thoughts, and helped determine his choices in the field of knowledge and in his later endeavours. The impact of a revolutionary, intellectual personality of such stature as Imām Khomeinī on the character of Muṭahharī was clear throughout his life, and right up to the time of the Revolution.

During this period, he also attended the classes of Ayatullāh Borūjerdī, the most prominent religious figure and the leading jurisprudent in Iran at the time. Ayatullāh Borūjerdī was the unequivocal leader of the religious *ḥawzah* in Qom, and it was during his classes that Muṭahharī became acquainted with Ayatullāh Muntaẓerī, who would later partner him in his intellectual journey and the course of his struggle.

In 1362 AH, Muṭahharī fortuitously met with one of the prominent scholars of Isfahan, Mirzā 'Alī al-Shīrāzī, and was able to attend his classes on the *Nahj al-Balāghah* during the summer of that year. This man transformed Muṭahharī's attitude towards the book, shaking his conscience and having a marked influence on his thought. The deep immersion in the inner meanings of the *Nahj al-Balāghah* and its mysteries that this scholar provided truly impressed him, and the book *Glimpses of Nahj al-Balāghah* was an outcome of this stage in his life.[2]

In addition to his unfaltering preoccupation with his research in Qom, Muṭahharī also had a study circle in which he gave lessons in logic, philosophy, theology, *Nahj al-Balāghah* and the principles of jurisprudence. He was an avid reader, and was particularly familiar with books on Marxism, which had captured the minds of his generation. Publications on Marxism were popular and readily available in Iran, and they left a significant mark on an entire generation of young people. He read the books of Arāni on the precepts of Marxism concerning man, existence, revolution and change, and was up to date with material published by the Tudeh Party. All this formed the basis of his subsequent thoughts concerning Marxism, and was the foundation for his later refutation of it in works such as *Society and History*, *A Critique of Marxism*,

The Fundamentals of Philosophy and *The Causes Responsible for Materialist Tendencies* amongst others.

Due to Muṭahharī's inclination towards the rational sciences, he began attending the classes of 'Allamah Ṭabāṭabā'ī, which focused on Avicennian philosophy and research into the Islamic philosophical heritage in general. Since his teacher was aware of Muṭahharī's deep interest in these matters, he organised an additional research group to contrast materialistic philosophy with Islamic philosophy, and the book *Fundamentals of Philosophy and Realism* was an outcome of these sessions.[3] Through the lessons that he gave for many years, and upon which he spent most of his time, 'Allamah Ṭabāṭabā'ī was able to open up Muṭahharī's understanding of the infinite dimensions of the Qur'an. In fact, this was an extremely rare opportunity within a religious institution that was mainly concerned with jurisprudence more than other disciplines.

During this period in particular, the religious seminary began to feel the effects of the intellectual milieu that had burgeoned within Iran from the beginning of the century, in addition to the growing call for reform. Both Ṭabāṭabā'ī and Imām Khomeinī were involved in this new and growing awareness. Sweeping changes in all areas served to kindle Muṭahharī's desire to identify the challenges confronting Iranian society and the wider Islamic *ummah*. As a result, he retreated in order to contemplate the facts and gain insight with an open mind.

Later on, he got involved in social and political activities run by certain progressive scholars in Qom. Since the religious seminary was not prepared to accommodate reform movements, let alone the idea of introducing Islam into the arena of reformatory legislation in the manner envisioned by Imām Khomeinī and those he had influenced, Muṭahharī subsequently left Qom and moved to Tehran.[4]

Muṭahharī arrived in Tehran in 1373 AH,[5] and married the daughter of one of the renowned scholars of Khurāsān. Later, he convened a special study circle at the Marwy School, where he delivered lessons on philosophy, jurisprudence and Qur'anic exegesis, which continued for a number of years. In 1374 AH, he published his first article in the *Journal of Hekmat* in Qom. In 1376 AH, he published the first part of his book *Fundamentals of Philosophy and Realism*.

In the same year, Tehran University invited him to teach at the College of Theology, and he duly accepted. In addition to his normal teaching responsibilities, he also sought to guide the young people by reviving the values of Islam and directing their concern towards the need for change. He spent nearly twenty-two years at the University of Tehran, which was to be the most fruitful and influential phase of his life.

At this time, Ḥosseiniyeh Ershād was the most prominent foundation of guidance in Tehran, and was the source of the initial sparks of change and reform. It was a platform for a considerable group of reform figures, such as 'Alī Davāni, Mahdī Bāzargān, Dr. Sahabi, 'Alī Sharī'atī and his father Muḥammad Taqi Sharī'atī, as well as Muṭahharī himself. Milestones of contemporary Iran's intellectual and political awakening were established within the walls of this centre.

During this period, Muṭahharī maintained contact with the developing movements within society, and as a result he faced persecution from the apparatus of the state. He kept abreast of various ideas, whether they were considered to be Islamic, as was the case with the ideas of Bāzargān and Sharī'atī, or of liberal, Marxist, nationalist or patriotic tendencies. From time to time he initiated heated debates, some generating agreement, while others resulted in differences and disputes. Yet Muṭahharī's ultimate goal in this respect was to amend the reformist tendency and guide it, so that it could reap the fruits of its struggle. Furthermore, he wanted to ensure that mistakes of the past which resulted in failure were not repeated.[6] Throughout this time he was in constant contact with Imām Khomeinī, who was in exile in France, thereby keeping the Imam informed of what was going on. Since Muṭahharī made no compromise by staying silent about the attempts to exploit Islam for worldly objectives, and thereby deforming its message, he never missed a chance to speak out in this respect. He subsequently became a permanent target of those who had such aims. As a result, in 1399 AH, nearly three months after the triumph of the Revolution, he was killed by an extremist religious group known as *Furqān*.[7]

This had been the richest period in Muṭahharī's life in terms of his endeavours. The realisation of the desired objectives of his cause and that of others resulted in the emergence of the Islamic Revolution. Furthermore, he produced a multi-faceted epistemological output that is unparalleled in the profound impact it had during this period of modern Iranian history.

2

INTELLECTUAL AND POLITICAL STRUGGLE

Muṭahharī's political cause went together with his intellectual work. Since his arrival in the city of Qom, the concerns of the moment had preoccupied him. Despite what he saw of the sorrows and failures, the beginning of a new era nonetheless loomed on the horizon. His determination was motivated by the firm belief he sensed in the person of Imām Khomeinī at this time of hope for the future, and in the inevitability of a victory over all the obstacles.[8]

The conservatism of Qom was quite often not an ideal environment for Muṭahharī to pursue his activities, for according to him, Islam was a reality that transcended far beyond the limits of lessons in jurisprudence drawn from a stagnant past and lifeless rites that were completely isolated from the affairs of life.

From the very beginning, he was keenly aware of the negative consequences of the isolation of the religious establishment from its responsibility towards reform, having abandoned its role in instilling Islam within society by guiding its course and responding to the challenges it faced. Muṭahharī was firmly convinced of the hazards brought about by a distorted and fragmentary understanding of the teachings and legislation of religion, especially at a time when foreign ideas, materialism and an overly liberal ethical outlook were sweeping through society. But on the other hand, it was a perfect moment for disseminating an Islamic perspective. Young people had a thirst for knowledge, and sought convincing answers to their questions. They needed a clear programme for defining a quest for justice and freedom, for their high aspirations of overcoming a bitter reality had been transformed by the tyrannical authority of the state into a submissiveness, without the will to determine their future.

Whilst in Qom, the first activities Muṭahharī participated in were those of the Shi'ite School, the Islam School and the School of Monotheism.[9] It was through these institutions that he published some of his works that essentially outlined the nature of his Islamic vision. He expressed his understanding of the role of Islam, and his profound perception of the tragic circumstances which had overtaken society. His lectures and activities revolved around two fundamental topics: the necessary comprehensive revival of Islamic teachings with active participation in response to the pressing issues of the time, and a thorough analysis of the causes of the present problems. Plans were to be drawn up for a complete awakening in the light of Islamic teachings, benefiting from experience and failure, and utilising the power of mobilisation. Large numbers of young people, academics and university students were responsive and firmly determined, and this would pave the way for an exit from the cycle of political tyranny, social degradation, and both material and moral poverty.

Muṭahharī's move to Tehran was a vital point in his political and intellectual career, for it was there that he realised his vision was correct, and he was to begin to find it translated into reality. He witnessed the cruellest form of political tyranny, but on the other hand, although failing to reach its desired goal, there was an active mobilisation for an overall regeneration.

Within such a turbulent climate and the many opportunities for action, Muṭahharī highlighted the strengths and weaknesses which could be factors of either success or failure. He had witnessed some of these first-hands, and realised that the atmosphere was still ripe for a fundamental change that could unify the existing capabilities, whose programmes needed to be defined. Consequently, he took upon himself the responsibility of instigating activities towards this end. In this regard, he delivered lectures, went to meetings, and organised debates for guiding the opposition groups. He also sought to educate the new generation in Islamic concepts and values, and challenged those intellectual and political currents – whether Eastern or Western – he deemed hazardous to the identity and values of his society. Moreover, he sought to remedy the false notions that exploited Islam for worldly interest and meagre benefit, which served neither the issue of reform nor the ultimate purpose of awakening.

Since he believed that individual action was neither feasible nor adequate, he valued those who shared his convictions and vision, and found them to be his foremost allies in his struggle. His aspiration was to form a large movement from this group of people, which combined all that was needed for recovery. This movement would lead the way and crystallise its vision through debates. In general, his relationship with these people was a real and effective partnership, which first began with the likes of Bāzargān, 'Alī Sharī'atī, Beheshti, Muḥammad Sharī'atī and Bāhonar. Later, it became an organisation for instigating activities through the Islamic Coalition Association, which comprised various religious currents. A distinct feature of this Association was the formation of gatherings that focused on instruction. Along with other scholars, Martyr Muṭahharī's role was to educate and deepen awareness, forming an organisation with a firm vision of its objectives and strategy.[10]

The well-known book *Man and Destiny* was a result of Muṭahharī's participation in this group. Since he believed that any successful movement must address contemporary problems at all levels, including the political, he therefore engaged in open confrontation with the political authorities. He fully recognised the danger of the state playing a negative role, and that any substantive change within society could not be realised in the shadow of a tyranny that stripped the people of their freedom and dignity, pushing them to the brink of moral and social breakdown, and spiritual ineffectiveness. Therefore, he began to be openly active in the wake of the decisive stance taken by Imām Khomeinī and his supporters against the Shāh in 1962, following the Faydiyya Massacre and the Shāh's earlier declaration of the referendum for constitutional reform. Muṭahharī formed the link between Imām Khomeinī and the movements that stood against the Shāh. He united the reform movements and the public at large through his speeches and statements, in which he would define a methodology of action.

During this period, the government recognised the danger posed by the reformist clergy that was threatening its existence. The state was astonished by the power set in motion by Imām Khomeinī's opposition, and in 1963 he was arrested. Subsequently, the state brought in a law imposing military service on the clergy as a means of suppression. Muṭahharī was included amongst them, and whilst serving at one of the military camps, he took the opportunity to propagate religious awareness within the ranks of the soldiers, by acting as a guide and educator. However, his activities were discovered, but he managed to flee from the camp before he was arrested. He then resumed his role, sometimes in public, at other times secretly. He led discussions on guidance, maintaining contact with the reformist cultural élite as well as the masses.

After the exile of Imām Khomeinī, Muṭahharī played an important role in mobilising the public in line with the Imam's movement. He continued doing this after the assassination of the Shāh's Prime Minister by the Coalition Committee – a movement that was directed by Muṭahharī himself – and the imprisonment of its leaders, despite the difficulties faced because of the Shāh's anger towards him and what was happening.

Notwithstanding the intense surveillance of Muṭahharī during this critical period, he resumed his activities in a different form, namely that of an intellectual confrontation. He challenged the atheistic tendencies, along with the materialistic, nihilist and nationalist currents within society. In addition, he confronted doctrines which advocated a false compromise between Islam and Western revolutionary ideologies, including other forms of Westernisation. He clashed with some groups that were in fact part of the movement of awakening, such as the People's Mujahedin of Iran, which had structured an ideology based on a distorted fusion of leftist Islamic revolutionary teachings and Marxism, and lacked an adequate understanding of the principles of Islam. Those who subscribed to this group were attracted by the ideas of 'Alī Sharī'atī.

The richest and most profound aspects of Muṭahharī's work, from their very beginnings, occurred during this time, and right up to the final days of the Shāh's regime. Upon the triumph of the Revolution, his efforts focused on organising the affairs of the Revolution, establishing a systematic framework and refining its structure and legislation through his work in the Revolution Command Council, to which he had been personally appointed by Imām Khomeinī to establish and preside over. However, during the early months of the Revolution his struggle came to end. He died a martyr on its altar, a sacrifice for its goals and principles.

3

THE ASPECTS OF HIS SCIENTIFIC PERSONALITY

His Educational Background

Through his structured education in both Mashhad and Qom, Muṭahharī was able to gain a firm and comprehensive grasp on the various Islamic sciences. He reviewed the resources of Islamic culture and familiarised himself with the foundational texts of Arabic and Persian literature. The sciences which he spent years studying can be summarised as follows:

> Important theosophical texts, Persian literature, such as the writings of Ḥafiz, Sa'dī and Jalāl al-Dīn al-Rūmī, and ethical Sufi poetry;
>
> A broad knowledge of historical and contemporary Arabic literature, and Arabic grammar, conjugation, expression and rhetoric. This enabled him to teach the language for many years, particularly in Qom.[11]
>
> Mastery of the Persian language, which was apparent in his many citations of foundational texts, his clear and fluent language with a beauty of style and simplicity of structure. As regards his vast knowledge of the Arabic language, it became apparent in his comprehension of its meanings and a deep understanding of its important texts, such as the Qur'an, Hadith literature and the Nahj al-Balāghah. Furthermore, he showed a great ability to

understand complicated and idiomatic Arabic philosophical texts written by writers of various affiliations.

An encyclopaedic knowledge of the Islamic sciences, the principles and interpretation of *fiqh* and contemporary Qur'anic studies. This was a result of the many lessons with prominent scholars during his education in Qom.

A shrewd understanding of Islamic philosophy, theology, Sufism, theosophy and ethics, as a result of the congregational sessions of 'Allamah Ṭabāṭabā'i – who was in charge of these sciences, especially philosophy – and Mahdī Ashtīanī. Furthermore, he immersed himself in the lessons of the Imām Khāmeneī in ideological and cognitive studies, and was known for his deep interest in psychology, as is apparent in his own work, which will be demonstrated later on.

Muṭahharī had a special way of dealing with these resources, that helped shape his education and intellectual development. He was aware of the unity of these sciences, and the fact that they belonged to a comprehensive structure of knowledge represented by the Qur'an and *Sunnah*, which contain the basic principles for all ways of life. Acquiring a comprehensive knowledge of the Islamic intellectual heritage is necessary for Muslim thinkers, as one cannot understand the essence and universality of Islam without it.[12]

In addition to his expertise in the principles of all the Islamic sciences, Muṭahharī was also familiar with their historical formation. He assumed that this was crucial for understanding their depth, and benefit from them by utilising them in the light of new developments.

Muṭahharī's comprehensive knowledge of Islam allowed him to face the Western trends that shook Muslim culture, boring into the minds of the people and affecting their existence. This was apparent in his writings, whether by allocating a section of it to a discussion of the Marxist view of the world and its social system, or by trying to disprove the materialistic and humanistic Western philosophies and their social, legal and political outlooks.[13]

Furthermore, in addition to all his sources of information, Muṭahharī had a sufficient knowledge of the various aspects of Western philosophy, sociology and politics, and the fruits of the relevant natural sciences and their protocols. In order to keep himself informed, he read the writings of cultured expatriates and enlightened intellectuals, and Persian translations of his preferred scholars, intellectuals and reformers. His unfamiliarity with Western languages put a renowned scholar such as himself at a disadvantage that one cannot ignore, causing his relevant views and arguments to be limited.

His Scientific Attitude

Muṭahharī had many scientific interests that set him apart, and which manifested equally in his teachings and activities, some of which are as follows:

> His deep faith in his vision and the principles he advocated and struggled for, and to which he firmly adhered without being exclusive or intolerant.
>
> The precise approach of his thinking and his methods of solving problems. He always reviewed the issues that preoccupied him in detail, in order to shed light on their history and accurately describe them, and establish logical connections between them. He took time to deliberate on his conclusions, with a noticeable ability to analyse, interpret and explain.

Muṭahharī had a penetrating mind that refused to blindly imitate ideas, even if they were firmly established and widely accepted as facts. He approached them with an astute and critical analysis, without falling victim to their power and charm or cohesive logic. He would neither accept nor reject an opinion without discernible proof.[14]

He had a unique way of reading and studying – a method he never strayed from. He would only move on from a book after the issues discussed therein had settled in his mind and he understood them, even if he had to read it several times in the process. Only then would he turn to another book on the same or a similar subject, which he would read in the same fashion in an attempt to learn more. He did this out of a conviction that one's mind was like a library, where books should be categorised for ease of reference. Otherwise subjects would get mixed up, making it difficult to organise them and benefit from them. This reading method enabled Muṭahharī to get the utmost out of his learning.[15]

It is worth mentioning that his writings dealt with topics much needed by society, considering the problems it faced, and they were approached in order of importance. He considered purely academic subjects, which did not relate to everyday life and solve its problems, to be an impractical intellectual luxury.[16]

Muṭahharī always reviewed his writings, adding or deleting where necessary. He also subjected them to the review and criticism of his students, colleagues or friends before sending them to a publishing house or distributing them. He felt no shame in retracting an argument if it were shown to be insufficient or false, which he would do with great courtesy and humility.

His style of language teachings was exemplary; both uncomplicated and eloquent. Even the most complex subjects were made easier to understand with each utterance or stroke of the pen. These attributes not only reveal Muṭahharī's linguistic and communicative skills, but also a comprehensive understanding of the ideas he taught, and the ability to simplify terminology in ways he could use however he wished.[17]

Muṭahharī was a great believer in freedom of thought, but he was not all words and no action. His beliefs were accompanied by action and a conviction proven by practice. He always emphasised everyone's right to announce their own views without being afraid or hindered, and the fact that Islam guaranteed freedom of thought, upheld good intentions and disapproved of deception.[18] Muṭahharī assumed that this was the best way to challenge the opinions of others, since suppression is self-defeating.[19] In addition, the vision of Islam can only be preserved by sciences that use logic, reason, persuasion and proof to challenge the opinions of others, and not through the imposition of its ideas and persecution.[20]

Muṭahharī also balanced the needs of the mind and those of the soul; he did not pursue matters of the mind to the exclusion of worship, self-discipline and ethics. When he recited the Qur'an or prayed, he was known to always do so with the commitment and responsibility that worship demands, and was attuned to the profound spiritual meaning it represents. All these attributes were part of his thought and work, making him a unique personality in his convictions, behaviour and goals.

4

THE INTELLECTUAL METHODS PORTRAYED IN HIS WRITINGS

It is not difficult to ascertain the concerns of Martyr Muṭahharī's thought and cultural activity. Despite their wide variety, they make up a comprehensive vision that serves the clear purpose of progress and reform. Muṭahharī presented his ideas in so many different talks and publications, that it would be virtually impossible to itemise them. They were inspired by his struggle, and formed by practical experience in the midst of tense and fast-moving events.

It is worth mentioning that Muṭahharī did not use his writings to compose an unrealistic theory. This was no futuristic vision that did not take into account the existing facts or something that might befall society without warning, for he could not forget the disappointing results of previous social experiments.

For that very reason it is difficult to define his intellectual output by category in order to itemise his writings under clear headings. They were generally written in answer to immediate philosophical and intellectual challenges. Yet they all served the specific purpose of defining the general direction of the reform movement. This created solid foundations for answering new challenges, and drawing together various objectives in order to benefit from a progressive experiment. This would allow it to reach its main objective with self-reliance, and transform words into action. Therefore, it would not simply remain a memory of an empty utopia, nothing more than a dream that brought hope to the heart, a vain theory lacking the cohesion necessary for its implementation, having neglected to realistically observe the changes within society.

Since the reform project occupied Muṭahharī the most and consumed most of his intellectual output, it is understandable that all the various other subjects are closely related to this issue in one way or another. They serve the same purpose directly or indirectly, whether in confronting the dominant intellectual trends, both Eastern and Western, facing the perverse use of religious concepts and the intellectual stagnation resulting from its isolation from reality, evaluating the renaissance processes witnessed at the end of the 19th century and the beginning of the 20th century in the Islamic world, or by reforming the Islamic sciences and developing methods for understanding them, so that they may serve the demands of the time.

If we wish to explain the events that had an effect on Muṭahharī's ideas, we would have to divide them into a comprehensive pattern and secondary patterns. As regards the comprehensive pattern, it would be the project of reform, which demanded of Muṭahharī a careful reading of the causes of the deterioration, and the stages of its negative effects. This would have to be done before reflecting on the obstacles that stand in the way of a comprehensive renewal reaching all the levels of society, methods by which the deterioration can be overcome, and realistic practical and intellectual conditions for guaranteeing success.

As regards the secondary patterns, they can be divided into three, as follows:

1. Recreating a comprehensive universal vision of Islam and its philosophical view of the world, and consolidating its position with regards to history and society, since it is an all-inclusive ideology that provides a clear vision of the purpose of our existence. This would be done by reviewing without prejudice the horizons of human knowledge, and calmly surveying the experiences of cultures and intellectual traditions of other nations, free of preconceived ideas. Furthermore, the legal system of Islam should be reformed in a way that ensures compliance with the complex conditions of an evolving society, enabling it to face the challenges of new and immediate questions, by setting free the principles of *ijtihād* and reflecting upon the universal laws of Islam, and challenging stagnation and insularity.

2. Confronting the misinterpretation of Islam and its teachings, the triviality with which its principles have been handled, the disfigurement of its legislations, whether deliberate or not, and the immediate and expedient application of its key ideas in the cause of freedom, justice, equality and human rights.
3. Impartially and unemotionally evaluating the authenticity of foreign imported ideologies and those who support them through calm, logical discussion and rational dialogue.

Each of these patterns required Muṭahharī to occupy himself with topics which contributed to the comprehensive pattern under which they could be effectively included, deliberating on them with extreme patience and penetrating insight, and a clear understanding of the potential results. This was a process that required a vigour and perseverance which one person rarely possesses. We will briefly discuss these patterns in light of their output, but we will deal with them in detail in the later chapters.

1. The General Pattern: Recession and Renewal

It is not possible for a vision regarding a project of renewal to exist without reflecting on the regression that has dominated the Islamic world for centuries, leading it to weakness and a disassociation that prevented it from actively participating in the progress of civilisation up to the present time. For this reason, the beginning of every project for an intellectual revival concerned itself with the issue of regression, whether broadly speaking or with limited connotations. This has been repeated several times during the last century, constantly asserting itself without losing its relevance. There is no meaning in a quest in which Muslims overcome their present conditions and cross over to a new one without providing this issue with an answer to the question of what were the conditions that contributed to its cause. Like all theorists and reformists, this question plagued Muṭahharī, dominating his being and driving him to come up with a visionary project through which he could identify the factors which generated it, and might give it coherence and stability.

Muṭahharī presented the outlines of his vision in many of his compilations, and expressly referred to it in a number of his lectures. We can find it in books such as: *Islam and the Demands of the Era, Man and His Destiny, Society and History, Glimpses of Nahj al-Balāghah, Immigration and Jihad, Martyr on the Martyr, Rationality of Islam, The End of Prophecy* and many others. But we will touch on their general characteristics as featured in the detailed introduction of his book, *Man and His Destiny*, or *Man and Predestination*.

He summarised the general factors for ensuring a renaissance of Islam in his research for *Rationality of Islam*. He did this also in his brief study of Islamic movements of the last century in his more comprehensive book, *Islam and the Demands of the Era*, where he identified the reasons for their failure. We shall restrict ourselves to the main ideas of this vision as presented in that book.

Muṭahharī starts by talking about deterioration in the Islamic world, and identifies the time when this problem started to preoccupy him, by saying,

> "I do not know precisely when I confronted the failings of Muslims, or when I personally first explored the topic, but I can definitely say that this issue has been lying before me for over twenty years, beckoning me to ponder it and read what others wrote about it."[21]

This subject had such a great hold on his thought that he began reading everything he could find concerning it and attending lectures.

However, this merely left him feeling dissatisfied, and he was consequently prompted to contemplate all the dimensions of this problem, and personally try to find methods that would ensure the present conditions of the Islamic world would change. He did this by carefully reading about the seeds of deterioration planted in the past, that had grown over the centuries, and remained alive in our present time. Muṭahharī briefly states,

> "Ever since then I would passionately read every book and listen to every speech pertaining to this topic. I was eager to accurately learn the opinions of each speaker and writer, because discovering a method of reforming the present conditions in the Islamic world is closely linked to knowing the past causes of this regression, and those that are present in our very time."[22]

Due to his deep foresight, Muṭahharī was able to perceive the many dimensions of this subject, which cannot be completely researched by a single person no matter what his gifts and qualifications. Even so, he insisted on pursuing the issue in an attempt to discover more solutions, and pave the way for others to contribute with their own opinions. In this regard, he said,

> "At that point, I had perceived the vast dimensions of this subject, and I knew that if I were to conduct a comprehensive scientific investigation regarding it, I would have to include a large number of topics. Furthermore, such an investigation is beyond the ability of a single person; or rather, it requires many years of research and thorough examination. Even so, I have decided – by way of a prelude – to mention the relevant studies in a categorised and summarised form, and investigate some topics to provide a sample study and enable others to do so."[23]

Over the course of many pages of this prelude, Muṭahharī attempted to present a general framework, while stressing on the importance of assessing the problem by subject, without concealing the facts no matter how bitter, and the importance of an unapologetic commitment to truth and clarity. This would be carried out while maintaining open-mindedness towards what non-Muslims say, dealing with their ideas and benefiting from their historical and intellectual efforts in order to acquire a clear view of all the parameters.

According to Muṭahharī, the study of this topic falls into several categories:

- Sociological research within Islam in the present era.
- Historical and philosophical research relevant to the rise and fall of civilisations.
- Determining the development of ideas from their inception and the accompanying conditions, and how these ideas affect behaviour patterns and serve the purposes of the Movement for Social Humanism, including the identification of how Islamic epistemology has shifted from its true meaning in matters such as predestination, ethics and faith, to a *Salafi* mentality and a cognitive impasse regarding religion.
- Analysis of the paradigms determining the growth of the Movement for Social Humanism and their resulting impact.[24]

In fact, Muṭahharī did not have the opportunity to conduct detailed research on all these levels. However, when discussing these matters, he would always stress that dealing with them requires special attention in order to get a comprehensive result. Despite its urgency, he unfortunately found that the project required more time, better conditions and greater intellectual resources than he alone possessed.

However, he did provide researchers with three themes relevant to social deterioration:

- The nature of Islam's role in this framework. Muṭahharī enters a profound discussion on an idea rooted in a philosophy of history that states that the relative strength of a civilisation is a cause of its deterioration. Islam was the basis of growth in periods of prosperity, but later became an obstacle to progress, and a direct cause of regression. He discusses this in various books,[25] in particular *Islam and the Demands of the Era.*
- The relationship between this project and the first of the alternative paths previously discussed. It is necessary to revive Islam, since it is an ideology that can be applied anywhere and at any time.
- The relationship between this project and Muslims and their effectiveness as a civilisation, the way in which Islamic principles and values are dealt with, and intellectual decline.
- The relationship between this project and other factors, such as political tyranny, the lack of free thought, colonialism, and cultural and intellectual dispersion.[26]

This was all about deterioration, but we also find that Muṭahharī focussed on renewal. Indeed, he gave it much attention, since it was the accompanying element in a complete vision of reform.

According to Muṭahharī,[27] Muslims have been familiar with revival for a very long time. This would happen when innovation began to appear, and the light of Islam grew dim in their souls due to the changing world around them, distancing them from the glowing source of Islam, and the Prophet himself. The concept of revival is fundamental, and is not directly related to the exposure of Muslims to the West and modern technology. It did, however, truly motivate them with a commitment to revival.

Furthermore, Muṭahharī considered religious revival to be an essential pivot for the reconstruction of an Islamic civilisation, since without it a comprehensive renaissance would not occur. However, one should not be under the delusion that this requires the repetition of past experiences. On the contrary, one should ponder the origin of Islam and thoroughly understand its values, whilst maintaining an open mind towards the concerns of the present. Furthermore, Islamic principles should be rid of the negative residues of time.

Muṭahharī describes the significance of these ideas by saying,

> "When I speak of these concepts, I must touch on a subject related to it – religious revival. I was once blessed with the opportunity to address a lecture on the topic, called *Reviving Religious Thought,* where I mentioned that religion, like anything else, can develop symptoms. I also said that religion is like water pouring forth from a clear spring, yet it becomes polluted the moment it joins a river, and must be purified in order to return to its pristine state."[28]

If religious revival is the pivotal root of a comprehensive renewal, this can be brought about in several ways, a summary of which is as follows:

- Affirming Muslim identity;
- Differentiating between one definition of civilisation and another;
- Determining the purposes behind every humanitarian activity;
- Freeing up individual and social activities;
- An emphasis on planning and organisation;
- The motivation of national potential and an awareness of the future.

Muṭahharī described the effects of loss of identity in the words, "Losing one's identity is *harām* (forbidden) ... blind imitation is *harām*, loss and disappearance is *harām* ...,"[29] and so forth.

Maintaining one's identity requires above all intellectual and cultural independence, in order to maintain a balance between stagnation and the very need for renewal. According to Muṭahharī,

> "Every society has a culture, and culture expresses the spirit of the society."[30]

That is why any cultural disintegration or loss of identity leads to collapse. Muṭahharī, in an overall investigation called *The Goal of Human Life,*[31] discusses the necessity of a comprehensive vision of every human activity. While this particular book deals with attitudes that give life meaning, Muṭahharī was devoting himself to a deeper understanding of a comprehensive vision from the Islamic perspective, and the importance of introducing such a vision into the consciousness of the nation. He brought all these points together under the title of *An Introduction to the Islamic View of the World.*[32]

A brief study of Muṭahharī's under the title *Rationality of Islam*[33] brings to light his introduction to a practical framework for future planning, in which he stresses the importance of social and political development. He believed that "readiness to confront and direct the future is an indicator of social development," and that this should be in conformity with established rules that effectively influence the demands of the present. Muṭahharī stated that,

> "Scientific predictability basically relies on acknowledging the effective influences and factors of the current time, because knowing the present plays a large part in predicting the future. In order to carry out developmental action, one must be aware of the requirements of the time. Those who are not familiar with these cannot predict or control the future."[34]

This study, despite its briefness, included many other aspects to be included under the banner of a comprehensive rejuvenation of civilisation. It also provided practical examples from the lives of Muslims.[35]

Muṭahharī hinted at the importance of future planning in his book *Islamic Movements in the Last Century.* He stated that without it human resources are wasted and unique opportunities are missed, and implied that neglecting the issue has led to the failure of many contemporary Islamic movements.[36] We shall expand on this when we discuss Muṭahharī's perspective on reform in later chapters, where we resolve some of what we have briefly summarised.

2. The First Detailed Path: The Universal Look towards Islam and its Legal System

Muṭahharī has written much on this important topic. He attempted to re-establish a new concept regarding the comprehensive monotheistic vision of Islam, using his deep knowledge of the Qur'an, Islamic philosophy and his own spiritual and ethical knowledge. He dealt with this topic independently in order to demonstrate its fundamental import for both the individual and the collective. Examples of this are *Man and His*

Destiny, *Man and Predestination*, *Man and His God*, *The Goal of Life* and *The Monotheistic Vision of the World*, as well as his theological works focussing on belief issues such as monotheism, prophethood, the imamate and the afterlife. He also discussed the issue with reference to foreign intellectual trends, both Eastern and Western, in *The Basics of Philosophy and Realistic Doctrine*, *The Philosophy of Morals* and *Motivation towards Materialism*.

In addition to a universal monotheistic vision of Islam, Muṭahharī was interested in presenting principles relating to Social Humanism, human resources and history, as outlined in his book, *Society and History*. He also included guiding concepts for all spheres of life, including justice, equality, freedom, asceticism, trust, worship, *Shahada* (the attestation of faith), and so on. Such concepts complemented his overall vision.[37]

Muṭahharī wanted to revivify an effective Islamic outlook based on its complex philosophical background. He devoted himself to recovering the Islamic heritage by analysis and clarification, and then developing it. He demonstrated this in his lectures and books, such as *Articles of a Philosopher*, his exposition of the Sabzwari system, and the metaphysics of Avicenna. Muṭahharī saw Islam as a timeless and comprehensive system of ideas, behaviour and law. He considered it imperative to re-establish the *shari'ah* in compliance with present needs, since it had become isolated from people's lives, causing it to lose its vitality.

In his initial outline, Muṭahharī formed an encyclopaedic analysis of the fundamental nature and methodology of *ijtihād* and its goals. As regards his second paradigm, he was very clear about the responsibility of the religious establishment for the consequences of atrophy and isolation, and discussed this in detail in *The Fundamental Problems of the Clergy*, *Ijtihād in Islam*, *The End of Prophethood* and *Islam and the Demands of the Era*, as well as in many lectures and articles.

If a revival of Islam were to be the stable foundation for rejuvenation, then it needed to be reintroduced to address the many questions related to the world, society and destiny. In addition, it should establish justice, equality and freedom in the lives of the people in compliance with the changes in society, its increased needs and complex problems.

3. The Second Detailed Path: Confronting the Systematic Damage to Islam and its Teachings

According to Muṭahharī, two negative factors stood in the way of his intentions. Firstly, there was a weak and superficial understanding regarding the principles of such a proposal, and secondly the systematic damage done to much of the religious legislation which alienated people from its meaning, rendering it ineffective.

While the first factor would be bad enough to impede a revival of Islam, the second was more pernicious, the reason being that those who had defined various social proclivities thereby encouraged superficiality. Their attitude was unconstructive, and was no different from that of those enlightened who bragged about revision, but were preoccupied with western modernisation and prosperity, all the while disregarding their own culture, distorting its principles and having the impression that Islam is an obstacle to building a Westernised civilisation. This was like a political authority digging a deeper divide between Islam and the minds of its followers in an attempt to assert power and establish hegemony. There was no effective opposition, and so it was easy to identify the risk such people posed in winning over the minds of the people at large without difficulty. It is a complicated task to confront intellectuals and scientists, who claim religious affiliation, speak in its name and defend its principles, in order to demonstrate their mistakes, even more problematic to return them to the correct path of righteousness.

'Alī Davānī[38] tells the story of a clergyman who had a book on monotheism (*tawḥīd*) published which stirred much controversy, and helped him gain a number of supporters who believed his writings to be correct. However, when his ideas were openly discussed, he displayed a narrow-mindedness which was exploited by non-believers. Muṭahharī surveyed the incident and its negative impact. At the start of the Revolution, a group was formed in honour of this clergyman, calling itself the Furqān Group, and adopted his book, along with a number of similar texts, as its charter, and was later responsible for Muṭahharī's assassination.

Muṭahharī's experience with Ḥusayniyeh Ershād[39] and the ideas of 'Alī Sharī'atī is well known. Despite Sharī'atī's appeal to young people and his efforts to faithfully instil hopes of liberation and renewal, from Muṭahharī's point of view, some of his ideas suggested a misunderstanding of the deeper meaning of Islam; but despite that he still respected Sharīʿatī greatly for his role, his character and his capabilities.[40]

It seems that by assessing Sharīʿatī's ideas in effect aided Sharīʿatī himself, by encouraging him to re-visualise the meaning of Islam and ponder its concepts. It also served the revival movement, by helping people discern between the truth and other ideas that were thrown at them, and preventing false notions and seemingly Islamic concepts from penetrating their minds without them being aware of the dangers.[41]

Muṭahharī realised that discussing the ideas of ʿAlī Sharī'atī in public decreased their influence on the young and diminished their power. He began to tackle them in his later books and lectures, discussing them subject by subject and analysing them with sound logic without referring to their source, in order to honour his status and avoid any negative effect such a controversy might have had on young people.

Similarly, there is another account recalling the split between Muṭahharī and the People's Mujahedin of Iran, which happened at a time when there had been a division among its ranks that resulted in the formation of the communist Peykār group. Peykār publicly denounced Islam, even though the main group used to present its ideas under an Islamic guise and attract many followers.[42] The writings of Muṭahharī greatly impacted on these factors by pointing out their negative influence on young people in the context of a renaissance movement. He published his well-known book *Mutual Services of Iran and Islam* to refute their ambitions, which distorted the history and experience of Islamic civilisation in Iran. He demonstrated the absurdity of the claim that Islam destroyed Iranian culture, obliterating the traditions of a golden age of Persian civilisation, and affirmed the benefits that Iran had gained from Islam. He also wrote *The Problem of Veil*, *Woman and her Rights in Islam* and *Sexual Ethics in Islam and in the Western World* in response to those who questioned a number of issues concerning the rights and status of women, such as modesty, dowry, inheritance and polygamy.

Muṭahharī spent much time speaking out against the negative use of Islamic concepts which the Islamic Marxist revolutionary movements were widely expounding. His books *Society and History* and *Criticism of the Marxist* were an answer to this challenge, as well as being a reiteration of many of his other ideas. Nevertheless, this was somewhat of a preoccupation for Muṭahharī, since if such perversions should proliferate, the renaissance project would surely meet with a number of obstacles which would ultimately lead to failure, as had been the case with so many similar projects.

4. The Third Detailed Path: Facing Western Intellectual Challenges

At the start of the century, a number of philosophical, scientific, psychological and materialistic trends spread throughout Iran and the rest of the Islamic world, having a profound impact due to their great appeal in the eyes of the people. They invaded the minds of young people and intellectuals alike, and even affecting the teachings in the *Ḥawzahs*.

Muṭahharī realised that this posed perhaps a greater risk than the superficial understanding of the principles of Islam resulting from the distortion of its teachings. This is because it causes a loss of identity, leading to dependence and exploitation. It would result in a nation with an ineffective global presence.

Muṭahharī concentrated his efforts on contending the ethics of a materialistic doctrine, and published *The Philosophy of Morals.* He also wrote *Society and History* in reply to the historical perspective of Marxism, and *The Criticism of the Marxist* to challenge the overall doctrine. *Motivation towards Materialism* was written to demonstrate the sterility of the materialist arguments and to refute the positions of some of the great Western thinkers, such as Russell, Sartre, Hume, Dewey and others. While reading Muṭahharī's works, one comes across discussions of their ideas in books such as *The Fundamentals of Philosophy*, *Woman and her Rights in Islam*, *Man and His Destiny*, *Man and Predestination* and *Divine Justice.* Just about all his books contain some sort of examination of Western ideas.

Muṭahharī was unable to study the foreign material in its original language, but Persian translations were available which were nonetheless adequate for him to use in his projects. We may now conclude this exposition of the background and general framework of Muṭahharī's thought and methodology.

Notes

1. Group of Researchers, *Muṭahharī: The Genius and Visionary* (*Al-Muṭahharī al-'Abqarī al-Risālī*), Damascus, Iranian Cultural Chancellery, 1993, p. 21.

2. Ibid., op. cit., p 14.

3. Ibid., op. cit., p. 14.

4. Ibid., op. cit., p. 15. 'Alī Davānī states that after the failure of Imām Khomeinī's movement against the Shāh, and after the Massacre of Faydiyya, the Imam's students and supporters in the clergy were isolated and boycotted, including Muṭahharī himself. The entourage of Borujerdi corrupted their friendly relationship, and despite the attempts of Montazeri to settle this problem, and taking a message from Muṭahharī to his teacher Borujerdi explaining his position, the latter refused to receive the message. Consequently, Muṭahharī decided to leave for Tehran. See: 'Alī Davānī, *My Memories with Martyr Muṭahharī*, Qom, Umm-ul-Qurā Foundation, 1417 AH, pp. 128-129.

5. Op. cit., pp. 130–131. The same was mentioned by Muṭahharī himself when talking about his dilemma in Qom after his participation in the activities of *maktab-e Islām* and his lectures in Dār al-Tablīgh. This was similar to Sayyid Ḥasan al-Qommi's dilemma, who was boycotted by the clergy and the seminary, despite being an Ayatullah. Thereafter he was banished by the regime to Karg, a remote place in Tehran. See: op. cit., p. 36.

6. *Muṭahharī: The Genius and Visionary*, pp. 16-17, and see in detail: 'Alī Davānī, op. cit, miscellaneous cites, and Group of Researchers, *A Journey in the Life of Martyr Muṭahharī*, Beirut, Dār al-Hādī, 1992, miscellaneous cites also.

7. For the nature and opinions of the Group, and the assassinations of many personalities under vain pretexts, including that of Muṭahharī, see: 'Alī Davānī, op. cit., pp. 126-127. This Group was directed by two unkown clergymen who were exploited by atheistic figures. They were later executed in Qasr Prison, op. cit., pp. 125 and 127.

8. *A Journey in the Life of Martyr Muṭahharī*, op. cit., p. 277, and *Muṭahharī: The Genius and Visionary*, op. cit., p. 17.

9. 'Alī Akbar Hāshemī Rafsanjānī, "*Muṭahharī Whom I Knew*" (*Muṭahharī Kama 'Araftoh*), in *Journey in the Life of Martyr Muṭahharī*, p. 120, and 'Alī Davānī, miscellaneous cites, and *Muṭahharī: The Genius and Visionary*, p. 16.

10. *A Journey in the Life of Martyr Muṭahharī*, pp. 128-129, *My Memories* by 'Alī Davānī, with more than one citation; *Muṭahharī: The Genius and Visionary*, p. 16. Muṭahharī was a major founder of the Combatant Clergy Association, (Jāmi'a-ye Ruhāniyyat Mubārez) which assumed the responsibility of leading the universal

advancement project in society and the project for the renewal of the religious establishment and activating its role. See op. cit., p. 16.

11. *A Journey in the Life of Martyr Muṭahharī*, p. 160; *Muṭahharī: The Genius and Visionary*, p. 11.

12. *A Journey in the Life of Martyr Muṭahharī*, pp. 147-149.

13. Ibid., op. cit., pp. 149 and 155-157.

14. Ibid., p. 256.

15. Ibid., pp. 180 and 257.

16. Ibid., p. 258. See also: *Muṭahharī: The Genius and Visionary*, pp. 17-18.

17. *Muṭahharī: The Genius and Visionary*, op. cit., p. 180.

18. Muṭahharī, *Articles about the Islamic Revolution*, translated by Muḥammad Jawad Mehri, Tehran; Revolution Information Centre, 1402 AH, p. 12.

19. Ibid., p. 49.

20. Op. cit., p. 16. Compare with *Muṭahharī: The Genius and Visionary*, p. 18.

21. Muṭahharī, *Man and Predestination*, translated by Muḥammad 'Alī al-Taskhīrī, Tehran: National Library of the Islamic Republic of Iran, no date, p. 5

22. Ibid., p. 5.

23. Op. cit., pp. 5-6.

24. Muṭahharī, *Man and Predestination*, pp. 9-15.

25. See for example: Muṭahharī, *The System of Woman's Rights in Islam*, translated by Abū Zahrā' al-Najafī, Tehran, Islamic Media Organization, 1987, chapter 4: "Islam and Life Renewal."

26. *Man and Predestination*, op. cit., pp. 11-15.

27. Muṭahharī, *Islam and the Demands of the Era*, translated by 'Alī Hāshim, Beirut, Dār al-Amīr, 1992, p. 258.

28. Muṭahharī, *Islam and the Demands of the Era*, p. 258.

29. Muṭahharī, *The System of Woman's Rights in Islam*, 1987, p. 95.

30. Muṭahharī, *Piramun Inqilab Islami*, Tehran, Sadra Publications, p. 45.

31. Muṭahharī, *The Goal of Human Life.*

32. Muṭahharī, *Monotheistic View of the World and Man and Faith*, (coming soon). *The Goal of Human Life* is part of this series of booklets, which are based on lessons.

33. *Rationality of Islam*, part of *Islamic Articles*, p. 94.

34. Op. cit.

35. *Rationality of Islam*, p. 95.

36. Muṭahharī, *Islamic Movements in the Last Century*, translated by Sadiq Abidi, Beirut, Dār al-Hādī, 1982, p. 97.

37. See for example: *Articles about the Islamic Revolution*, pp. 11, 15, 16, 49, 57, 58, 64 etc.; *Freedom of Faith or Freedom of Thought: Jihad and its Legitimacy in Islam*, Arabic translation, pp. 37-38 and 44.

38. *My Memories with Martyr Muṭahharī*, op. cit., pp. 118-127. Sheikh Gūdarzi. They were the cause behind two fanatical groups, "Hope for the Weak" and "Furqan Group" which assassinated a number of important figures in the struggle.

39. Hosseiniyeh Ershād in Tehran.

40. 'Alī Davānī, op. cit., pp. 79-106.

41. Hosseiniyeh Ershād, which was initially supervised by Muṭahharī, Rafsanjani and Bahonar, published *Understanding Islam*, *Muḥammad the Final Prophet* and 'Alī Sharī'atī's *Caliphate and Imamat*, which stirred much controversy, op. cit., p. 83. Sharī'atī's ideas ignited strong arguments from traditional clergymen that affected Muṭahharī himself, which is why he left Hosseiniyeh Ershād for the al-Jawād Mosque in Tehran.

42. *My Memories with Martyr Muṭahharī*, op. cit., p. 88.

CHAPTER 3

REFORMATION AND ISLAMIC THOUGHT RENEWAL

PREFACE

In order to breath life into the overall framework of ideas and legislation, the Muslim thinkers of the beginning of the last century included a revival of Islamic thought in their projects for social change. This would reconfigure spirituality and ethical values of the Muslim character as an inspiration to reorganise society and plan for the future. It would be the basis for a comprehensive renaissance and the escape from the negative cultural predicament that had spread to all walks of Islamic life and deprived the nation of its authority and potential, and led it into a deep slumber. Without a comprehensive overhaul of perspective, a renaissance would be impossible.

This was something reformists became aware at the beginning of the century; Abul Alā Maudūdī, for example, said,

> "It has become futile to call people to Islam by evangelism, even if prophets beckoning people to adhere to Islam and fear Allah were circulated throughout the day. What kind of practical gain would we acquire by affirming that Islam is valid for all times and places, and that its benefits are incomparable, through writings and public speaking? This era requires a practical display of these benefits in the real world. The claim that Islam is the answer cannot solve the materialistic problems of the world; the personal value of Islam must become foremost in a dominant practical system that enables people to see its power and reap its benefits. We live in a world that is built upon conflict and struggle, where speaking and preaching would not have much effect; only revolutionary struggle can do that."[1]

In his book, Renewal and Revival of Religion, Abul Alā Maudūdī clearly identified the process of renewal, by stressing the importance of diagnosing the malaise from which Muslims suffer, and classifying the specifics of corruption and seeking a radical reformation in the light of Islam, both intellectually and practically. In order to do this, full rein must be given to *ijtihād* in confronting all the dangers, both internal and external, that threaten the nation, and comprehensively reviving the Islamic system.[2] Muḥammad Iqbāl wrote his well-known book, *The Reconstruction of Religious Thought in Islam*, in order to introduce these principles.[3]

Martyr Muḥammad Bāqir al-Ṣadr, states:

> "We can say that the Islamic theory behind the Prophet's mission is that of a revolutionary coup d'état, because it lays down primary rules that define the way in which one's spiritual and intellectual character takes shape, unaffected by a general outlook towards life and the universe, or a higher practical standards in life, or a general rational way of thinking. Then, upon this character a society is established. The issue from Islam's perspective is creating a character with spiritual and intellectual characteristics that enable it to carry its message to the world, and not just a matter of repairing and transforming the social aspect of the personality. This takes into consideration the theory adopted by Islam, however it may be specifically implemented in its course, for the enduring details in all situations and under all conditions are yet to be decided. This is how we know that Islam is revolutionary in its theory, and flexible in its practice, and must shed a clear light on confusions and conditions, and the requirements of the general legislation."[4]

According to revivalists and reformers, a comprehensive revival of the concepts of Islam is the primary condition for bringing about change, and showing the way out the dark tunnel of dependency and regression. Muṭahharī was well aware of this, and he understood the dimensions and implications. He probably knew something of the nature of the efforts of these reformists, and adopted some of their ideas on the subject. Their opinions influenced him, and he fully understood the increasing decadence of Muslims and the causes of it, and for that reason he introduced his book *Revival of Thought in Islam* with a brief review of the contents of Iqbāl's book, *The Reconstruction of Religious Thought in Islam*, ranging from his ideas to the practical steps Iqbāl assumed to be the milestones of a comprehensive renaissance project. This situates Muṭahharī's efforts within the overall framework of the reform experiment in the Islamic world, despite differences in details of his vision of modern Iranain society.

1

REVIVAL AND RENEWAL: THE MEANING AND THE JUSTIFICATIONS

Muṭahharī assumes the laws and legislations of Islam to be alive, and anything but outmoded or dead. When we say "revival" or "renewal", we do not mean a revival or renewal of religion itself by changing its rules and guidelines and abrogating its teachings. Rather, what is meant is a renewal of the act of thinking about religion, that is to say, a revivification in the soul of the follower. Moreover, it would the reintroduction of its ideas into people's lives, so that it accordingly influences the direction of their action.[5]

According to Muṭahharī, this operates at two levels, the first being a comprehensive formulation of Islam, including divesting it of concepts that are the residue of false experience. This would include the ambiguous comprehension which deformed many of its teachings throughout the years and gave it a false image. He says,

> "This is an addition to what we mentioned with regards to revival; we have made it clear that it is a revival of the ideas of the nation and a correction of its attitude towards religion. The life of religion is dependent on the life of the nation, and vice versa; just as a science dies with the death of those who practise it."[6]

These words may cause some to think that Muṭahharī believed in a stable path of Islam, to which any type of renewal would not apply, irrespective of any outside influences that may affect it. Rather, these outside influences affect those who have strayed from its path, so that the revival takes place in their souls and actions.[7] Hence, they are the ones being renewed, not Islam. This is a common thread in the thinking of many reformist intellectuals in the modern Arab world. They believe that, since Islam is from Allah, it cannot be "renewed", and refuse to develop the Islamic sciences and *fiqh* to conform with the changes of the era. They instead opted to Islamise society and pull it out of its state of ignorance. Amongst other examples, this line of thinking is found in Sayyid Quṭb's books, *Signposts on the Road* and *Islam and the Problems of Civilisation,* and *Muḥammad al-Bahi*'s *Modern Islamic Thinking.*[8]

Yet the reality is this: in the general context of Muṭahharī's views on rejuvenation or his discussion of the requirements of the era, his real meaning is not what it seems, for he is not a revivalist like Qutb and his peers, to whom he attributes stagnation and intolerance. On the contrary, he believed that an Arab renaissance failed only because it turned to an intolerant and moribund Salafism, which he was undoubtedly trying to avoid.

Consequently, Muṭahharī distinguished between firmness and adaptability in Islam, so that the fundamental principles remain, but are flexible enough to adjust according to circumstances.[9] This might require the provisional suspension of a law until the cessation of whatever required such a provision. He also believed that a text can be understood in various ways, and a new approach in the light of developments would be legitimate. This may be done with due consideration of the paradigms of Islam and the sources of *ijtihād*, so that models seemingly never having appeared before remain faithful to the transcendent meaning of the texts. This would neither refute the basic tenets of religion, nor cause a confusion between what is permissible and what is not.[10]

According, while it is necessary to revive the spirit of Islam in the souls of the people[11] so that they may build their lives upon it, part of the process involves passing over the deformed understanding that had a hold on Islam for many years. An attribution of sacredness to a petrified interpretation made it impossible to distinguish between the true teachings of Islam and a perverse understanding. According to Muṭahharī there were many such cases.

A rejuvenation of Islam could not be achieved other than by filtering out earlier concepts that have burdened and weakened it, deforming the minds of its followers and causing them to engage in false practices.

Furthermore, the reality of Islam must be determined in the light of world events. A systematic application must be built upon fixed principles, resurrecting Islam in the souls of Muslims and enlivening the community.

If this is the meaning of revival, then something needed to be done about the prevailing conditions for work to begin on practising it and occupying oneself with the aforementioned issues. For a long time now, Muslims have for many reasons[12] stopped interpreting the teachings of their religion as the basis of a lived experience. It ceased to have an effect on their souls, and its glow diminished in their minds. On the level of practicalities, much of its legislation was deformed through malpractice, whilst many heresies were introduced on the level of thought. Through caprice, bigotry and self-interest, many concepts had been altered from their original Qur'anic meanings, causing the loss of the most important cultural pillar supporting Islamic society throughout the years. It had been a river of strength, the sustainer of authority and power that secured unity, progress and creativity, and active participation in the course of world history. But people had been left like feathers in the wind, a nation torn and plundered by others, devoid of life and activity.[13]

When describing contemporary Islamic society, Muṭahharī drew inspiration[14] from the Qur'an, which declares that a lifeless person or society cannot benefit from change or warnings:

> *So that he may warn anyone who is alive* (36:70),[15]
>
> *And is one who was lifeless, then We gave him life and provided him with a light by which he walks among the people, like one who dwells in a manifold darkness* (6:122),[16]
>
> and *O you who have faith! Answer Allah and the Apostle when he summons you to that which will give you life* (8:24).[17]

According to Muṭahharī, the greatest attributes of life are awareness and activity, and they are each opposed to stagnation, intolerance and weakness. If Islam, as confirmed by the Qur'an, is what breathes life into a nation and guides it to wakefulness and rebirth, then it is deviation from its teachings that causes society to become lifeless and without direction. Therefore, bringing a nation to life, instilling awareness in the minds of the people and guiding their path, requires a revival of the light of Islam in their souls, in order to direct them and free their minds from the residues of perversion, innovation and the effects of malpractice.[18]

Muṭahharī does not settle for this brief demonstration when describing the nature of the reality in which Muslims struggle today. Rather, he tried to evaluate some of the elements involved. He had a clear understanding of the undisputable fact that Muslims had drifted away from their religious concepts. He had not the slightest doubt, having directly observed their practices, and recognising the abyss separating what they conceived as Islamic from its ideal. Thus, he found it necessary to explain their materialistic tendencies and the false concepts they had held throughout the years, in order to direct them in accordance with sound Islamic concepts and fundamental religious principles. There upon, he demonstrated how human actions affect the destiny of the people, according to his view of the concept of work that Islam has emphasised, the contents and breadth of which he sought to clarifying and linked the human actions to the historical course of society. In this regards, the Qur'an states,

> *And that nothing belongs to man except what he strives for* (53:39),[19]

> and *So whoever does an atom's weight of good will see it, and whoever does an atom's weight of evil will see it* (99:7-8).[20]

This began to encourage people in becoming self-reliant and responsible, and investing their abilities to the maximum. According to Muṭahharī, the first generation of Muslims understood this concept in all its dimensions, and the idea of the connection between action and destiny became deep-rooted within them. An extraordinary confidence erupted within their souls, and they faced the struggles in their lives with fortitude, unafraid of obstacles or dangers. However, over the years the concept of working towards one's destiny became unclear, until Muslims began to believe in luck and coincidence, and thought little of personal effort in this respect. Realistic ideas regarding happiness through Islam, generated by self-effort, were replaced by false ideas far from reality.[21]

From Muṭahharī's point of view, the deviation of the concept of work from its Qur'anic implications began when the notion of procrastination appeared in people overcome by sin, and was consequently adopted by the political authority, which started to differentiate between faith and work, praising the former and deriding the latter. This notion became dominant in the minds of Muslims. There had been an organised programme in support of it, including the efforts of scientists who dedicated themselves to its cause, and the ambitions of the authorities. It spread throughout the nation and affected its awareness for many years. As a consequence, many

Muslims became apathetic and hesitant, abandoning work in all its forms, and wasting their potential through narrow-mindedness and weakness.[22]

Reliance and asceticism are two false concepts which left a mark on Islamic society. Reliance was a judicious concept in Islamic culture, which Muslims benefited from in the best way possible. It was a living concept that urged Muslims to move forward, overcome difficulties, lift their spirits, and both strengthened their confidence in Allah in the field of work and action, and honed their fortitude when weakness struck. The Qur'an urges Muslims to reliance in situations that require patience, resolve and a firm will:

> *And we will, surely, put up patiently with whatever torment You may inflict upon us, and in God let all the trusting put their trust* (14:12),[23]

Also:

> *Indeed [malicious] secret talk is from Satan, that he may upset the faithful, but he cannot harm them in any way except by God's leave, and in God let all the faithful put their trust* (58:10).[24]

However, in the Muslim awareness this theme shifted from its true meaning to that of relying on the efforts of others, neglecting self-motivation and submitting to defeatism.

Asceticism is another false concept, for it means forsaking that which one naturally desires. In its essence, it formed a moral guarantee that prevents a Muslim from violating the rights and possessions of others and satisfying the desire to possess, appropriate and dominate. It also generated responsibility towards the needs of others as well as one's own, endurance in the face of loss, and a defence from the bedazzlement of worldly attachments.

Those who have this gift are people who are capable of helping others, and serving life and society, without merely satisfying their own whims. Unfortunately, however, this perception changed to that of something which caused an indifference to work, making people negligent of their responsibilities, encouraging them to abstain from having any influence on the functioning of society, and fettering them with idleness and isolation. This has affected many Muslims right up to the present time.[25]

This deviation from the true meaning of asceticism has affected a number of other important Islamic concepts, so much so that they have almost vanished from the lives of Muslims. One example is that of altruism, which encourages the individual to put the interests of others before his own. He does not monopolise things by keeping something for himself which other people need, when he is capable of giving it away.[26]

Other examples are consolation – the stirring of compassion towards the suffering of others – and liberation or emancipation, which lifts a person from the clutches of selfish desires to effective will and a calm awareness.[27] According to Muṭahharī, the result of deviating from such concepts did not stop with a direct practical impact on individual awareness, for it grew to such an extent that it became stabilised in the intellectual and religious mindset, which to a certain extent supported it. This had a destructive effect,[28] for this trend found fertile ground for spreading its roots and acquired enthusiastic supporters and small-minded admirers, who became so important that it was difficult to confront them. This only started when they began to promote their ideas under the guise of reform,[29] which earned them a certain perceived legitimacy which established their appeal. According to Muṭahharī, plenty of examples in this regard are to be found in both ancient and modern history. No era is exempt from its presence and influence, examples of which are Populism, Wahhābism, and the Khārijite, Akhbāri and Ash'ari theologies. In his opinion, they are pernicious, narrow-minded movements that have had a powerful impact on the history of the nation, causing it to fall backwards and constantly fail on many levels.

2

REVIVAL AND RENEWAL: METHODS AND TOOLS

According to Muṭahharī, revival is not just a strict reclamation of the Islamic heritage that has accumulated over time, a straightforward imitation of the thoughts and actions of our ancestors, or merely a sophisticated recovery of the collections of codified laws and principles which were applied to past events. Such a revival would be akin to a form of narrow-minded stagnation, stepping away from life and settling for isolation and surrender. It does not lead to renaissance, progress and development. It is incapable of being a stepping-stone in the revival of Islam in the souls of its followers. The reason is that the time has changed, along with its requirements. People are bombarded with pressing questions, new and complicated situations that require a re-examination and a new understanding for any revival to come about. These concerns need to be addressed in a compatible way. In Muṭahharī's view, whilst firm in its principles, Islam is quite flexible in its interpretation.[30] It is dynamic, but stable in its foundations. With a broad and clear vision and a comprehensive methodology, it answers to the needs and challenges of time.

Two factors are required for an Islamic revival. The first is the faith that Islam can respond to all contingencies, that the flexibility of its principles ensure the ability to keep astride of the latest developments. The second is to be confident in the face of the changes that affect society, the complications that alter its conditions and the recent requirements that impose themselves upon civilisation.[31] The lack of either of these two factors weakens any attempt at revival, damages expectations, and may even have the opposite effect. Both factors are needed for success. Many of those who have devoted themselves to the Islamic sciences have lacked one of them. In other words, they believed that the meaning of Islam is fixed,[32] and that time does not change, so that new events are merely a repetition of what happened in the past. Such people have not been able to actively participate in a revival of Islam in the present, spreading its ideas into the heart of life, so that it may be used as a foundation for a vision of the future.[33]

Due to his confidence in these two features, Muṭahharī stepped forward to defend the possibility of a renewed Islam for the changing times. He did this by emphasising the principle of *ijtihād*[34] as a method of examining the dimensions of *sharī'ah* according to its fundamental constants and comprehensiveness. The principle of *ijtihād* is twofold. It is to draw from the Islamic legal tradition that which has not been applied in practice before. It also involves the assessment of a particular understanding in order to develop new methods that were perhaps not required in the past.

First: The Importance of Ijtihād

According to Muṭahharī, Islam revealed guidance regarding the prospect of *ijtihād*. It opened up the possibilities of *ijtihād* through a balanced deliberation on the hidden allusions within religious texts, which only reveal themselves by astutely employing the many recognised legislative tools which guarantee a universal implication.[35] Our forefathers established this method in the heyday of their civilisation, confident of the ability of Islam to critically assess the heritage of the nations, whilst maintaining its own integrity.

In Muṭahharī's view, *ijtihād* is the tool for recovering the important meaning of religion in life, and actively supporting society in the midst of its vicissitudes. It is able to return the sparkle to Islam, so that it may efficiently respond to changing events. The intention of *ijtihād* is to gain insight into the matters of religion and its laws as evidenced in the Qur'an and the *Sunnah*.[36]

From Muṭahharī's perspective, *ijtihād* is of two types, the first of which is disparaged on account of it inferring theories that have no source, whether from books, the *Sunnah* or from logical thought. But the second type is commended, since it is indeed established in accordance with the aforementioned pillars, that is, the Qur'an and the *Sunnah*. The first kind is a blind imitation with no due consideration, or in other words, merely the unthinking acceptance of deep-rooted convictions that conform with accepted customs. In several places the Qur'an has disparaged such an imitation. The following is an example:

> *We found our fathers following a creed and we are indeed following in their footsteps*[37] (43:23).[38]

The commended form of *ijtihād* is when someone uninformed in shari'ah consults someone who is, and thereby gains an awareness of its implications and benefits through examination.[39] This is a condition of its legitimacy.

As regards the *mujtahid*,[40] Muṭahharī assumes him to be a person with an adequate aptitude for studying Islamic belief and law. In this he should be actively practising Islam, have a sure comprehension of its significance, and have a wide knowledge of the Islamic sciences and the work of those who specialise in theology and law. He must also clearly understand through personal insight the problems of society. All these things reflect his understanding of Islam. As an example, there is a vast difference between a jurist who knows little of events in the world, and one who does, who is familiar with different cultures and traditions, and the intellectual trends influencing the world around him. Nevertheless, both types are putting their energy into an attempt to draw rulings from source material, and striving to reach the best level of *ijtihād*.[41]

The intellectual perspective of every jurist affects his standpoint, along with his view of the world and events. There are many new and changing laws that affect the work of the jurist and challenge his abilities. This is because there may not be a text that explicitly identifies a problem. This consequently requires the jurist to identify what is needed by referring to the universal principles that govern the law in general, and the implications that can be found within it. If such things are not grasped, it is impossible for a jurist to take a clear religious stance regarding legislation.[42]

In order to make things easier for jurists and open up a modern and efficient *ijtihād*, Muṭahharī proposed the division of legislation into several specialised fields, and that all capable jurists knowledgeable in the details of *sharī'ah* should devote themselves to one of these fields. Distributing skills in this way would be more effective, and allow legislation to keep track of new events and develop to the point where can cover all recent requirements. This would make it more creative and flexible under pressure.[43] Muṭahharī was driven to such a proposal due to the complicated needs of society which were constantly increasing. This presented the jurist with many difficulties which might exceed his competence.

The Islamic sciences have complemented each other over the years and are constantly expanding, and because of the successive developments it is almost impossible for one person to be acquainted with them all. Practice and observation is required for their comprehension. Islamic jurisprudence began initially in a simple fashion, suitably adapted for conditions of life at the time. As time went on, jurisprudence evolved, becoming more complicated as the difficulties of life increased. In former times, one would not have thought it possible for human problems to increase the way they have, pushing jurisprudence to limits that would have been previously unknown. And the changes in jurisprudence have an inevitable effect on the sciences and other branches of learning.[44]

What is more, Muṭahharī had a proposition he regarded as beneficial; that there should be cooperation between the various specialities within each discipline, since nowadays one's person's ideas are of little overall value in getting good results. The exchange of theories between various specialists would enable them to share ideas which could be discussed and refined, thus achieving better results.

Much to Muṭahharī's dismay, however, these particular ideas of his were not pursued, and this later proved to be an obstacle that needed to be overcome in order for society to be transformed. In his opinion, there was no other way for jurisprudence to shake off its legacy and develop in accordance with contemporary society.[45]

Nevertheless, if unawareness of the needs of the times is detrimental for *ijtihād*, as Muṭahharī believed, over-enthusiasm for a liberated *ijtihād* is equally harmful, if not more so. Many of those who advocate reform have resorted to this type of *ijtihād*, and have fallen victim to two ambiguities. The first is an ambiguity within their minds, for they consider it an improvement upon tradition and a new understanding.[46] The second is an ambiguity regarding contemporary requirements, in assuming that every new thing is right and compatible with the truth, but unable to distinguish between what is ethically suitable and what is simply false.[47] In relation to this, Muṭahharī says,

> "Some others who are interested in the issues of the era and think of the horizons of the future use Islam rather too excessively. They consider the modern requirements of the era and the soul to be a standard for Islam itself. For example, they believe that dowry is unnecessary because it contradicts the spirit of the era, and that polygamy and the *ḥijāb* are but residues of the time of slavery, etc. And since Islam is a religion of reason and *ijtihād*, then *ijtihād* allows us to make such judgments."[48]

He remarks on the nature of this trend by saying,

> "Nevertheless, the trend of excessive renewal actually expresses what happens when non-Islamic concepts are introduced to Islamic ones, and when Islam has departed from its true meaning for the sake of modernising it and making it compatible with the requirements of the time. This trend is an epidemic that threatens a new beginning."[49]

This pattern of understanding introduces us to a third element of *ijtihād* whose meaning is neglected. Muṭahharī expressly referred to it when speaking of reality the life and death of a society, and is the confrontation of *ijtihād* with reality. It has been ignored very often in the past, causing the relevant rulings to be abstract and unable to respond to reality through a lack of flexibility in its interpretation. This has often happened, and continues to do so. Muṭahharī stresses the importance of this issue, apart from his other concerns. The concerns of modern life have to be considered, without either ignoring them or rushing to embrace them in an attempt to justify them and then apply a religious interpretation to them. One must understand what is going on, and guide it by trying to manage it efficiently. Then one can benefit from it through legal applications that are not just theoretical, but have a practical framework. Jurisprudence would then be complete to the extent that open-mindedness, comprehension and practice coincide.[50] It would be suited to present reality and be able to manage life according to its priorities. This methodology takes into consideration the fact that the religion does not specify conclusive formulae for different patterns of life, but rather laid down universal indicators as general guidelines with occasional interventions to prevent society from making mistakes, thus leaving the applied form of religious practice dependant on time and place. This is apparent in many religious concepts that do not have a strictly specific application. For example, excessive laughter is traditionally frowned upon, but who can precisely determine what is excessive? The respect of elders is a good thing, but who can determine the form respect takes when it varies between different customs and societies? Very often such issues determine an applied form of a religious concept, without departing from its meaning. Such a distinction between a concept and its applied form liberates the concept, animating it so that it can be rid of past practices imposed by it under conditions different from our own. Perhaps the most obvious example of this is the concept of the veil, which was associated with earlier norms of dress. People were accustomed to these norms to the extent that the concept became specifically linked with them, even though Islam specified the concept without specifying its form, leaving that up to the customs of the people. The responsibility for this lies with the jurists, and is an indispensable part of *ijtihād* as envisioned by Muṭahharī.[51]

Since Muṭahharī aspired to an efficient *ijtihād* based upon stable Islamic principles and answering to contemporary requirements, it was necessary for him to examine various ambiguities. He sought harmony between them and the *sharīʿah*, in such a way that the *sharīʿah* could assimilate from the confusion of irrelevances what was authentic. Muṭahharī dedicated his book *Islam and the Demands of the Era* to this particular issue. A close look at some of the contents of this book would complete our picture of Muṭahharī's view on the true nature of *ijtihād*.

Second: Ijtihād and the Demands of the Era

As Muṭahharī saw it, the modern world is continually overflowing with new and complicated developments, imposing conditions never dreamt of before. Some are due to scientific and industrial development, some are the result of social and political change, while others stem from contact with Christian thought in Europe. In the midst of such a world, a Muslim must not only have a correct understanding of Islam and its social philosophy, but also be aware of what is going on in the world at large, avoiding dangers and establishing a stable path for himself.[52]

We must recognise that man has generated much of this himself. Constant research has helped him easily satisfy his basic needs. He inventions have brought what was far away closer to him, made the difficult easy, and helped him satisfy his desires with little or no difficulty. Man is different today than he was before. He has a different way of life, different ideas, behaviour, ideas and goals.

According to Muṭahharī, Islam was not revealed in order to inhibit human activity, nor is man meant to live in a cycle of monotonous idleness. Rather, one is encouraged to be dynamic in the pursuit of discovery and creativity, opening up the future so that it may be fashioned according to requirements. Islam set down foundations that ensured success. It proved to be capable of leading people forward if they remain loyal to its principles, while taking into consideration new needs and the heavy burdens imposed on them by time.[53]

Muṭahharī claim that it is unfair for someone like Gustave Le Bon[54] to claim that time is evolving, while Islam remains fixed in its original state, causing Muslims to feel that they must abandon their religion if they wish to keep up with developments in the modern world. It is alleged that clinging to the teachings of Islam has only hindered them, leaving them in a state of weakness for some time.[55]

Such views swept away many Muslims. They were convinced that it was necessary to discard many religious traditions they saw as incompatible with modernity. This happened for two reasons: an insufficient knowledge of Islam, and the inability to discern between what was good and what was bad about the changing world. For example, the chaos and corruption that happens when man considers himself free of any rules and values. This inevitably lets loose a disorganised desire for gain and the exploitation of power.[56] These people just took it for granted that that kind of attitude was simply part and parcel of progress, and that it was necessary in order to achieve the kind of superiority which others have achieved. Since out of ignorance they saw Islam as stagnant and unchangeable, and unable to keep up with modern developments,[57] they assumed there had to be a conflict between Islam and modernity. They decided to sever their ties with Islam, as the West had increasingly done with Christianity since the Renaissance, and keep it only as a distant memory which had helped them in the past, and thereby move forward, unhindered and liberated, into modernity.[58]

Muṭahharī considered that a sufficient knowledge of Islam enables us to distinguish between the universal laws and the flexibility of their application. This is an inherent quality of the legislative system that qualifies it to respond to the needs of every epoch in ways that surprise even those who do not believe in it, but are aware of the Islamic heritage. The system can adapt when there is a clear understanding of the meaning of *ijtihād*, for it has kept pace with an expanding Islamic civilisation for many decades, finding solutions to the problems presented with the broadening of the relationships affecting society. It can perform efficiently even in the most precarious situations.[59]

Islam is a religion that is attuned with natural laws, and works with human needs, ethics and developments. The innate paradigm of the law is an eternal truth. Change only occurs in details that are applied to given circumstances, but which are nonetheless harmonious with the permanent law. In this way the law encompasses all the movements and profound changes in history.[60]

Muṭahharī realised that Islam's ability to respond to the changes in life did not really need to be affirmed, since one may find a clear explication through a thorough reading of Islamic legislation. Moreover, the experience of history has verified this in a way that leaves no room for doubt. The theoretical complexity and magnitude of Islamic jurisprudence is a good indicator of it being put into practice. However, Muṭahharī was also aware that it was not so easy to distinguish between the good and bad aspects of progress. This becomes apparent by taking a look at the fundamental nature and requirements of man, and comparing them with developments over time. Only then can one distinguish between the essential and the unnecessary, or progress and decay. Accordingly, man is social by nature, and lives in an organised society that ensures that his needs are provided for through mutual cooperation. His basic nature also gives him the freedom to develop methods and laws which facilitate his happiness quickly and safely. This is in contrast to the animals that enjoy living in herds, but fulfil their basic needs according to fixed laws in accordance with instinct.[61]

Man has a consistent nature that remains unaltered with the changes of time and circumstances. Yet he is able to develop his life and move forward, using his capacities to create, imagine and innovate, and his reason to distinguish between the good and evil. This self-nature has burdened man with the responsibility to perfect himself, using his skill to advance himself and develop systems which serve his interests and needs. Moreover, this is the purpose of his existence, and he must choose those things which comply with his conscience and reason. He accordingly tries to adapt to his surroundings, respond appropriately to the requirements of the time, and harmonise with their increasing complexity.[62] As for animals, their lives are governed by rules that regulate their relationships and fulfil their needs, and which force them to abide by them. They have followed the same patterns of behaviour imposed upon them by their nature since the beginning of time. They cannot change, or go beyond their natures.[63] Man, however, has been given the gifts of reason, intellect and imagination, the attribute of free will, and skills with which to create and innovate to fulfil his needs.[64] Therefore, the transformations that have affected man and society throughout the years may be considered as natural; they relate to his constitution, and link up with his self-will, skill and capacities. Thus he has had to take responsibility for his actions in his advances and decline, since this stems from his ability to make choices and decide his fate as best he can.[65] Since the beginning of time man as made his own history. His free will affects all his actions for better or worse, in his ideas, creations and growth, as well as those that lead to his downfall.

The changes throughout history have not always been for the good, and cannot always be regarded as an advance, for change in itself does not always serve his best interests. Man has indeed fallen many times. Some of the failures of the past are unforgettable, and the horrors of his deeds can be haunting. Cruel, dark scenes do not belong only to the distant past, since similar things in recent times have happened, and the memory still lingers in the most prestigious societies. They illustrate an important point regarding man's destructive capacity.[66]

But what is the standard by which to distinguish between what is good and what is to be avoided? According to Muṭahharī, man must use his reason to come to a conclusion about his corruption and decline. Sound reasoning would quickly guide us to the fact that over the years man has used his abilities to serve goals which were counter to his nature. He did this to fulfil reckless ambitions and satisfy erratic impulses, and resulted in the collapse of his schemes, the decline of nations and the enslavement of society. In our own times, it has led to disaster and war, eradicating what man has suffered for and struggled to build for centuries.[67]

Many things these days indicate man's creative abilities. Yet industry and technology could very easily become a disaster that threatens mankind itself. Will this not prompt us to reflect, and divert our path away from concerns such as personal gain, wealth, convenience and comfort, so that we can shed some light on that which gives us life and determines our abilities?[68]

For Muṭahharī, the value of development lies not only within forms and appearances, but also in its essence and meaning, i.e. the way humankind uses it for good.[69] This should be used as a standard, since, for example, it is not enough to cite advances in science and technology, or multiple choices of lifestyle for satisfying whims, when considering a society to be developed, for such things are not what true development is all about. Rather, it is the profitable use of imagination and achievement in things which serve man's legitimate aims, in compliance with the perfection his natural state and the purpose of his existence.[70] Over the course of history, we find many nations that were creative and innovative, and had immense material wealth, but which lacked the basic principles that direct man's actions and ensure the good use of his capacities. They also lacked the ethical principles that would guarantee the good use of his capacities for his own benefit and that of other people. This unavoidably led to division and eventual ruin.[71]

This is the standard by which to judge the essence of advance and decline. Any examination of our own times must be in accordance with it, since this is what truly concerns us and the issue of progress in harmony with the principles of Islam. The modern world tempts us with the various signs of its progress, achievements and urbanisation. It also causes us to wonder about our heritage and renewal. What, then, does Muṭahharī say in this context? According to him, moderation and regularity are attributes of Islam that are emphasised in the Qur'an. They are neither frozen and intolerant, nor do they fluctuate wildly with changes of circumstance. Throughout the history of Islamic, each of these two positions can be witnessed, the former having a negative impact on society, while the latter gave free rein to innovation and various forms of corruption, also having an adverse effect.[72]

As for the response of these two positions to modernism, we also find an intolerance that refuses to change and clings to deep-seated norms, as well as trends that have been swept away by the styles of Westernised civilisation with its accompanying beliefs and behaviour. Both are fatally wrong, and contradict both the balanced moderation and vitality of Islam.[73]

Nowadays, Muslims are required to acknowledge their responsibility in the midst of many intolerant, corrupt and declining points of view. They need to define their position regarding the demands of the present and the means by which Islam may respond to them, a position characterised by balance and moderation.[74]

According to Muṭahharī, the demands of today have various characteristics. So how do we decide which are genuine and reliable? Also, out of all the aspects of Westernisation we see every day, which are those that are compliant with Islam and illustrate realistic changes compatible with the needs and purpose of human life?

The requirements of one phase in the process of history differ from those of an earlier phase. Through our experiences in life, we come to realise that man feels compelled to meet the needs of these changing requirements, despite having values and patterns of belief that he may have to change. Machines have contributed to the process, and have as a consequence led to changes in the clothes we wear and the food we eat, as well as relationships, customs and norms.[75]

However, this is not the right way to evaluate the demands of the present, i.e. these newly generated aspects do not exemplify an advance, for they are nonetheless still what could be described as basic needs of humankind, as previously mentioned. They are more likely to be the result of caprice, false aims or wild impulses, and be symptomatic of a decline.[76]

If Islam is to fit into the picture, then it may need to accommodate certain aspects that are contrary to the fundamental nature of mankind, things that do serve man's real interests and fall short of realistically serving the purpose of human life, or even bring harm and lead to both moral bankruptcy and the devastation of nature. If all change within civilisation are to be regarded as signs of progress and prosperity, then how do we explain the reform movements that emerge every now and then, which mourn the decline of mankind's values and the degradation of man's dignity and will? These reformers reflect upon[77] the prospects of a society engulfed by corrupted patterns of behaviour. They seek to emphasise how man's attitudes and actions, and the systems he builds, are not all in his best interests. They do not lead to true progress, and will undoubtedly become corrupt and fall apart. How can we expect Islam to conform with this scenario, no matter what?[78] It is first of all necessary for man to use his reason in order to discern what is beneficial to him and will grant him happiness, so he may try to accommodate them to Islam, give them meaning, and find ways to use them which serve his interests in compliance with his fundamental nature. Needless to say, he should also distance himself from those things which could lead to chaos and decline.[79]

The other thing to bear in mind is that which in every legitimate reform movement refers to the basic, unchanging needs of human activity. These requirements are innate and necessary for the survival of mankind. Man has always sought to satisfy his needs by inventing ways of doing so that make things easier by removing obstacles in the path to progress.[80] Man has to use the tools of development correctly for his inherent needs to be fulfilled. These tools are constantly evolving through the use of man's skill. He does this of his own choice, and thereby the complexities of society increase. His inherent needs are fixed, and only the means by which they are satisfied are changed. Consequently the system of administration also has to develop in order to ensure these things are put to good use.[81]

These means are requirements imposed by the development of all aspects of society. They are not simply a passing phase, but true requirements that impose themselves in order to guarantee that basic needs are satisfied. According to Muṭahharī, Islam's position regarding such secondary needs is positive. It sets guidelines, and encourages man to use his skills to develop the means and use them well, in order for them to be of benefit to mankind.[82] Islam only objects to an excessive obsession with searching ways to satisfy unnecessary needs.

The normal man adapts himself to the demands and complications of his time by devising useful ways of dealing with them in a sober fashion.[83] He has fundamental needs, and as his skills develop, he invents suitable tools. Life later became more complicated and different circumstances presented themselves.[84] Tools considered useful at one time may not be of any use later, and are usually replaced by something better which saves energy. Man may also find that some tools or methods turn out to be of more harm than good. Throughout history, experience has taught man to evaluate his discoveries before developing them.

Consideration of the demands of the time is unavoidable, and Islam has laid down foundational principles that identify the best ways of employing one's creative abilities. There are a number of universal guidelines that ensure the good use and benefit of those things which man has full authority to create.[85]

Since Islam accepts that times change, it is perfectly in order for *ijtihād* to move forward and discover new pathways within the fixed principles of the *sharī'ah*. This ensures that new possibilities conform with the principal needs in man, and prevent any deviation in mankind's development.[86]

Muṭahharī did not fail to notice that Western technology and thought was not just a matter of its usefulness. It includes a vast system of knowledge concerning man and the universe, nature and existence; it involves a philosophy of life based on empirical knowledge which is alien to traditional metaphysical and religious views. It seeks to explain reality in terms of scientific discoveries that reduce everything to particles.

A confidence in experimental science has led to the popularisation of its methodology outside its original framework, and infiltrated the consciousness of the general public. The framework of experimental science, through observation and ratiocination, seeks to explain the phenomena of the whole of existence, and thereby gain the ability to predict future phenomena by discovering the rules that govern them.[87]

The accumulation of scientific achievements created an ideology which claimed to have an explanation of the human soul and civilisation. In other words, a scientific existential philosophy, which maintains that there is a scientific explanation for the principles that govern the universe, phenomena and society. It is a form of knowledge built upon an exclusively scientific view of the world and nature.

The expansion of these considerations raises the question of the compatibility of technical and material innovation with Islam. The spread of modernity has generated a value system based on the conviction that experimental science is invaluable for the understanding of existence. This is in addition to technical and industrial progress, and the desire to likewise find means of overcoming difficulties by the same methods. How can all this be evaluated in order to form an Islamic response to these issues?

Muṭahharī stepped away from the comfort of his books to examine this scientistic ideology, and reviewed Islam's position. This will be discussed in the following section, and the fourth chapter of his book.

This insight led Muṭahharī to believe in the necessity of returning to the concept of *ijtihād* in its traditional sense. A popularisation of *ijtihād* is necessary for examining the practicalities of a different way of life. New requirements call for the creation of an interpretation of *ijtihād* that ensures the good use of the theoretical and technical knowledge that has come out of the Western world. This is so that *ijtihād* may expand to include this knowledge within the intellectual framework of Islam. This kind of *ijtihād* involves more than simply deliberating over texts. It would be the construction of a methodological vision. This would free *ijtihād* from a static traditional concept, and its hierarchical practice in both the Sunni and Shi'ite paradigms. It would result in a transformation into a method of analysis that uses the existing texts as an inspiration for understanding new concepts, and creating a new form of practice. Thus it would embrace the spirit of the *shari'ah*, while remaining in complete harmony with reasoning and the ambitions of human society.

Third: Revival and Renewal: Elements and Beginnings

Preface

Muṭahharī was well aware that a religious revival would not have a positive impact on society unless Islam is seen as a comprehensive ideology. One cannot assume that a revival of the *shari'ah* is enough to answer the questions regarding people's immediate response to emerging events. Rather, a comprehensive revival is needed, an all-inclusive vision according to the *shari'ah*, which would determine the responsibility of man in the face of materialism.

Therefore, a revival involves the entire Islamic system as its starting point. If we consider *ijtihād* to be the method that would ensure a reconstruction of the Islamic legislative system, then it also allows for a comprehensive redefinition of its philosophical position in the light of the many recent developments.

Muṭahharī is generally considered as completely open-minded in his methodology. He assiduously devoted himself to experiencing things that could help him achieve his universal vision. He wanted to invest in all the rich creative diversity of the Islamic heritage as it was in its prime. He likewise attempted to find within both Western and Eastern philosophy ways to serve his purpose, as well as in different scientific, psychological and social trends. His assumption was that knowledge is not the prerogative of one section of humanity, but is the culmination of man's various attempts throughout time to identify answers to the universal questions regarding his existence. This was the foundation of all movements throughout history. However, Muṭahharī took care to ensure that everything was included in an Islamic vision, which he saw as the pinnacle of human achievement.

In *An Introduction to the Islamic Universal Vision*, a concise text detailing the outlines of this comprehensive vision, Muṭahharī presented the deep philosophical position of Islam regarding the world, which is found in many of his books and lectures. He provides us with a harmonious vision as the foundation for a new Islamic standpoint in the light of the tensions of the present time, and a world whose vision is clouded by overwhelming questions.

1. Reviving the Universal Monotheistic Vision of the World

According to Muṭahharī, a universal vision should be a comprehensive system of belief and understanding regarding existence, its inception and destiny, its laws and relationships – a complete philosophy of life and all its activities. No religion, or any sociological, psychological or scientific outlook, lacks such a vision upon which it depends. He states,

> "Every outlook on life must be built on a specific beliefs and systems of evaluation, interpretation and analysis. Every principle has a particular way of pondering the universe and existence, which are the foundations and intellectual background for such a principle."[88]

In his view, a universal vision is not simply a physical observation of the universe. Rather, it is primarily an epistemology of reality in all its relationships;[89] a cognitive stance based on three sources: science, philosophy and religion. Accordingly, each of these three categories embodies a universal vision. Muṭahharī aspired to combine these elements in a comprehensive universal vision, which is why he dealt with each of them as parts of an even bigger picture.

A. The Scientific Position

Science is based on both hypothesis and experimentation; a scientist who aspires to uncover a universal phenomenon that has caught his attention one way or the other attempts to do so through a hypothesis that he tries to test. Should the hypothesis prove to be cohesive and realistic, it is accepted as a scientific fact and acquires a value for as long as it is not disproven by another theory supported by experiments and characterised by coherence and rationality. This can lead to a diversity of theories, and one theory may give way to another for reasons decided by the rationality of science itself.[90] Accordingly, science progresses in the analysis of phenomena. Muṭahharī believed that this methodology has some advantages. It offers us much information about material things and how we may benefit from their use, and to a certain extent it enables us to both visualise whether or not things will work, and therefore prevent damage before it occurs.[91]

However, science has many flaws. It is limited in the scope of its research, and it only touches upon the essential nature of phenomena. This means that it does not extend beyond the framework of its own vision, and is unaware of its limitations. Despite its achievements, science knows little of the surrounding world and the nature of existence, which is mostly still shrouded in mist. No matter how much it advances, the question of why things happen remains forever outside its remit.[92]

It is also unreliable. At one point, science may come up with a satisfying explanation for something or other, only to have it overthrown by subsequent research, and this will continue to be the case for as long as the scientific method endures. Its knowledge has a temporary value, and for that reason one cannot have any firm convictions about it.[93]

The efforts of scientists have revealed that data obtained from experimentation does not result in a system of general laws for reality; rather, they only uncover partial elements through observation. Instead, the human mind conceives of the laws of reality in accordance with a transcendent and philosophical system, which the outlook of contemporary science cannot but confirm. If not, then how do we happen to come by a philosophical position pertaining to universal reality, when experimentation fails to supply it?[94]

Muṭahharī believed that the results of scientific research only serve man within a practical framework; i.e. they supply him with enough knowledge about the world for him to benefit from it in a practical fashion. However, this is not enough to be the foundations for a universal vision, meaning that it does not portray reality in its entirety, and it does not inform us about our place in existence.[95]

In this regard, Muṭahharī was strict about his position. He does not simply evaluate science as such according to his own opinions, since many who have believed in it and dedicated their lives to it, such as Bertrand Russell,[96] admit that science has no ultimate theoretical value, for it neither offers a comprehensive explanation of existence, nor does it provide us with a stable and finalised vision of the world and the universe. It is for that reason that science is incapable of being a universal epistemology. It cannot answer the fundamental questions about existence and the universe required by such a vision. Furthermore, it only offers explanations of a practical nature, but reveals nothing of ultimate value. Thus, science on its own is not fit to provide us with a comprehensive and stable theoretical vision of existence.

B. The Philosophical Position

The philosophical position suffers a similar problem to that of science. However, it is different in that it has a kind of certainty due to its reliance on intuitive roots that the mind can realise through demonstrative evidence that deals with existence as a whole, rather than physical matter alone.[97]

Therefore, the philosophical position is capable of providing existential answers constituting a basis for a universal vision.[98] Science is capable of providing useful knowledge regarding how things work, and philosophy does so in a different way; it affects our standpoint on things, how we regard our surroundings, and influences our overall attitude. It can either give a meaning to our existence that we can use to shape the world and our convictions regarding it, thus giving life value, or else cast us into confusion and meaninglessness.

C. The Religious Position

The religious position can exist harmoniously with the philosophical position in one dimension, despite their different cognitive foundations; the former being based on revelation and the latter based on ratiocination. However, it could almost be said that Islam expresses its vision in a way similar to that of philosophy by the inclusion of the natural abilities of the human mind. It is also similar to philosophy in that it is an application of theory derived from a higher framework, due to its dependence on a transcendent principle that Muṭahharī refers to as "holiness." Regarding this, he said,

> "This vision has the attributes of a universal philosophical vision – stability and comprehensiveness. Furthermore, it is characterised by an attribute that both science and philosophy lack, that is, holiness, which dominates its foundations."[99]

Perhaps Muṭahharī meant to say that every universal vision is worthy of some kind of acceptance, and does not necessarily require completeness. It is not the attribute of comprehensiveness that brings it out from the context of being a partial and narrow, like the scientific view, which is trapped within change. But rather, it is the attribute of holiness expressed in religion. According to him, a universal vision cannot be the basis for an ideology or grounds for faith unless it has a religious quality.[100] In this way it combines the depth of philosophical thought and the holiness of religion.[101]

A universal vision defines man's position regarding material things, the world, his own values, and an awareness of his goals. Hence, it is not only an intellectual position, but also a psychological one. That is to say, it is not enough for a universal vision to generate only a cognitive position on the world, but there should also be a psychological position, or at least one interpreted as such. For this reason, Muṭahharī set a specific standard by which one can identify whether a vision is beneficial or not, as follows:

A sophisticated universal vision is that which combines the following attributes:

The ability to be proven by logical conclusions;

The ability to give life a meaning, and abolish the absurdity and meaninglessness that bring about the squandering of energy;

The ability to engender hope and motivation;

The ability to attribute transcendence and holiness to human goals;

The ability to engender feelings of commitment and responsibility in the soul.[102]

According to Muṭahharī, the first attribute is that of clarity, coordination and harmony, and the third makes it attractive to its followers and gives it strength and ardour.

As to the fourth, it encourages believers to surpass their own selves in order to aspire to higher and goals, whereas the fifth instils in the conscience of man responsibility for his own self and his actions towards others.[103]

Muṭahharī believed that these attributes can only be found together in the universal monotheistic vision. So, what are the fundamental principles of this vision?

D. The Universal Monotheistic Vision

The universal Islamic vision is based on two essential foundations that a comprehensive vision cannot be complete without: one is the idea of a Principle, and the other a goal, or destiny. This vision places man at the centre of things, where he uses his monotheistic understanding of the Principle to shape his awareness and his relationship to destiny.[104]

The Principle (Allah) Monotheism Man Orientation Purpose

←——— ———→

With this perception established, man would be expected to achieve three levels of science and knowledge. The first level comprises his acknowledgment of the Principle, namely Allah, His truth, His existential status, His power and His attributes. The second level involves his knowledge of the purpose or destiny that his existence struggles to achieve. As to the third, it is about the knowledge of his own self in the context of the other two, as well as his capacities,[105] his existential status, the conditions that determine history, and the material and moral laws that surround him and affect him and his surroundings, in other words, the world that constitutes his home.

Muṭahharī was convinced that knowledge does not generate action if it lacks motivation.[106] He believed that it is necessary to transfer this knowledge from the level of reason to the level of emotion and instil it in the consciousness, while perceiving its meaning in the depths of the soul, for it is man who determines a practical position in this regard.

In this case, faith emerges as a deep feeling that takes over the soul and allows man's heart to accept the Principle and experience it in all its depth, acquire its qualities and be inspired by its creativity. It also opens up his destiny, so he feels a responsibility to achieve it and make available the realistic conditions that lead towards it, and is reflected in his emotions as tranquillity as a result of knowing the meaning and implications of his existence, and the value of his own self. Faith, not intellect, brings about motivation. It is the only thing that inspires man and gives him the chance to transform his knowledge to an experience based on the most profound meaning of the Principle. This establishes the elements of commitment and work regarding man's ultimate purpose, the exalted goal of his life, activity and experience.[107]

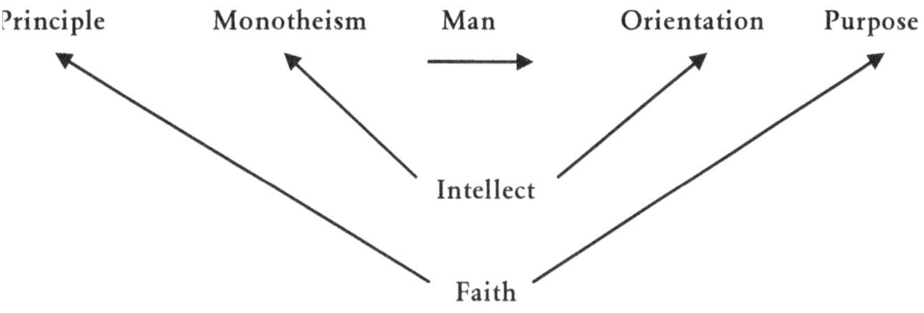

Muṭahharī decided that, in the monotheistic vision of the world, man reaches an understanding of the Principle as the source of the universe. Moreover, this is also known because of the awareness of the perfection of the Principle – It is oneness, power, transcendence and so forth, all of which are concomitant with a universal vision. His understanding of destiny revolves around the end towards which all history inexorably moves. With this understanding well established in the mind and will as a firm belief, the heart and soul is instilled with profound meaning. Commitment and responsibility are generated in man, which direct his moral strength and his potentials towards his destiny.[108]

In a series of books under the title *An Introduction to the Islamic Universal Vision,* Muṭahharī discusses his standpoint within the framework of this vision. He identifies the nature of man and the idea of the one Principle, His oneness, attributes and power, and the relationship of the Principle to existence. Muṭahharī also discusses destiny as the definitive conclusion of the course of existence, before moving on to faith, its meaning and how it develops, and the effect it has on man's relationships with both the Principle and destiny.[109]

E. The Material and Moral Dimensions of Man: "On the Existential Status of Man"

As in all his studies, Muṭahharī also stresses how man differs from all other living creatures by having unique qualities. Although man is a creature very similar in many respects to the other animals, he has characteristics that make him quite different from them. These characteristics are apparent in his cognitive skills and his achievements in the world, and can be summarised as vision and motive.[110]

Vision is manifest in man's consciousness and perception, whereas an animal views the world from one perspective – its senses through which it seeks what it needs as dictated by instinct.

The animal's inclinations are directly proportional to the range of its perception.[111] Although creatures such as bees and ants live in a social environment, their lives are still determined by instinct rather than free will.[112]

The range of perception in man is superior and far more comprehensive, since man's knowledge of the world touches the depths of phenomena and the laws governing them. This does not stop with the surrounding environment, but extends far beyond to the whole universe. Man can also comprehend the changes in time that envelop the past, present and future.[113] The mind of man can also explore spiritual concepts such as infinity, immortality, good and evil, permanence and change, logic and the soul, the invisible and the visible, and so on, and by his free will he may affirm his superiority over nature by guiding his abilities so that he may benefit from them.[114]

Man's inclinations accord with his perception and knowledge. Unlike the partial perception of animals, man can rise above the materialistic framework to the boundaries of meaning. They also extend beyond the individual to include the society, and beyond the present to the past and future. Man diligently searches for the meaning of phenomena, to make sense of their rhythms, and seek the perfection that lies beyond the boundaries of limited dimensions. He does so above all else with utter devotion. His hopes, dreams, visions, discoveries and laws, are all an undeniable proof of this.[115]

Man acquires experiences through the application of his many qualities, using his strength, vision, belief and values to achieve his goals in the surrounding world. He has a natural disposition for freedom, an ardent will, and the awareness of success and failure. As a result, he has been able to form a vision of himself, the surrounding world, his existential status and his fate, and managed to design a layout for his movements, organise his abilities, identify relationships, and regulate his system of life with legislations. Muṭahharī was able to find his long sought-after definition of man's nature and status in a Western philosophical vision, which supported his way of thinking. Muṭahharī recounted Descartes' ideas regarding what distinguishes man from other creatures:

> "It is obvious that each of these qualities is correct, and if we wish to define the basic qualities, we could say that man is an animal, who differs from all other creatures by science and faith."[116]

Accordingly, authentic human motivation is both materialistic and moral – both complement man's nature and determine his experience. Through observing his motives, man is able to ascertain his existence and achieve his purpose, perfect his character and exercise his free will[117] in a progressive integral movement that places his material needs within the framework of his visions, concepts and ethics, and forms the infrastructure that enables him to achieve them.[118] Such a vision proves that man's reality is independent, and that he seeks the perfection that determines his ultimate destiny and urges him to continue moving through life.[119]

F. On Man's Relationship to the Principle: "The Cognitive Efficiency of Monotheism"

The human universal vision based on the assumption of an exalted Principle is the most cohesive of all. Upon such a vision materialistic and moral motivations can be built, leading man to his hopes and goals. He can achieve what he wants and organise his relationships in a way that corresponds to his natural requirements. Islam, as we have just mentioned, has made the One and Only Allah the pillar – or rather, the core – of a universal vision that corresponds completely to all the above. It traces all historical changes back to a single comprehensive source, which regulates the rhythms, guides the paths and establishes the laws and framework, while leading towards a necessary destiny of ultimate perfection.

Monotheism (*tawḥīd*) is the most refined approach of man towards this Principle. It constitutes the most exalted cognitive relationship between his nature and the essence of his existence, and leaves a great impact on the lives of the individual and society. When faith is instilled in the consciousness, it guides one's relationship with the world and other people. Here, Muṭahharī elaborates on the meaning of monotheism and what it requires of man's understanding.[120] According to this monotheistic vision, the whole world is a creature that relies on an Almighty Creator for its existence and its laws. The primary Principle has limitless power; He manages the world with His infinite wisdom and firm judgment, and sees all things no matter how small. Nothing can escape the perfect law He has laid down for the world, or go beyond its defined goal. This law forms a framework of relationships that includes man's freedom of will, and makes of him its effective agent. The creative Principle has all the perfect attributes that stir within man a desire to imitate them, and embody them in his moral formation and actions.[121]

Monotheism has several levels. It asserts the belief in the divine, which is elevated to the level of unity, uniqueness, adequacy and supremacy. Almighty Allah is the One and only, with neither an equal, nor a consort. He is the first, and creates, envisions and predetermines everything; He created all creatures and brought them into existence by His own will:

Nothing is the likeness of Him (42:11),[122]

Nor has He any equal (112:11),[123]

Say, Allah is the Creator of all things (13:16).[124]

This monotheistic vision of Allah is reflected in the realisation of the singularity of the world in which the oneness of its creation and destiny is depicted:

Verily to Allah do all matters return (42:53).[125]

It is also a monotheism of attributes. The Divine Self gathers in its oneness all the attributes of perfection without exception, where no attribute is above another, and no perfection is preferred to any other. It is only the "Self" that holds all the attributes of perfection.[126]

Likewise, it is a monotheism of actions. Everything in existence is a direct result and consequence of His actions – all things, relationships, systems and laws. The world only exists because of Him, and it relies on His management. It moves because of the power of movement He made available for it, and renews itself by way of the principles He instilled in it. It is perfect because of the fundamental perfection upon which He established it (*Whatever Allah wills, there is no power but with Allah*).

These are the theoretical levels of monotheism, that is, the knowledge appertaining to monotheism.[127] Reflection of this monotheism in action makes it a practical monotheism, which will be discussed when we address the meaning of faith and its effect on the world.

G. Man and his Relationship to Destiny: "Objective Efficiency of Monotheism"

The purpose of human action is perfection. According to Muṭahharī, it is man's destiny. He changes nothing of what has been established in Islamic literature. He links this perfection to man's strength and capabilities, whether physical, rational or spiritual. Man devotes himself to everything he does in the name of perfection and struggles to bring it about. In order to do so, he uses his reason and experience to guide him.[128]

There are many who do not believe in such things, assuming that man has no ultimate purpose in life, and that he does not have the power to direct his abilities to that end. However, man's experience implies otherwise. Since the beginning of his existence, he has always tried to find the means that would enable him to reach his purpose, while organising his actions to facilitate the process.[129] However, whenever man has relied on his own management or appraisal, sometimes he has succeeded, but often he has made mistakes, either basking in the joy of his success or struggling with the consequences of his mistakes. Man needed guidance[130] to reduce the effects of the deficiencies inherent in his nature.

Monotheism is a regulator and a guide. It defines a clear goal and codifies the use of his and abilities, setting out a framework of universal laws that ensure his attainment of perfection. They can be relied upon in order to regulate the rhythm of his life and integrate him in a relationship with the world and what it contains. This always arises from the direct intervention of the Principle in the framing of practical legislation by sending prophets to guide and instruct. This regulates the rhythm of human action and uses man's freedom and will in the best way possible while employing the laws worldly affairs and conducting their facilities and potential for the sake of ultimate human perfection[131] and complete happiness.[132]

This understanding requires of monotheism one other type of efficacy: an existential efficiency, or in other words, the clear identification of the existential relationship between man and the surrounding world. How does monotheism establish this relationship?

H. Man and the World: "On the Existential Efficiency of Monotheism"

Through his intuition, man realises that he is not alone in the world; he shares his existence with all the other things he interacts with and benefits from. Since the beginning of existence, man has associated himself with the surrounding world, and he set out to search, identify and explore it, while investing what he saw and experienced with attributes in the hope of closing the distance between him and them, and thereby build a sentimental relationship. The monotheistic vision of the world has instilled within his existential status certain qualities that cause him to constantly need something to manage.

These qualities include those of limitation and impermanence, and these are related to both time and change, and change implies a lack of stability. There nothing in the world that can avoid engaging with its surroundings in a precise symmetry. Furthermore, there is a need arising from these association, and the fact that there is a relativity. Things do not acquire their attributes without being compared to other things; a thing cannot attribute perfection to itself by itself.[133]

When man ponders these limited attributes and reflects upon existence, he realises that behind such a world exists a Reality that does not have limited attributes, does not lack what man lacks, and does not need what he needs. Such a Reality is absolute, unlimited and unconditional, and nothing compares to it or can be associated with it. The world relies on It for its existence, movement and survival,[134] and through It ascends within the limits of its own self and its own perfection. This Reality guides the world towards Itself, so it may be in its own self a sign and an indication of the greatness of the sole Reality, Its holy authority and comprehensive will. In such a way, the world not only becomes a place for reaping benefits or satisfying curiosities, but rather it becomes a symbol – a place of contemplation and understanding.[135]

According to Muṭahharī, the Qur'an instilled in man this vision of the world and his place in it, so it may become a principle that mankind can rely on and follow to reach the truth, and eventually perceive it in the world. The Qur'an states:

> *Indeed in the creation of the heavens and the earth, and the alternation of night and day, and the ships that sail at sea with profit to men, and the water that Allah sends down from the sky – with*

which He revives the earth after its death, and scatters therein every kind of animal – and the changing of the winds, and the clouds disposed between the sky and the earth, are surely signs for a people who apply reason.[136] (2:164).[137]

Man's relationship with the world is characterised by perception, reason, discovery and knowledge. In other words, it is a conscious intellectual relationship. Man also has emotions and sentiment with which he reacts to holy signs, indicators of God's infinite power and omnipresence. This relationship between man and his world manifests itself in compassion, love, glorification, respect, and feelings.[138]

I. Man and his Faith: "On the Psychological and Social Efficiency of Monotheism"

The monotheistic vision can only be reflected in actions through faith, because the mere thought alone cannot bring about motivation, commitment and responsibility. Rather, it is produced by the firm belief in the idea, and illustrated the experience of its dimensions, which are part of man himself, his conscience, his deep and innermost feelings, and his psychological and spiritual strengths. This belief enables the idea to endure and be experienced, and eventually penetrate the essence of man and manifest in his actions through responsibility and commitment.[139]

Faith may become manifest itself as *tawḥīd* in the psychological framework of man.[140] It is expressed in the essential spiritual connection between man and Almighty Allah, man's devotion to Him and imitation of His superiority and holiness, which encourage him to perfect the attributes of his personality and rise above his limitations. These limitations can impose their own rules, demand to be followed and overshadow man's freedom. But *tawḥīd* brings forth a boundless liberation in one's self and grants man a unique access to the absolute and the infinite, consequently generating the power to overcome one's impulses and frivolous inclinations, and a feeling of deep commitment and responsibility.

According to Muṭahharī, the pre-eminence of this connection expresses itself in acts of worship, which represent the tendency towards a direct relationship with Almighty Allah, a unique dialogue with His holiness, and the imitation of His attributes.[141] Muṭahharī says,

> "The first impact of Allah in man's life is a psychological influence and feeling of safety, which both manifest themselves in the unity, consistency and harmony of the soul. In the context of life, the only similarity to Allah is the psychological consistency of man's soul, and He is the only deliverer from the division between Him and man's soul."[142]

This is the significance of worship in monotheism. It is the expression of the monotheism of the soul and its attributes in absolute devotion to Almighty Allah through worship and obedience. Its residence is the deepest depths of the soul. Such a connection produces unity, harmony and consistency within man's soul.[143]

Muṭahharī says,

> "... monotheism in accordance with Islam must be applied to man's existence; the presence of Allah in the imagination and the thoughts is but the beginning. The first effect of monotheism is unity – the unity of the world which proves the unity of God: *Had there been gods in them other than Allah, they would surely have fallen apart* (21:22).[144] This verse depicts the oneness of the soul, as it implies that the unity of man's soul is similar to a world controlled by one authority; because otherwise they would both lose their unity, harmony and consistency, consequently corrupting their presence, threatening their order and paralysing their capacities."[145]

Faith in monotheism manifests itself in society in a stable interdependent and collaborative fashion. The psychological unity of man and the inner consistency of his personality become harmonious with his surroundings, the world and the rest of humanity. This is a normal and stable interconnection based on integrity and benevolence, and the commitment and responsibility towards other people's welfare in acts of compassion.[146]

Muṭahharī also says,

> "A sound social life is one where people treat laws and the rights of others with respect, honour and justice, and share love and friendship. It is one where people rely on each other in an interdependent and collaborative fashion, feel responsible towards each other without any greed or ingratitude, and treat one other as if they were a single body comprised of symmetric

and complementary organs. Religious faith, above all else, causes rights to be respected, justice to be sacred, hearts to be amicable, individuals to be trustworthy, piety and chastity to penetrate the conscience and moral values to be alive, and grants courage so that oppression may be defeated, and unifies individuals into a single unit."[147]

J. Man and his Faith: "On Psychological Efficiency and Orientation Dynamics"

Believing in Almighty Allah and His oneness leaves an impact on the soul and society, causing them to merge into an organised unit in which different abilities complement each other in a wondrous harmony with efficient consistency. Similarly, believing in the orientation of the world towards a single destiny also leaves an impact on the human soul and society as a whole. The functioning of society, with its activities, values and traditions, all become included within a comprehensive vision of the unity of the world and nature, and their systems and laws.[148]

As for the psychological impact, it is apparent in the optimism resulting from the impressions man has of the universe and its creation. Pessimism, nihilism and emptiness are alien to him.

> *And whoever disregards My remembrance, his shall be a wretched life* (20:124).[149]

Man is given hope for the future.[150] Religious faith in destiny brings about tranquillity, and feelings of purpose, significance, value and usefulness, since everything that exists in the world has a meaning and a purpose.

With regard to action and motivation, belief in orientation[151] urges man towards activity, and encourages him to use his full potential for the sake of serving and accomplishing his goals, while organising his abilities in the best possible way and putting any tool, machine or mechanism at their service. It also motivates man to understand and invest in his surroundings, and strengthens his will and determination to improve his life and overcome its obstacles.

This is what Muṭahharī has offered us as regards the monotheistic universal vision, by identifying its elements and clarifying its qualities. He assumed that such a vision achieves many goals, for it connects man to Almighty Allah and uplifts his soul, exalts his rank, deepens his understanding of his existence in the world, and engenders a feeling of responsibility. It also unifies society by investing it with high standards and relationships based on communal welfare, happiness and justice. It illustrates to man the exalted purpose of life, guides his strengths and skills, and helps him endure the transience of time so that he may reach his final goal. He also has hope, peace and contentment, which enable him to experience the deep meaning of life and the significance of his actions.

Hence, this universal vision builds the character of man in all the degrees of his existence. He is able to perceive the oneness, power and omnipresence of the Principle and the meaning of creation, and how creation endures for the sake of reaching its designated end. He can sense the unity of existence, the world and nature. This vision helps restore his soul and abilities to a cohesive unity. It also modifies his behaviour and manifests itself in his actions, in which he invests all his potential to serve the universal purpose of existence with all the means at his disposal, while all the time being conscious of the results of his actions.

Alone, man is unable to establish a connection with the Principle that ensures the unity of his self, and cannot rely on himself for building a consistent, balanced and harmonious system in which he unifies his inner capabilities. By himself he does not have the ability to discover the guidelines he needs to help him achieve the purpose of his existence and reach the end of his path. He gets some help by managing his behaviour according to its consequences. But he has a limited perception and the possibility of his inferior impulses and desires unconsciously controlling him, and consequently destroying the cohesion of his soul, incapacitating his strength and abilities, and diminishing his connection to the world. For this reason, man needs to regulate the rhythm of his psychological and behavioural activity, and distinguish between what is right and what is wrong. He needs a principle to define all these elements, and offered to him through a comprehensive legislation delivered by chosen men who are characterised by purity, exalted souls, sound minds and perfect attributes. They are the ones who are able to guide and introduce the appropriate legislation, explain its methodology and arouse in man the interest to adhere to it. Such legislation makes it possible to define the connections the soul should have with the Principle. Laws of this kind define how we worship and conduct our lives, which in turn set the standards for efficiency, effort and change. Laws thus formed constitute a system that regulates mankind's activities in all fields and ensures that they achieve their ultimate purpose by the safest route. This is done by making the best of our abilities, and building relationships in accordance with the balance of justice, moderation and integrity between ourselves and others, and between society, nature and the world.

Muṭahharī believed in rediscovering the elements of a universal vision and the revival of that vision. By revival, he means renewal. This implies that this vision had become deformed, and many of its elements – whether knowledge, psychological efficiency, behavioural efficiency or historical changes and adaptations – had become paralysed.

Throughout the ages, our vision of the primary principle and destiny as presented by Islam have become distorted, disturbing our ideas and beliefs. Believing in such deformed principles has affected our psychological and spiritual makeup, the balance of our inner capabilities, our actions, our overall way of life, and our behavioural patterns that determine our relationships.

It is clear that the false concepts we have formed over years have transgressed against the monotheistic vision of the world, man and existence. They have corrupted our understanding of creation, predestination, divine justice and the divine attributes – whether knowledge, ability or will – as well as our understanding of the divine authority over the world, our understanding of our destiny and the Day of Judgment, the connection between our life and the hereafter, our understanding of prophethood and the Prophet himself (as), and the nature of revelation, divine law and the Holy Book.

Muslims have changed this comprehensive Islamic vision of the universe into a mere rational system of thought, ignoring its psychological, social, historical and cultural import. They have ignored the impression it leaves on man's life and actions, and the spiritual and practical benefits of the belief in monotheism an example is spiritual and practical believe in monotheism, or believing in Judgment Day and destiny and its role in the social life of man and his relationship with the nature The vision has turned into either a rational system of beliefs, an abstract vision, or a collection of bleak and dry concepts, and arguments that lack guidance. This has consequently disrupted both the soul and society.

Therefore, revival involves the revitalisation of our thought and belief and being rid of false ideas. It involves the revival of the universal vision in the depths of our consciousness, in the ideas and convictions experienced in our hearts and given life in our actions. How does

Muṭahharī portray this revival? What are its rules and methods? This is discussed in the next section.

2. Renewal of the Science of Kalām: "A Look into its Methodology and Vision"

A. Kalām and the Incentive for its Renewal

Kalām (scholastic theology) is the use of evidence based on logic that was initially used to defend Islamic beliefs against the heresies and false creeds that occurred within Islamic society.[152]

At first, this practice was employed in many well-known confrontations, and preserved the cohesion of Islam. However, during its later development, it began to become a collection of ideas and logical religious and philosophical concepts presented in the form of basic principles, without which one could not become a Muslim. This practice started taking shape at the time of the first political differences within Islam, the introduction of Hellenistic philosophy, and the formation of different groups and creeds. It was used as a tool in intellectual and sectarian disagreements, and as a means by which each sect affirmed its legitimacy. The different sects developed methods to defend their points of view, using theological and philosophical knowledge acquired from different sources. Despite all that, *kalām* managed to preserve its connection with the foundations of religious faith, even though it included some exclusively philosophical themes. It never focussed exclusively on philosophical themes divorced from theology and metaphysics. Its standpoint always pertained to the existence and attributes of Almighty Allah, predestination, revelation, prophethood, Judgment Day, the Imāmat, governance, and other relevant themes. Therefore, monotheism remained the basis for all the other themes were built, and for this reason *kalām* became regarded as Islamic theology.[153]

During its development, there remained the single question as to what extent were its interpretations purely theoretical, and how could they affect the individual and society?[154] *Kalām* began to lean towards objectivity. It was deeply reliant on dialectic and a paradoxical theoretical methodology that produced inert concepts that barely related to everyday life. It also tackled nonessential issues, and changed from being a practice for establishing a clear system of Islamic belief to something dry and lifeless, and ceased to have any impact on the personal life of the Muslim and his relationship with Almighty Allah. Muslims could no longer understand the meaning behind statements such as "Allah is Absolute and Self-subsistent," "Allah is All-knowing," "Allah is the Living," and other statements argued over by the *mutakallimūn* (scholars of *kalām*).

The ambiguity of the approach of *kalām*[155] regarding the scope of divine action and the limits of man's activity had a great impact on Muslims. The argument did not depend entirely upon dialectical arguments, but rather the simple question of the relationship between Allah and His creatures. The question led to a fork in the road. The claim that Allah is the absolute agent was the first route, and its supporters felt that their actions depended on the divine Will. He is the one whose authority encompasses the entire world and whose knowledge guides it to the correct path. But this raises many questions regarding man's responsibility. As a result, those involved in the controversy sought to provide every justification possible to support their claim.

The alternative route stated that the centrality of humanity in creation endows man to govern his actions. Its supporters intended to affirm man's responsibility for his actions, which justified the *sharī'ah*. The claim that Allah is the agent of all actions alarmed them, for this would include everything man did, whether right or wrong. They believed this made the principle of ethical obligation redundant, and so they used every possible justification to establish man's responsibility for all his actions.

However, despite this controversy, *kalām* was of no use in the everyday lives of Muslims. There is no doubt about the social and psychological effects of the principle of monotheism. Theoretical dialectic does not need to penetrate our general awareness in order to demonstrate the living consequences of faith. In general, such themes did not reach beyond scholarly discussion, and furthermore their effect as motivating principles in the social conscience is virtually nonexistent nowadays.

The dialectical nature of *kalām* often sought to confute adversaries rather that establish the truth, and this set the scene for heretical views that distorted the image of monotheism. When such a heresy touched upon the principle of divine efficiency, it became coercive, giving man a passive, resigned attitude – a helpless creature with no will or determination. The result was a monotonous, inert society, surrendered to its fate, and liable to submit to a tyrannical authority. What is more, it infiltrated the principle of justice, causing disorder and political, social and psychological regression. *Kalām* began as a means of defending the faith and guiding mankind, yet it ended up by almost toppling everything, and the influence of religion withered.

After *kalām* had become merely an objective practice that presented its arguments in the form of explanations and footnotes, Muslims had to wait for the emergence of modernity before they could search for a fresh approach to work out the ambiguity they faced. This new *kalām* restores the basic function of Islam as it is stated in the texts. This should liberate man and his potential, and revive his efficiency in managing the rhythms of life, free from the problems of complicated dialectical arguments. Furthermore, living practice revitalises the soul and motivates man. It sustains his freedom in building his present in the light of his ultimate destiny and provides him with hope.

Muḥammad Iqbāl[156] was the first to attempt such an approach, after he saw the necessity of reforming *kalām*. Instead of only affirming the absolute knowledge of Allah, man should build a relationship that provides an inner motivation that revivifies man's heart, thus granting him victory over indolence and inertia.

We also find this trend in the work of Mālik Bin-Nabī. In his book *Destination of the Muslim World*,[157] he stressed that,

> "Our issue does not lie in proving the existence of Allah. Rather, it lies within our ability to sense and experience His presence, as He is the source of all life, power and action, and the origin of will, determination and resolve."

We cannot expect traditional *kalām* to do this, since it glorifies discussion and displaces cultural and psychological efficiency with theoretical ideas about the existence of Allah.

This is what has drove intellectuals towards a restoration of *kalām*, so that it could have some influence on the personal lives of Muslims. However, there was another reason. In the world's haste to modernise, there was a proliferation of many different ideas and philosophies, and an unprecedented interaction between the cultures and religions of the world. Monotheism needed to unveil its potential to assimilate and to respond to matters that Muslims had not experienced in the past. The most important issues were to do with progress and civilisation, and new outlooks and discoveries which aroused curiosity and overshadowed religious belief. Yet other problems arose as a result of changes in educational, social and political systems.

Jamāl-al-Dīn al-Afghānī was the first to attempt to recreate the perspective of monotheism, in the hope that it would respond to the demands of progress. In his criticism of atheistic doctrines, he focused on the belief in the Principle and the one destiny of all creation – their gathering for judgment on the Day of Reckoning – and its positive effect on man's values and sense of responsibility for his actions.[158] He considered those two points;

> "Powerful restraints that curb the desires of the soul and prevent it from being destructive, whether in a passive way or actively. They are radical and strict; they erase the effects of treachery and remove fraudulence; they are the best way to attain justice, put an end to prejudice, and achieve security and comfort." Without them, "mankind's unity cannot be achieved, civilisation cannot come to life, reciprocity cannot become sound, and human relationships cannot be free from impurities and problems."[159]

He believed that this could help civilisation advance, and consequently engender happiness and spiritual perfection in man.[160] In order to bring this about, the distortion that had accumulated over the years had to be cleared away. This referred directly to the coercion which had left man helpless,[161] and the principle of predestination, which no longer possessed the meaning that Allah had decided for it.[162]

The work of Jamāl-al-Dīn al-Afghānī led to more, and Muḥammad 'Abduh presented us with the most important vision of Islamic thought of the time in his book *Theology of Unity.* Despite its comprehensive resumption of traditional dialectical and philosophical ideas, and a rationality that clearly reminds the reader of *Mu'tazilah* in its prime, his book used it all in a new framework of thought on the social efficacy of Islamic belief and other monotheistic principles. Muḥammad 'Abduh stressed the effect of conscience as much as that of reason. He decided that man is not merely rational, but has an awareness of his dependence on the might of Almighty Allah, who gave him everything, has power over him, and enables him to carry out his activities. The book provides enough examples for these matters to be understood, and it encourages man to ponder the meanings and implications through sermons and lessons that revive his soul, awaken his conscience and subdue his inferior impulses.[163]

'Abduh considers unity to be a liberated energy, because it uproots agitation and purifies the mind of delusion and false beliefs. It gives man dignity and freedom, and liberates him from subjugation to any false authority and his own whims. It teaches that mankind was created equal, and encourages people to compete in knowledge and virtue, and to work together at the social level. It also situates multiplicity within unity, and explains how rivalry and differences should be harmonised. Just as monotheism attributes all beliefs to Allah's one religion, it also traces societal differences back to unity, and as a consequence results in the independence of man's will, his ideas and opinions. Thus humanity is complete, and the happiness that has been prepared for him by Allah can be achieved.[164]

Muḥammad 'Abduh was eager to respond to Hanoteau and Farah Antun and assert the value of these principles for mankind and society. However, he admitted that many Islamic beliefs had been distorted during the regression that Muslims had experienced over time. It had a destructive impact on their lives and led to decline – something which the first Muslims did not experience. Hence, Islam declined in proportion to the decline of the believers.[165]

At the beginning of the 20th century, Muḥammad 'Abduh's work was considered the best of its kind. It left an impact on many scientists and thinkers, such as Ḥossein al-Jisr (who attempted to emphasise the agreement between Islam and science in his two books *Al-Ḥusūn al-Ḥamidiya*[166] and *Al-Risāla al-Hamidiya*[167]), 'Abd al-Qadir al-Maghribī, Shakīb Arsalān, Ṭanṭāwī Jawharī and Muḥammad Jamāl-al-Dīn Qasimī. They adopted its ideas and used them to formulate various different perspectives. However, their work resulted in new ambiguities that could have been resolved on the same basis established by Muḥammad 'Abduh, but instead they were dispersed throughout the Arab world, and by the end of the century had had an impact unlike that of the start, resulting in directing Islam along new paths.

B. Methodological Foundation for the Renewal of Kalām

Muṭahharī's motive for renewing *kalām* did not differ from that of those others who recognised the dilemma of it losing all relevance for the personal lives of Muslims. He could clearly perceive the turning point where *kalām* became a dry rational practice. He attempted to gather together a series of writings which he had originally planned for the study of subjects such as monotheism, justice, prophethood, the Imāmat and the Day of Judgment, so that he might retrieve what he could of *kalām* as it was in its prime. Monotheism, being the principle and foundation of these issues, got the largest share of his research. He attempted to recover the glow of its meaning and implications, stressing the important role it plays in knowledge, science and society.

Muṭahharī was an expert in all the sources of *kalām*. This enabled him to test their usefulness in reforming its practice – especially its views on monotheism – and generally renewing it. There were some philosophical and metaphysical schools of thought that had remained alive around the world.[168] Muṭahharī clearly asserted the importance of reforming *kalām* in accordance with a firm logical and philosophical methodology that excludes all dialectical influence and all elaboration. In this way it would have a more cohesive structure to ensure its firm methodological and logical coordination and rid it of all possible perversions. Otherwise it would be distorted by nonessential or unrelated issues.[169]

Muṭahharī could see what the outcome might be. He legitimised it and defended it against doubt and suspicion so it might remain alive in the consciousness of the people. He set out to free *kalām* from transcendence and stagnation by simplifying its terminology and freeing its arguments from objectivism, and applied them to conscience and emotion. A preoccupation with dialectic has often turned the principles of monotheism into lifeless and complicated concepts. The Day of Judgment has stirred up many debates on logic, but they have produced any stimulation for the mind or a sense of responsibility. These have always been closed logical arguments that did not take into account the effect they would have on the rest of society.[170]

The Principle and destiny are the foundation of the existential experience of mankind, and for that reason Muṭahharī stressed the importance of transferring them from the level of the intellect to that of faith, where they would have some kind of psychological efficiency. This would then affect the soul, regulate the rhythm of its emotions, assert cohesion within it, and instil it with virtue and compassion. This latter gives man a sense of responsibility regarding the outcome of his actions and reap the benefits inherent in his nature and be happy. There would be no disorder, regression or indolence; man would be in complete harmony with the surrounding world. The psychological makeup of monotheism allows the soul to advance towards perfection, and encourages it to utilise its strength in mutual cooperation with others.

If we wish to summarise the realistic impact of these two principles in a Muslim's personal life, we would say they unshackle the mind from delusion and falsehood, and beliefs that restrain the will. They elevate his abilities to the highest degree, and enable him to overcome his vain impulses. Furthermore, they give him freedom and deliver him from the errant forces which trap him in their vortex. All this encourages people to set about competing in the fields of work. This in turn results in a victory over inertia, while evoking the presence of Allah so He may accompany and guide man along his way, and act as a source for his strength. Society then becomes cohesive, and assists man in achieving happiness.

Like Jamāl-al-Dīn al-Afghānī and Muḥammad ʿAbduh, Muṭahharī was aware of the perversity that plagued Islamic beliefs, distorting its meaning and having disastrous results in people's souls. Over time it gradually corrupted our culture and subjugated us to despair, until eventually all our power, with which we had once ruled nations and spread knowledge, science, civilisation and prosperity throughout them, was dissipated.

Muṭahharī began to list the false notions that had distorted Islamic belief. One example was the false interpretation of predestination as surrender to an inevitable fate that life imposes on us against our will. Another example is the concept of dependence, which was changed to mean dependence on other people. A third is the belief in the absolute competence of Allah, thus cancelling all man's freedom and responsibility for his actions. This paved the way for the steady dismantling of *sharīʿah* as the regulator of action. Another example is the principle of asceticism, which turned man towards an isolated, passive life free from any sense of responsibility towards society. Those who have perceived this dilemma are responsible for ridding the doctrine of impurities by instilling a pure and virtuous image of Islam and confronting the challenges generated by the changes of time. Muṭahharī realised that the need for modernisation affected this task, and that the new sciences and knowledge[171] of our era made the responsibility greater, since they tended to overshadow the attempts to revive religious doctrine. Modernisation also forced upon the doctrine the challenge of assimilation – something which traditional *kalām* could not offer.

Upon reading Muṭahharī's writings, one can see his concerns. The lectures he gave resulted in his books, and allowed him to meet others with and modern scientific knowledge, and who were well-acquainted with ideas that had appeared throughout the century. These meetings[172] forced Muṭahharī to completely reconsider the matter of faith in view of his newly acquired knowledge. He was open-minded about modern science, and the knowledge acquired during this era, having introduced previously unknown questions to the issue of faith. Those involved in such matters were obliged to engage in this work, and to use it as an inspiration for finding solutions to use as a basis for reforming the march of civilisation. In the midst of all this, Muṭahharī remained firm in his belief[173] that;

> "The principle of monotheism – with its deep meanings and dimensions – alone can ensure that mankind will build societies upon deep-rooted foundations."

This also included the development of civilisation and the use of man's abilities in a comprehensive system that will lead them surely and steadily to their own happiness. Furthermore, it alone can promise Muslims a return to their former glory, increased development and prosperity, and their participation in building the future. It also ensures them influential participation on the world map once again.

3. The Religious Response to Modern Science

We have stated that, during modern times, civilisation has seriously challenged the principle of monotheism and the entire Islamic system of beliefs, which they had to respond to one way or another. The nature of modern science – with its outlook, methods and discoveries – was one of these challenges. In general, we have seen how Muslims understood this challenge at the start of the 20th century, and how they sought different ways to reach a balance between scientific and religion.

In Muṭahharī's writings, we come across topics pertaining to the separation imposed by the nature of this era, the goals science pursued without restraint or guidelines, and the immense capabilities it discovered, which in turn aroused concerns regarding its unrestrained use. We also come across two stances, the first being the stance towards the separation of science from faith, and the second is the stance regarding the scientific philosophical attitude towards nature and the universe. From this perspective, we find that science has expanded our perception of nature, the elements and the laws of the universe. It has opened our eyes to worlds that had been previous unknown, and for that reason, Muṭahharī formed a framework by which he could contemplate the divine presence in the universe, and discover the infinite power of the Creator and the diligent management of His creations; a domain which adds depth to the issues of religious faith.

A. Faith and Science: "The Prospects of Integration and the Ambiguity of Separation"

According to Muṭahharī, the idea of a contrast between science and faith had become deep-rooted in Christian nations in the light of a statement mentioned in the Book of Genesis of the Torah which connected knowledge to death. It states,

> *And the Lord God commanded man, saying, "Of every tree of the garden you may freely eat. But of the Tree of Knowledge of good and evil you shall not eat of it, for on the day that you eat thereof, you shall surely die."*

This statement is repeated in two other places. Because of this notion, people believed that religion wanted man to remain ignorant about good and evil, because this ignorance allows his life to be put right, and that if he achieves knowledge he would perish. It also led them to believe that man can only achieve knowledge through disobedience, which is the reason for his expulsion from Heaven. Accordingly, evil lurks in knowledge; it is the source of perversion, corruption, disobedience and rebellion. However, Islam glorified the truth, and those who bore it were uplifted to the highest ranks. The Qur'an informs us that Allah taught Adam all the names, and then ordered the angels to bow down to him. The *Sunnah* taught us that the tree Adam was forbidden to eat from only represented jealousy, greed, selfishness and other attributes related to the lowest nature of man, i.e. the level of his animality, not his humanity. Satan only tempts in order to satisfy the whims of the soul, and not to fulfil what is supported by logic and knowledge. For that reason, Satan has always represented the impulses in man that enticed him towards evil, immorality, treachery, injustice and corruption.[174]

Based on biblical understanding, Western history can be divided into two eras: the era of faith, and the era of science.[175] On the other hand, the Muslim understanding of Islamic history is also divided into two eras: the era of openness and prosperity, which is also the era of science and faith, and the era of regression, which is the era in which both science and faith deteriorated.[176]

The deviant biblical idea resulted in losses for both science and faith that cannot be recompensed. In truth, the tackling of the relationship between science and faith should be different. It should be in accordance with a scientific methodology that examines the nature, essence, impact and foundation of both fields.[177]

According to Muṭahharī, science is composed of discovery and experimentation based on theory and practice. He had previously clarified the characteristics of discovery, stating that it is limited to known phenomena; it progresses every time it uncovers something new; and has narrow horizons – it can only experiment on what is apparent in the world and cannot go beyond that. Furthermore, it is characterised by impermanence, meaning that what it may offer at one point is but an acceptable explanation of some phenomenon at the time, but later developments may uncover new things that overthrow it or reduce its value.

Science may be useful in terms of work, for it provides man with the ability and the instruments to benefit from natural phenomena in building his life and exercising his capabilities. It could also help him in acquiring material means to improve his lifestyle and fulfil his material needs. However, it does not provide him with a comprehensive view of man and his abilities, or a deep understanding of the nature of existence. Neither does it enable him to satisfy his moral and spiritual needs.[178]

Only faith can do that, because it deals with existence in its entirety instead of just tackling parts of it by experimentation. However, this difference means that science and faith both complement each other, as well as help each other achieve their goals. Muṭahharī identifies the nature of this connection with reference to its results by saying:

> "Science gives us discovery and ability, while faith gives us hope and enthusiasm.
>
> Science creates production methods, while faith pinpoints the goals.
>
> Science gives ability, while faith gives us good will.
>
> Science explains things in our existence, while faith inspires the nature of the task.
>
> Science is an external revolution, while faith is an internal revolution.
>
> Science subjugates nature, while faith creates man.
>
> Science is the beauty of the mind, while faith is the beauty of the consciousness.

> Science gives detached strength, while faith gives connected strength.
>
> Sciences provides external security when its keeps us away from dangers that know and helps us makes use of what benefits us, while faith provides internal security and psychological tranquillity.
>
> Science creates harmony between man and nature, while faith creates harmony between man and himself ..."[179]

Each of these two fields provides man with things that complement aspects of his existential efficiency. It is impossible to limit man's experience to only one of those fields, i.e. one cannot replace the other in terms of its accomplishments.[180] On the other hand, each of these fields serves the other in achieving its goals through sound methods, while prompting man towards his goals via the best and widest routes. Muṭahharī says,

> "Obviously science cannot replace faith and provide us with love and hope by increasing our demands. It cannot remove the individualistic and self-centred hopes and dreams inherent in our instincts and nature, and instead provide us with goals revolving around love, forgiveness and altruism, by turning to methods that change our essence and quiddity. But faith can fill the void left by science, by offering us knowledge that unveils the nature, abilities and potential of the elements, as well as their connections, movements, changes and development."[181]

In order for faith to bear its fruits, it must rely on science to be efficient, and to motivate, prompt and guide it. This reliance prevents it from becoming stagnant and blindly intolerant, going round in circles and unable to lead man on the path of life.[182]

Science without faith is like a drunken man with a hatchet, or like a thief in the night with a torch in his hand.[183] But coupled with faith one can consider it the greatest way of enabling man to achieve his goals by the shortest of routes.[184]

According to Muṭahharī, the man who possesses strength is always driven forward to search for tools and methods that aid him in reaching his goals, but he needs to nurture this with faith. This is so that his abilities do not lead him to destructive, materialistic and individualistic goals that harm him, destroy what he has built and damage society.[185] He needs another kind of power; one that causes his hidden abilities to overflow and become more defined, that brings about a revolution in his conscience and creates directions for him. Such a power cannot be acquired through scientific discovery; rather, it is the product of the sanctity of exalted souls, resulting from venerated motives generated by a unique awareness and a comprehensive universal vision. This cannot occur in test tubes or be discovered by measurement or deduction.[186]

Muṭahharī lamented the destructive results that have left their imprint on the soul of mankind over recent time. Nevertheless, innovation has provided many ways to lead man to impressive results in material life as regards his immediate needs.[187]

In the midst of a complete lack of faith, this led to conflicting outcomes. On the one hand, it has driven man towards employing technology in order to fulfil most of his pleasures and desires. It has led to oppression, destruction, monopolisation, greed, deception and trickery.[188] On the other hand, it urged those who have perceived that science does not offer them tranquillity and security, or give meaning and purpose to their lives, to seek sanctuary in literature, poetry, mysticism, asceticism, magic, sorcery, psychology, or in nebulous religious and spiritual doctrines. It has also led them to mental and spiritual disorders, which in turn took them down the road to drugs and passing pleasures, which they recklessly and hastily seek in their need to forget, pushing them to the edge of nihilism, from where they have leapt to their deaths.[189]

It was not difficult for Muṭahharī to assert the disastrous results of divorcing faith from science with examples that are repeated almost every day in Westernised civilisation. But he also stressed that people in the West are also aware of the dangers of a materialistic society.

He recounts Will Durant's grief over what had become of civilisation in a striking passage, where he says:

> "The old world differs from the new one not only by its methods and goals. What can we say when all our progress is restricted to fixing those methods and instruments and does not care for the soundness of the aims and goals?"[190]

He goes on to say,

> "The revolution is exhausting, and logic and wisdom is but a feeble and cold light. As to love, it warms the hearts with the indisputable power of God."[191]

Muṭahharī remarks on this by saying,

> "Most people have realised that the purely scientific route is unable to nurture a perfect man. It creates an able man, not a good man. This man has only one dimension instead of many."[192]

Muṭahharī also recounts what Russell said in this context:

> "Actions that are meant for pure gain do not produce useful results. In order to get these results, we must carry out actions that hold a faith in a being, or a wish, or a goal."[193]

He also quotes a passage in which George Sarton says,

> "Science has advanced in an immense and curious way in some fields; however, in the fields pertaining to mankind's relationships with each other, it is still cause for mockery and ridicule. Art brings out beauty, and it is a source of joy in life. Religion brings about love, and it is the music of life. Science relates to truth, honesty and logic, and it is the source of human awareness. We truly need all these three things ... science is absolutely necessary for life, but alone it can never be enough for man."[194]

Inspired by a deeply-rooted belief that science and faith should remain together, help and nourish each other, and serve each other in achieving goals, Muṭahharī began to tackle in detail the issues of faith in the light of science, its developments and discoveries. He also dealt with the issues of science in the light of faith, devoting himself to the study of every book that dealt with an issue of faith or a religious principle.

B. Monotheism and theological exploitation of the results of scientific knowledge

This section does not intend to elaborate on the evidence Muṭahharī presented to prove the existence of Allah, which is the subject of his book entitled *Monotheism*,[195] where he describes the three methods for reaching that realisation: the instinctive method, the cognitive method, and the logical method. Rather, this section clarifies the method by which Muṭahharī employed scientific discovery in forming these proofs and in reconstructing its format, especially that pertaining to instinct, or the distinct order in all creation and the guidance that governs its movements.

Along science progresses, it uncovers the importance of these two things in the visible universe.

According to Muṭahharī, the intellectual evidence for the existence of Almighty Allah is based on an inherent feeling in man that attracts and guides him naturally and willingly towards Allah, this inclination having been proved by the Qur'an and many scholars. Muṭahharī, in his aspiration to benefit scientific discovery by instilling in it the principles of belief, examined a number of opinions given by the era's greatest scholars who have devoted themselves to the experimental sciences. Among such scholars is the American philosopher and psychologist William James.[196] Muṭahharī quotes the following from him:

> "Whatever the motives and urges behind our tendencies and desires that have resulted from the natural world, we will find that most of them have emerged from beyond the natural world."

Muṭahharī comments on these words by saying:

> "He means that the roots of our tendencies and desires are not in the natural world, because we have more exalted tendencies that emerge from truths more glorious than matter. Proof of that is the impossibility of explaining many of these tendencies in terms of materialistic considerations, i.e. the proof lies in the light of the underlying benefits of these tendencies, which caused us to adhere to this higher realm more than this tangible realm."[197]

Muṭahharī also recounts words by James that stress the effects of piety, where he says,

> "Each state that is considered pious is associated with tranquillity, dignity, passion, kindness, love and selflessness. It distances man from stupidity and fortifies him against doubt. I have found a manifestation of this state in my experiences. I am strongly convinced that the heart is the source of the religious life and inclination, and that the scientific, philosophical and religious visions and methodologies are but translations of facts written in a different language."

Muṭahharī remarked on these words by saying,

> "These words are important and profound; they make known a truth which states that cognitive, scientific and intellectual activities did not create religion, piety and religious tendencies; rather, they were brought about by the evidence of religion. They are the product of man's heart and instincts."[198]

He has also benefited from the famous physician, Albert Einstein. He recounts a vast number of texts from his book called *The World as I See It.* We shall convey something of these texts here to show how Muṭahharī used them to stress the deep-rooted religious tendency in man, and the impulse to adhere to an invisible power that encompasses and guides the world. He describes Einstein by saying,

> "The author of this book is one of this era's best scientists, and his research is very accurate."[199]

Muṭahharī summarised the introduction of Einstein's book, as he found that it benefited his aims. He says,

> "He [Einstein] began his book with an introduction that I will summarise in a few words. He said that love and hope are the driving force behind man's actions, and they are acquired through religion and piety. He also said that the nature of the feelings and self-motivation towards religion are various, and cannot be constrained. However, there are at least three types of religion in terms of their foundation and the nature of the religion itself. The first is the religion of fear, known by primitive people; the second is religion born from social and moral factors, man's need for a moral sanctuary; and the third is a religion present in all peoples in various degrees of purity – it is the religion born out of an inherent feeling in man regarding his existence."[200]

According to Muṭahharī, Einstein assumed that each of these forms is definitely beneficial, as they rescue man from corruption and regression. Even though the first two religious forms depict Allah in an anthropomorphic manner, as in Judaism and Christianity, Einstein believed that we should not ignore those few people who have perceived the true meaning of the existence of Allah amidst all these misapprehensions. Their perception of Allah is characterised by profound ideas which set it apart from the others.

Einstein considered that those within that particular group deemed the ambitions of man insignificant, and instead experienced the wonder of things beyond our existence. They see ordinary existence as a kind of prison, and try to break of the shell of their bodies in order to comprehend the oneness of existence. According to him, religious men of earlier times were characterised by the brilliance of this exalted form of religious sensibility, and recognised the greatness and glory of Allah.

Einstein rejected the Christian concept of Allah, which he found distorted His image, and found that only art and science can convey a profound religious message to the masses. He thought that it was the task of these two disciplines to stimulate this refined religious sense and keep it alive for those capable of benefiting from it.[201]

Therefore, science should support that inherent sense in man which guides him to Allah, since that sense constantly needs stimulation and a means by which it can develop. Even if science can to some extent contribute in such a way, it is does not explain the source of that certainty which mankind has had for all time. Science is able to develop such an inclination by revealing particular aspects of the greatness of man and the world, when they are perceived in terms of their universal harmony.[202] This brings us to what Muṭahharī called the scientific-philosophical proof, which reiterates the guidance found in the Qur'an and elaborated upon by Muslim scholars. This is what Muṭahharī wished to reconstruct in the light of new scientific discoveries.

This scientific-philosophical evidence is more than just empirical evidence, because he believed that science on its own does not reveal the existence of Allah; but it can help us indirectly by providing an initial introduction for developing an instinctive sense of religion, and prompting us to contemplate marvels of the Creator.[203]

Scientific evidence illustrates the order of the universe, and indicates that everything is established on the basis of an efficient cause. In other words, nothing happens by chance, and must be referred to a cause that guides the order of the universe for a specific purpose,[204] and which originates in knowledge, awareness, a will and judgment. Muṭahharī said,

> "What he means is not limited to the fact that a cause is needed for every effect, and an actor for every action. Everyone acknowledges this simple fact, for it applies to matter as well as to divine occurrences. However, it is important in this inferential path to recognise a different origin, because assuming

the existence of efficient order – that is, the existence of enough power to bring about an act – is not enough to prove the existence of a universal organiser. Those who use order in nature to prove the existence of Allah observe the existence of a will and a choice, because nature always faces different choices at every stage, and it always makes the most appropriate choice. Choice is the basis of all the transformations in this world."[205]

Muṭahharī did not refer to Martyr Muḥammad Bāqir al-Ṣadr at all, but he used the Law of Probability in a way that reminds us of him. Modern science has relied on this law, and adopted it as a methodology, and this regard Muṭahharī said,

"A monotheist may come to the realisation of Allah by means of modern methods of inference, especially the Law of Probability and its mathematical basis. He [the monotheist] says: Scientifically, we cannot admit to the existence of an order [in the natural world] without admitting to the existence of an aware and perceiving organiser, and we have no choice but to submit to the existence of said organiser. The probability of two successive events usually equals the result of multiplying the probability of the two events occurring at separate times. If an illiterate sits before a typewriter and punches in a letter, the probability of the letter being "B" equals 1/32. Nevertheless, the probability of him punching in a "B" followed by an "N" equals the result of multiplying 1/32 by 1/32, which is 1/1024. As the probabilities increase, they gradually become more improbable."[206]

Upon observing the natural world, we find that order prevails throughout in a way that goes far beyond that of the typewriter. Thus, the probability of there being no connection between its parts, and the probability of its source being unaware or without intention, is almost zero, which is sufficient evidence for believing in the existence of Allah.[207] Muṭahharī considers the Law of Probability to be one a significant discovery of recent times, for everyone, in speaking about monotheism, begins their argument with it.[208]

According to him, in the light of such a law, we can perceive that the world reveals a powerful knowing and guiding cause. He believed that the perception of order in the world wears out, and intuition and simple observation no longer clearly perceive them. But others have been discovered by science, for science has clarified certain aspects of creation and formation, and laws which govern the motion of the universe.[209]

In addition, the world reveals something else besides order, and that is guidance. One can use order to infer that the Creator of the world is rational, organised, wise and perceiving. But in addition, guidance illustrates that this Creator motivates His creations, through their different potentials, towards a definite and inescapable destiny. To perceive this one need only observe the flow of nature. This flow is not the mere result of the components of matter reacting with each other; rather, it reveals the existence of a kind of gravitational pull that leads all things along their respective paths towards an ultimate goal.[210]

Muṭahharī believed that these two evidences of order had previously been expounded by Fakhr al-Dīn al-Razī, who used the Qur'an to illustrate how they proved the existence of Allah. The skill alone required to create everything in existence reveals the existence of a Creator, but the study of nature reveals something else as well; for all things act and react of their own accord by relying on a special form of guidance.[211]

In order to prove the accuracy of the methodology in which he uses these two things as evidence, Muṭahharī studied a large number of books on science, nature and psychology explaining the laws governing and guiding the movement of all creatures. Thus, he shifted the issue of divinity from a metaphysical philosophical and theological context to an existential one, by applying the principle of divinity to historical records, and discovering it in all corners of nature and the laws of the universe, all the while perceiving the immutable greatness, power, knowledge and skill of Almighty Allah in all its aspects. He then combined all this within the context of a direct consciousness that prepares the consciousness and sentiments for His presence to engulf the heart and soul, so that it no longer remained a dormant objective concept.[212]

In order to benefit from the work done by Muṭahharī to assert the existence of Allah through science, we need a clear cognitive position to explain the ambiguities that surround it. An example of this is Darwin's theory, which some have relied on to assert that the order present in the world can be explained by the principle of evolution as expounded by Darwin. Another example is the theory of Lavoisier, which states that the existent cannot not exist, and the nonexistent cannot exist, thus completely denying the idea of creation and a Creator. We are going to tackle Muṭahharī's position on both theories in chapter four, while discussing the themes of the intellectual confrontation in Muṭahharī's reform project.

C. Dialogues Between Science and Religion: A Sample from Muṭahharī's Work

An example of Muṭahharī's methods of dealing with the discoveries of modern science may shed some light on his views on it. His three books, *Monotheism*, *Prophethood* and *Judgment Day* have many such examples, and they give us a comprehensive picture of the discussion between science and religion. These books are actually a collection of lectures given before a number of intellectuals, scholars and engineers, all of whom were well acquainted with various fields of science, as well as Islam and religious faith. One of them was Mahdī Bāzargān, whose books – which were mostly attempts at using scientific evidence to reassert and understanding afresh religious faith – stimulated Muṭahharī's ideas, and whose input enriched these lectures.[213]

The following is an example of the nature of this discussion, which is presented in the form of a dialogue:[214]

Muṭahharī: Mr. Engineer [Bāzargān] in his explanation has elaborated on what the ancients had to say with regard to matter and power, but he has done so in his own way. Actually, one could say that he has rephrased the words of the ancients in modern language, and has fortified these words with what supports his methods. However, he did so for another purpose that he wished to achieve.

I will review some sections of his book *The Infinite Entity* which I have noted. He writes,

> "Modern science only knows two bases: matter and energy. Science wants the whole world and its contents to fit into these two elements, plus the framework of time and place. On the other hand, even though the Qur'an acknowledges these two elements (unlike some *mutakallimīn* and philosophers who did not refer to them215), we find that it introduces a third element, thus indicating the presence of other possibilities.
>
> It is only normal that the Qur'an does not speak of this third element in many sections; it is limited to where it speaks of special events, death and moments of transformation.[216]

> In the light of this Qur'anic elaboration, we must find out where the truth lies, with the vision of the Qur'an or with modern science. Is the natural world (which can only have one explanation) made up of two or three elements? Contemporary science is unable to assess the world using two elements in the framework of time and place; it is unable to explain and justify many things that have occurred, or will occur, using the aforementioned elements."

I have mentioned that this position resembles, in terms of evidence, the position of the ancients. They did not know of "energy"; they only knew of matter, but they believed that it alone is not enough to explain the world. If no other component (they did not refer to it as "element", since this expression implies fabrication) were comprised in the essence of existence, we cannot attribute power to matter, because that would cause a similar ambiguity. Therefore, we must refer power to the essence of matter, not to matter as inert material.

In the same fashion, Mr. Bāzargān is supported by modern science when it speaks of matter and energy, but reports that science is unable to justify the existence of the world based on these two elements, and that there is a need for a third element. However, the third element Bāzargān speaks of is the same as the second element spoken of by others.

However, Bāzargān has employed some inferential methods that the ancients did not use, but which we deem feeble. He first goes on to say,

> "Concerning this is the initial creation of the world. Should the universe have a beginning, its first cause would have to be thermodynamic, that is to say something which would disturb the fixity of matter and energy. The theory of two elements is obliged to make the world infinite."

This is not to remonstrate against those who believe the world is made up of two elements, for they do not have to assume that the world is an accident in order to fall into such an ambiguity. In other words, we do not have to prove that the world is finite to say later that the (theory of) the universe based on two elements cannot explain to us the meaning behind existence and the beginning of the world. Those who believe that existence comprises two elements also believe in the infinity of existence, so we cannot present it in the form of an ambiguity or a conclusion, but it should be part of our claim, but in itself is insufficient.

The second clarification mentioned by Bāzargān comprised a good explanation. He says,

> "As to the characteristics and properties of these elements, or the way bodies are structured and the significance of change, this all leads to the following questions: Why aren't the forms and states of matter from which the world is formed stable? Why do these raw materials not remain in one state? What is the source of these transformations? If these movements, changes and events result from characteristics found in the nature of things, then this cannot be considered a form of association, but rather it indicates a purpose and a unique order, or movement in a specific direction."

This is the same proof that philosophers have mentioned in reference to power. They say that if the characteristics differ, then why does that happen? What is the origin of this dissociation and similarity? What is the origin of the differences in characteristics? Our research revolves around the source of different characteristics.

This proves the soundness of Bāzargān's explanation. It is similar to that of the ancients, but only differs in presentation, for he says,

> "There has to be a purpose or a unique will in action and order, so that these general and determined characteristics can be attributed to the dimension of the elements, and so that there may be an overall system that regulates our existence. Should interference from a specific agency be lacking, then the elements that make up the world must be in a similar situation to that of all the attributes and conditions."

The use of the word "will" should not raise objections, since an explanation using this expression would be correct.

The ancients believed that the evidence proved the existence of power. Since it cannot be an self-subsistent (i.e. have the characteristic of matter itself), then it has to be in contradistinction to the essence of matter. The two things are not separate from each other; but rather they join and share a form of union, meaning that they are a single entity (i.e. they are two aspects of one entity). As long as this power changes the characteristics of matter (for if a power did not exist, then all things would be the same, meaning that power is the principle behind the variety and diversity of things), then it would be called the "diversifying power" or "the qualitative method".

The third evidence presented by Bāzargān is to do with life and its emergence, for the phenomenon of life itself only appears after it first emerges. In this regard, Bāzargān remarks that research has not yet been able to solve the issue of life's first emergence. However, should it claim to be able to do so, then Bāzargān was right in saying that the appearance of life for the first time has nothing to do with the issue, because no matter how life appeared, our research does not take into account the source, but rather the means.

He writes,

> "This method contradicts *entropy* (decay and decomposition), or in other words, it contradicts the second law of thermodynamics, which is associated with the principle of aging."

This is a very valuable point. However, in terms of evidence, we find that it is similar to the first evidence, which claims that we have found something else other than matter, and so it cannot be considered independent. It is only logical that we do not consider them two pieces of evidence, for they both are represented by one evidence for which many examples have been given.

As regards the important issue of life, the ancients spoke of it in another manner, and said if we created a machine or a building, it began to decay and decompose from the very first day. However, a living creature heads towards perfection from the moment it appears, before finally starting to decompose. It appears that they do not deem this decomposition realistic, and instead they believed that the power that seeks perfection cannot be exhausted and decompose, but rather, its association with a particular being is cut off.

In their opinion, this proves that life itself is a reality that controls matter.

Bāzargān writes:

> "As I have mentioned in *The Young Islam,* the manufacture of a living being (i.e. changing simple metallic bodies to sequential or annular cells to form a living robotic being, which would be an extremely complicated process) is scientifically impossible from the perspective of the Law of Probability and entropy (the law of

> decay and decomposition). This is because the formation, detail and specialisation required by living components and the functions of organs and tissues are considered inconsistent and incompatible with what is required by the increase in entropy (the law of decomposition).
>
> The decomposition, decay and death of living things comply with the Law of Probability and the law of entropy. Furthermore, the appearance of life and living things, whether at the first moment of existence or through reproduction and renewal, does not comply at all with either the laws that govern matter and energy, or a world that is comprised of only two elements."

It is as if this text says that there are two laws in this world: life and death. On the one hand, matter and energy in all the aspects of existence are the biggest factors regarding death. In addition, the third element that controls the world is the factor behind life and renewal. The third element represent life and renewal, while the elements of matter and energy represent decay, decomposition and death, because it is inevitable that things decay and die. From the point of view of the cycle of life and existence, decay and decomposition become most prominent, whilst in the other point of view we find life and renewal.

Should the third element not be explained in this way, then renewal in life cannot be explained by matter and energy.

The researcher then moves on to the study the source of integration and the appearance of humankind.

Bāzargān: This is not the first time Shaykh Muṭahharī refutes the "the denial of the soul." I have always stood in the interrogation box, even though I have written in the footnotes of page 61 of the third edition of *The Traversed Road* the following: "I am not determined to disprove the existence of the soul." For I have never aimed to disprove the existence of the soul in *The Traversed Road* or in *The Issue of Revelation* or in any my other books. However, I have always focused on two issues in this context.

As it has been noted, *The Traversed Road* was only meant to offer man an explanation of this line of enquiry. The idea was to show how much mankind has perceived and understood of what the prophets have showed to them.

In all the books, the theme supported what mankind believed, and by that, we mean people living in the contemporary world.

In this context, nobody can deny that many scientists have tried to deny the existence of the soul. *The Traversed Road* could not attempt to support the existence of the soul, for it had to go in the opposite direction and blend in with the convictions of those others relating to the inexistence of the soul. By doing so, we have insisted on two issues, and we have mentioned the following on page 160:

> "As regard the Day of Resurrection, the Qur'an did not depend on the theory of the soul at all, and it does not contain a single verse that indicates that the soul will remain alive."

As to the circumstances during the writing of the book, they were burdened by the pressure of challenges from communists and materialists. Many of those teaching mathematics and the natural sciences (communists or otherwise) arrived at class bearing books written by Dr. Arrani and his peers, to use as evidence for uprooting the theory of the soul.

On the other hand, many *mutakallimūn* depended on the existence of the soul to prove the existence of Almighty Allah and the Day of Resurrection, to the extent that it seemed as if they considered the soul to be an auxiliary mathematical component; especially when they said something like, "Yes, man dies and nothing is left of him in the world." Physical bodies decompose and vanish, but as long as the soul remains, it is not impossible for it to return and resurrect man.

However, the approval of resurrection in such manner immediately disapproves it by multiplying the fundamental root of the Day of Judgment.

This book is the response to the communists and materialists of that time. The basis of its logic is as follows: All right! Let us assume the correctness of your claim and say the soul does not exist, so what does this have to say about the resurrection, if the Qur'an does not specifically mention the soul?

The Qur'an has expressions such as the *Day of Reckoning* (*al-Qiyāma*), *the Hour* and the *Day of Judgment*, yet it does not mention a Day of Resurrection, although this is used more commonly, especially since it appears in a traditional context at the root of the doctrine, in the context of monotheism, prophethood, justice and the Imāmat, followed by the

Day of Resurrection. Till now nobody has answered this dilemma just because they have not discovered a verse with the following implication:

> *"O people! Your soul is alive, and the soul remains alive even after you are undoubtedly dead."*

As to the final part of this day, which refers to *al-Qiyāma*, I have tried my best to include naturalistic evidence from the Qur'an, because when it asserts *al-Qiyāma* to make us aware of it, it uses completely natural examples, such as the Spring and the Earth. It explains the reviving of a dead land and its being filled with greenery brought about by the straightforward assistance of rain and other elements:

> *Likewise will be the resurrection [of the dead]* (35:9),[217]
>
> *Likewise you [too] shall be raised [from the dead]* (30:19),[218]
>
> and *When He calls you forth from the earth, behold, you will come forth* (30:25).[219]
>
> The Qur'an does not mention the soul anywhere in these verses.

Thus, we find that one does not need to believe in the soul to believe in *al-Qiyāma*. In such a way, the book attempted to assert two things. The first is that the Qur'an did not prove the genuineness of *al-Qiyāma* through proving that the soul exists, but rather it used material evidence, and the second is that in our research we do not need to depend on a theory that claims that the soul exists.

From the point of view of terminology, the Qur'an does not in this case mention the soul. Usually it refers to something adjacent to the body, thus implying movement and life are made up of two components: the body and soul. But as for affirming that when the body dies, the soul dies as well, the Qur'an never once gives this impression when talking of the soul.

Thus, as is mentioned in the book, we arrive at the following:

> "Breathing life into the soul is an act of perfecting; the soul comes from the Divinity after the creation of the form of man and establishing his posterity (or after the completion of the forms that must be present in a sound man). Therefore, the soul is unlike that of which the Greek philosophers speak, and unlike the common belief that is known as the essence, the source of life, and the centre of sense and perception."

As such, it proves that the soul was not denied in *The Traversed Road.* We have also mentioned in *The Infinite Entity* that the soul, the command and the will are similar and scientifically approved of, and that this is emphasised in the Qur'an.

Muṭahharī: Some of the things you have said relate to the part played by *The Traversed Road* and the vision it was based upon. Of course, these are acceptable introductions, and the book – as far as I know – had a positive effect on those who deny religion. It has played a guiding role and performed a useful task.

Should there be any criticism, it is based on something else entirely. As long as Mr. Bāzargān does not insist upon the issue, and claims that he was not attempting to deny the existence of the soul, there is no need to discuss the philosophy of the book.

This leaves us with a remark mentioned about the Day of Resurrection, but I will discuss it in detail later on. What you have said about the Qur'an and the fact that it has not referred to *al-Qiyāma* as "the Day of Resurrection" (in other words, when souls are resurrected in their bodies) is a very valuable point, and it is a brilliant concept of yours. However, it is an intellectual concept that has been discussed in the past.

3. Instilling Values and the Comprehensive Nurturing of Mankind's Capacities

A. Instilling Values

It is worth noting that the contemporary understanding of "values" is absent in the Islamic heritage, whether in *fiqh*, history or education. Throughout the years, scholars have used other terms when speaking of the virtues, graces and morality, included here under the broad title of "values," that cover a wide range of characteristics pertaining to human behaviour. As to the motivation behind behaviour, it has always been associated with the pillars Islamic pillars of faith and the ideas of piety, worship and retribution. Accordingly, this places values as such under the banner of Islam, as it is a doctrine, a *shari'ah* and a way of life, which manages the affairs of the individual and society, and integrates all the activities of life with the hereafter.[220]

The universal Islamic vision mentioned earlier comprises a belief system from which emerge ideas about man, the world, nature and destiny, and a system of laws governing one's actions, behaviour and relationships. Furthermore, it comprises a system of values which defines the motivation directing action and behaviour.

The word "values" (*qiyam*) is often mentioned in the Qur'an in different forms. Allah is The Ever-Living (*al-Ḥayy*), The All-sustainer (*al-Qayyūm*), He who can exist on His own without partner; He who makes and controls things, knows everything about them, preserves them and watches over them.[221] It is also mentioned in connection with the upright religion (*al-Dīn al-Qayyim*), which steers towards all that is good without deviation.[222] Another example is the clear, straight path (*al-ṣirāṭ al-mustaqīm*)[223] that leads towards man's goal, without difficulty, effort or deviation, aberrance or squandering.[224]

Furthermore, the Qur'an guides to that which is most upright (*li-llatī hiya aqwam*)[225] in terms of beliefs, legislations and morals. In addition, precious books whose value is priceless are described as *al-kutub al-qayyimah*. Allah has created man in the best of forms (*taqwīm*),[226] whether that of body, mind or soul. Furthermore, the Arabic word *qiwām* refers to moderation, temperance and rationality in all matters.[227]

This shows that in the Qur'an, the meaning of values (*qiyam*) refers to the concept of an order which guides all phenomena along a clear, straight path in preparation for judgment, perfection and completeness; for the whole universe is built upon a system that rectifies its matters. The rectification of man's life is through a system of values that determine his ideas, tasks and relationships, both apparent and hidden. It sets him on a path towards righteousness, moderation, perfection and harmony, and allows him to set straight his strengths and abilities and organise his deeds so that they may be put to good use.[228]

In the context of the Qur'an, the word "value" has many implications which impart to it several wide-ranging attributes whenever it is used:

> *Some refer to weight, benefit, worth and good: They are the ones who deny the signs of their Lord and the encounter with Him. So their works have failed. On the Day of Resurrection We will not set for them any weight (18:105).*[229]

Others refer to firmness, stability and tenacity:

> *Indeed the pious will be in a secure place (44:51).*[230]

While some others refer to care and responsibility, since those who are in charge of a ward are responsible for caring for them and managing their affairs:

Men are the managers of women (4:34);[231]

Allah, there is no god except Him, The Ever-Living, The All-sustainer (2:255);[232]

So, is He Who sustains every soul in spite of what it earns (13:33).[233]

Yet others refer to righteousness and integrity: And [Allah revealed] that if they had remained straight on the path [of Allah] (72:16).[234]

Either way, believing in Allah, and the inevitable destiny expressed by the universal vision of the world that guides and moves towards, requires a two-way relationship between Allah and man. The rectification of this relationship needs a system or order, which cannot be built without principles and values; for they are the foundations of man's thought, feelings, conscience and desires and impulses, whose rhythms they regulate and guide along the path of moderation and righteousness. In this way the soul may reach unity and harmony, and man's work and behaviour may be in accord with it. Thus, the principles for regulating and guiding human behaviour are formed, so that mankind may inherit the Earth and establish civilisation upon it.[235]

Islam has asserted that the roots of these values are inherent in the man's nature, and that man perceives their virtue by way of improvisation and common sense. However, they are often distorted, or deviate from their natural state because of conditions and circumstances, and this indicates the need for their significance to be clarified, developed and preserved. Islam has also stressed the importance of these values and encouraged them, and explained how they can be developed through worship, nurture, guidance and education.

On the subject of upbringing within Islam, Muṭahharī noticed the harmony between true Islamic values and intuition, which allows man to form his own self in the light of his relationship with Almighty Allah, and develop the skills to use in his life for creating his own history and civilization in accordance with his destiny. However, he also saw that these values have become fragile, and the average Muslim is barely conscious of them. They have little impact on his personality and his actions, or on the way he treats other people and the world around him.[236] The new values and principles that man has adopted from Western culture

– which do not relate to a universal principle and destiny – have replaced the old ones. They are part of a materialistic vision that uses experimental science as its inspiration and foundation and places man in charge of his existence, while putting the values that guide him within a comprehensive framework that has nothing to do with a divine principle or a comprehensive, universal purpose.

Such principles became gradually instilled in the souls of Muslims through habituation, upbringing, and the direct influence of being surrounded by an attractive technology which developed an unparalleled urge in man to assimilate it, until our current standards and behavioural patterns became enormously distanced from Islam and its values. They took over our ways of thinking, until traditional Islamic values were either erased from our minds or became a lifeless principle with no impact or efficiency.[237]

Recent times have prompted us to embrace overpowering but unstable values, which change with the times and suit the needs of technology and modernity. Muṭahharī discusses this issue in the fourth chapter, which speaks of the relativity of morals in Western thinking, and the consequent impact on man's behavioural patterns.

The only way to return to comprehensive and stable religious values and moral concepts is through a good upbringing and a complete awareness of what is going on regarding the changes, values, behavioural patterns and lifestyles within society. In Islam, upbringing and nurturing is an important time of development and guidance for the mind, soul and body. It is a form of education and practice that builds the soul and the will. Should Muslims wish to turn over a new page, they should remember that nurturing is a building-block of renaissance. A revival of Islam, along with its universal vision, principles, legislation and ethical values, must occur with proper upbringing and a comprehensive educational programme with specified principles and a governing vision. And so, how did Muṭahharī envision this path and show us its steps?

B. The Comprehensive Nurturing of Human Capacities

According to Muṭahharī, man's nature has two essential dimensions: one is a spiritual, mental and psychological, while the other is physical, and each of them is made up of a number of potentials, strengths and motivations. The physical dimension involves the impulses of the body;

the desires perceived through the senses and the organs. As for the spiritual, mental and psychological dimension, it is has different and more exalted tendencies relating to society, rather than animalistic ones.

Following the example of William James,[238] Muṭahharī divided these tendencies into four categories in his book *Religion and the Soul*: the intellectual and mental dimension, the moral dimension (or moral conscience), the religious dimension (or religious sense), and the artistic and gustatory dimension.

Muṭahharī believed that these tendencies are inherent in man, and that they appear or fade in accordance with the surrounding circumstances. However, their elimination is not possible, for they react to stimulants and factors that exist around man. Since Muṭahharī assumes that man has a formative dignity of stature, which causes him to feel superior to all other creatures, it is because this spiritual, psychological and mental dimension distinguishes him from other creatures. It is because of it that he has a strong will and unique abilities.[239]

These tendencies within people have manifested themselves throughout the course of time. They have defined their fate in history, and enabled them to create their identity, live their experiences, establish civilisation and visualise their destiny. All the activities of man, whether spiritual, psychological, intellectual or physical, are initially determined by motives that require fulfilment and satisfaction, and become apparent in behaviours that comply with a vision that has been formed in accordance with these tendencies.[240]

Man is the only living creature who possesses free will; he is able to act in accordance with his motivations in all kinds of different ways. However, his tendencies may develop in ways that do not serve his own goals or those of mankind as a whole. This has a negative effect on his life by making it disturbed and chaotic, thus ruining the happiness and well-being he could achieve.[241]

For this reason, many nations have striven to establish educational systems based on doctrine and a true vision to ensure the development of man's potentials. This has to be a deep-rooted vision that takes into account man and his nature, strengths, stature and destiny, as well as his function within society.[242]

Islam is a comprehensive system of beliefs; an existential vision that has an intellectual system, legislation, clear goals, as well as a comprehensive understanding of the movements and laws of the world, and man's place in society. Thus, it is only natural that it should comprise a system that ensures the development and integration of the man's potentials to help him achieve his goals and use them in the best way possible. This is so that he can build his life and civilisation in his best interests.[243]

C. The Fields, Principles and Elements of Nurturing

Despite the consistency of the system which Muṭahharī here refers to, it takes into consideration its consequences for the many dimensions of the nurturing of mankind. For that reason, the system of nurturing in Islam has been able to detect these various domains and accordingly create methods compatible with them. Muṭahharī placed these domains in four categories: the mind or reason, the self, the soul and the body. He classified meditation as the nurturing mechanism of the mind, worship as the nurturing mechanism of the soul, piety and beauty as the nurturing mechanism of the spirit, and work as the nurturing mechanism of the body.[244] However, he did not neglect the mutual effect of these methods on the dimensions and actions of man; each one of them leaves an imprint on all the dimensions, even if that imprint is refined in one area. For example, worship leaves an imprint on the soul, the body, the spirit and the mind as well, and the same applies to piety, meditation and work.

In order for these methods to reap benefits, they need to be coupled with knowledge and habituation. Knowledge[245] enables man to perceive the nature and consequences of his actions, thus stirring into motion his will and determination. As to habituation, which is the product of will and knowledge, it instils the actions in the mind as an experience, giving them a greater impact and causing them to be more beneficial, while also strengthening the soul's resolve so that it may not ignore them for any reason.[246] Habituation also puts these actions at the service of the soul, so it may execute them without difficulty. Muṭahharī calls this an "actual habit," because it arises from man's will and awareness, unlike "declamatory habits," which arise from the influence of the surrounding environment or imitation.[247]

D. The Effects and Results of Nurturing

According to Muṭahharī, the nurturing of the mind has many effects:

It frees the mind from the common, deep-rooted notions and customs of society and popular opinions that lack proof.

It leads to creativity, innovation, renewal and transcendence, and builds a connection with the future wherein man might foresee the consequences of actions.[248]

It develops the cognitive soul,[249] which means that man should be impartial in his search for the truth and his attempts to discover meaning, instead of using his previous convictions and biased views. Should man adhere to impartiality and preserve the cognitive soul, his liberated mind would guide him to the truth, and depart from intolerance, bias, stubbornness and arrogance.[250] According to Muṭahharī, this soul brings about humility in the face of the truth and what man perceives of it, because it enables him to realise that the knowledge he has is but a small portion of what he seeks to acquire, thus motivating him to constantly seek the truth and realise how little he has acquired and discovered. Muṭahharī believes that Islam has strongly encouraged learning, defended the mind and its freedom, and assumed that prudence is one of the best and most efficient ways towards discovering Allah.[251]

It brings about analysis, criticism, research and *ijtihād*, which eradicate stagnancy and indolence, and allow the mind to become a scale that is able to distinguish between the logical and the illogical, right and wrong, truth and falsehood, and the beneficial and the harmful.[252]

As regards the many results of nurturing the soul through worship, they are as follows:

It constantly reminds man of his place in the world, his relationship with the Principle and his fate, and stirs a sense of responsibility within him towards his own self, his society and the world. Islam has considered worship a complete educative programme that nurtures the qualities of the soul and a way of life that includes a responsibility towards others. It develops tranquillity, confidence, calmness and discipline, and respect towards the possessions of others, since it states that prayer performed on land that has been seized by force is not accepted. It also develops good habits, such as purity and cleanliness, along with self-control, a strong will, control over impulses and desires, patience and tolerance, as is the case with fasting and hajj.[253] Prayer also helps man organise his time and make the best use of it, as it is should be performed at certain times of the day and night.[254]

> Islam specified an orientation[255] for prayer to inspire the concept of unity in man. It is as if this one location that man turns to face during prayer always inspires him to feel the unity of his capabilities, his society and the world around him, thus developing a sense of harmony between him and society, and causing him to treat others with compassion and respect. It makes him aware of the unity of the world, so that he may feel greatness and beauty in all its aspects, and treat it with kindness and reverence.[256]

It develops a sense of purpose and sincere intentions, because one needs to be aware of the effectiveness of worship before it is performed, and one needs to be conscious that it is imposed for a specific purpose. In this way, one does not attempt an act without perceiving its true nature, and receive its effect, for better or worse, with a pure intention and strong determination. It also enables man to control his self, direct his capabilities, and determine the nature of his actions.[257]

The results of nurturing the self[258] are a strong will, dignity and a sense of one's capabilities. This enables man to control his tendencies and desires and employ them to achieve happiness and well-being.

The many results of nurturing the body by way of work are as follows:

It steers man away from indolence, which nullifies his capabilities and sabotages society, surrendering him to impotence and inefficiency and pushing him to the brink of decline.[259]

It releases capabilities and opens up ideas and imagination. For work is a kind of laboratory, a place where experience and efficiency can be tested. It acts as a doorway for these capabilities to enter the world and reveal themselves in the many areas of life.[260]

It causes man to think logically, because it shows how each task has a result. Furthermore, it leads him to his goals in a definite fashion, by way of logical relationships.[261]

It brings satisfaction and a sense of calm. It causes man to become aware of his value as a productive being, a living component that leaves an imprint on the course of history, whereas idleness causes him to feel upset and agitated, and can lead him to violence, desperation and nihilism.[262]

It preserves man's independence and self-sufficiency, and preserves him from submissiveness, humiliation and subjugation for the sake of satisfying his basic needs and desires.[263] Islam has stressed the importance of work, and stated that work is the only way by which people can depend on themselves and create the necessary dynamics of life. This idea was instilled in the first generation of Muslims, who were convinced of its direct connection with their destiny, resulting in a surprising confidence that had them marching to the fields of work and *jihad*, unafraid of any power or authority.[264]

Islam has encouraged the moderation of man's capacities and potentials, meaning that nothing should be developed at the expense of something else. It emphasises the importance of the equal development of all the aspects of man, so that he may be complete in all his dimensions and the act of nurturing may reap the desired rewards.[265] If this becomes apparent to man, by the correct application it will lead him to happiness, and make available a methodology for enabling him to build his life and undertake the burdens of society. It also gives him the adequate sufficiency for him to create his history and build his future by his own will and reasoning, in accordance with the universal vision in which he believes. In such a way, he would be able to achieve revitalisation and prosperity.[266]

According to Muṭahharī, Muslims should undertake the task of education if they wish to revive their lives, establish a basis for the future and a renaissance in the present, for education is the only way to achieve it all. Without it, they can neither prosper nor progress, and the principles of Islam would remain distanced from their experience; it would be absent from their consciousness and their work in both the present and the future.[267]

Fourth: Revival and Renewal: The Hindrances and Obstacles

Preface

Muṭahharī's work enabled him to uncover the defects that plagued his society, causing disruption and reducing efficiency. His affiliation with the social experience and intellectual movements of his era and his proximity to the ideological and sectarian trends, allowed him to perceive the faults in all aspects of society. He was always engaged in the search for a clear prospect of renaissance, and passionately began to analyse all the factors. He learnt about times of prosperity and decline in Islamic history, in the full awareness that every project seeking progress and change cannot go far without realistically identifying the problems and examining them. Otherwise, no matter how cohesive its vision, precise in its methodology and deep in its perception, every project will fail once put into practice. It will be counterproductive and turn into a lifeless dream, an almost impossible hope, whilst also deepening the hole in which society finds itself. This has happened in many Islamic countries in the past centuries, with movements for liberation with honest leaders, known for their noble motives and enthusiasm to push their society forward along the path of revival and progress.[268]

Muṭahharī believed that it is not enough just to call for the revival of Islam as the rule of life, make people aware of the possibilities, or identify a system of education that would be able to revive the creative abilities and hidden potentials of society and use them in the best way possible. It is also not enough to let loose the imagination so it may perceive religion by way of a liberated act of *ijtihād*, or offer an explanation for the regression that has affected the lives of Muslims, or to merely foresee the dangers that surround them on all sides. One must also be aware of the real obstacles and difficulties that stand in the way and try to overcome them. One must face these things with wisdom and logic, and distinguish between the internal and external obstacles brought about by changes in relationships throughout the world and the centralisation of places of power and authority, whether these are new and immediate, or old and established.

It is worth mentioning that, whilst in the midst of all this, Muṭahharī had the courage to speak out and to act. He was well-acquainted – in a discernibly different way to other revivalists in contemporary Iran – with what was required of a project for the renaissance of Islam. He was also familiar with practical examples from history of the problems faced by different movements that had upset their balance and what should be brought forth into the new progressive era with its many horizons.

Muṭahharī focused on the internal obstacles to the renaissance project at two levels: the first being the religious institution, what it required in the present, the problems that surrounded it and limited its efficiency, and the crises that have shaken its very foundations, which together affect the nation and its understanding of Islam in a negative way. And secondly, the tyrannical political authority which controlled the fate of the people, their wills and their minds, oppressed their potentials and stole their freedom and rights. This authority had had such a devastating effect on society, that it was almost lifeless; it was crushed and incapable, with no control over the present or the future, and no identity to define it.

Muṭahharī found that the external obstacles comprised three things. The first was foreign colonisation by way of economic and political control. The second was the cultural and moral invasion of society, and the values and behavioural patterns it instils, which contradict our cultural and religious values. The third was an ideological and intellectual incursion that distorted our view of ourselves and the world, destroyed our identity and independence, and made us victims of alienation, weakness and annexation.

Furthermore,[269] Muṭahharī mentions drawbacks to the renaissance movement itself, such as the absence of a plan and a comprehensive vision. This would inhibit its progress and cause it to become apathetic. There was also a lack of comprehensiveness; it focused on one aspect at the expense of others. It was also too idealistic, and the enthusiasm had become overwhelming at a time when the project as a whole was still unclear, and its foundations, development and goals were undefined.

1. Obstacles within the Renaissance Project and the Crisis of the Religious Institution

For many years, the religious establishment in Iran was one of the decision makers in the country, and an influential actor in the political and social life. To some extent it preserved an effective connection with the collective awareness of the people, and a sentimental association that allowed it to play a very important part in society and leave an imprint in many fields.[270]

However, for several reasons – some relating to the cognitive approach of the religious establishment in the past few years, and others relating to developments which shook society – this institution retreated to the shadows and became a mere observer. Not only was it unable to take a lead in the renaissance movement, but it became an obstacle in its path.[271]

This retreat of the religious institution took the form of a complete isolation from life and its events; it secluded itself and existed independently. It became intellectual inactive in many ways, longing to return to the past and cling to it. This included a disgraceful failure to confront the many complicated concerns stirred up by the changing times.[272]

This led to the legitimisation of a form of knowledge that could not be utilised, which was undesirable and lacked the ability to develop. It was rooted in a religious knowledge that adhered to empty, traditional notions that did not address experience, but was constantly repeated despite its lifeless and meaningless content. For that reason, the religious institution withdrew from history, and stopped being a sanctuary for people to approach in order to calm them amidst upsetting events and fortify their minds against the pressing questions of fast-moving events, the influx of human knowledge and the worrying complications within society. As mentioned earlier, Muṭahharī believed that the only cure was the revival of *ijtihād*, for legislative knowledge to reflect in such a way that new capabilities might be used in life, undiscovered potentials compatible with the questions of the time. Furthermore, the religious establishment should be reinstated in society to stir the awareness of the people in the direction of Islam and its principles, encourage them with its values, and shape their consciousness with its vision of mankind, the world and existence.[273]

Not wishing his words to remain mere speculation, he contributed to a number of reforms, which included:

- Breaking down the legislative methods in order to acquire more depth and comprehensiveness, by forming a jurisprudential council for an exchange and of opinions regarding current events, and identifying the priorities that required the most attention;

- Organising systems of knowledge in a way that brings them up to date, whilst also developing their methods and language to make them compatible with contemporary scientific developments;
- Instilling freedom of thought away from traditions, common practices and the political authority, so that it may rise above the prevailing stereotypes with their vacant appearances and empty titles which impart an illusionary and offensive superiority that distracts the mind and destroys creativity;
- Changing the religious career from a paid job to being a cognitive responsibility for seeking guidance and direction; from being a way of acquiring fame and social status to a flexible mechanism for the return of Islam to the perception and activities of the people.[274]

Muṭahharī spared no effort in tackling the issues, and he approached things with a pure and open mind, and a clear view of reality. This was during his attempts to bring the religious institution from its retrograde state of isolation, and into society as an institution contributing to the renaissance.[275]

2. Internal Obstacles and the Dominance of Political Tyranny

Political tyranny was not a new thing for Muslims; they did not suddenly come across it during their attempts to build the foundations of a modern society. It has been a part of their experience for a long time, they were aware of its destructive effect on man and society, and they knew its mechanisms[276] and the tools it used to protect itself.

In the past, tyranny relied on religion to legitimise itself, establishing its authority by claiming that power and domination should be in the hands of a theological institution – or to be more accurate, a divine institution – as was the case with the Umayyids, the Abbasids and those who followed. However, it has appeared in a different form in current times, either in the methods used or the origin of its power. The foreign colonisation of society have brought forth political élites that have associated closely with it, discovered its purposes and submitted to it completely, as well as powerless nations engulfed by poverty, ignorance, decomposition and inefficiency.[277]

Even after the colonisation faded, it had given the political élites everything they needed to seize the reins of power. It provided them with a wide knowledge of how to establish their presence, manage their authority and spread their influence. They did not rely on a divine idea to affirm their legitimacy, but instead took possession of the idea of progress and renaissance, and boasted of their ability to uplift society in their own way, in order to catch up with the standards and prosperity of Western civilisation. While they pushed society in that direction, they reformed its institutions, removing their traditional outlook by gaining inspiration from the Western influence; they severed the ties with religious values, deciding that they were backward and were responsible – along with the Islamic law – for the regression, disruption and idleness of society.[278]

Iran was not safe from all this, for a westernised[279] political élite took over the country at the beginning of the century. They invested in it a process of renewal representative of the West in all its domains, by imitating its activities and borrowing its values, cultural and legislative principles, and systems of management and governance, and then forcefully imposing it upon the country. This closed the door to any objections that threatened their authority or rejected their opinions. This enslaved society, which by now lacked will and independent thinking, and was powerlessness and defeated. It became a society whose fate was in the hands of a group of dictators and executioners, who controlled it and basked in its benefits. This came about at the expense of countless needy people with no spiritual, intellectual or physical power, so that the few could be free to make their plans in accordance with what would preserve their authority.[280]

These élites started forming the political, economic, social, educational and administrative institutions in ways that served their own goals. These institutions became pawns in their hands which they could direct however they wished, at a time when there remained for society no efficient will to give it its freedom, no enlightened mind to save it, and no purposeful vision to guide it.

Muṭahharī believed that the governing authority could be confronted in two ways:[281] the first was by uncovering its purposes, and the destructive effect on society. The second was by freeing the educational institutions from its power, which was the greatest threat to present society and to the future, because the universities and colleges had the living and efficient potential for aiding any project of reform and the elimination of tyranny. In his work, Muṭahharī pursued both these channels; he challenged the intentions of the dictators, and uncovered their falsity and the dangers they posed. He tried to enliven the awareness of young people in the universities and educational institutions, and to make these places platforms for the freedom of thought; he wanted to create a vision that incorporated the capabilities of the new generation for changing the present and building the future. Along with others of a similar mind, he managed to get results in both these directions, and young people – who began to sense their importance and perceive the corruption within the system – were being motivated towards the overthrow of a power that regarded them as nonentities, controlled their fate, nullified their capacities, distorted their identity and destroyed their independence.

In both cases, Muṭahharī expressed the vast potential that members of the clergy had for reviving society, and the psychological efficiency they could ignite in the awareness of the people. This included the impact religious concepts could have on society and their aspiration to change, despite the difficulties that stood in their way.

3. External Obstacles and Cultural Invasion

In the Islamic world, the local political authorities generally made up the framework that enabled the earlier colonisers to preserve their interests and their influence. For that reason, the former colonisers tried to provide everything that would ensure their permanent presence, and interfered directly in order to do so. They were unconcerned with the tragic reality of the subjugated nations, or their legitimate rights, such as political participation, freedom of thought, the right to live safely, the right to learn and their right to freedom, and so on. They were only concerned with protecting their influence in areas they considered vital and indispensable, where they could acquire resources, and where they could establish some sort of control in the fight over power and interests. These localised political authorities served their masters in a way that guaranteed all this at the expense of their own people, until they became powerless satellites with no control of their own.[282]

Political and economic control was only the outward expression of endless foreign interference, which internally became apparent in the form of an irreversible influence on society.[283] Our nations became prey to a blind cultural and intellectual subordination, an empty and meaningless imitation of the lifestyles of Western civilization. They walked down a foggy path, unable to see where they were going.

In addition to the political élite that held power and subjugated the people to a Western political and economical influence, a westernised cultural élite was dismissing cognitive intellectual trends. They began to talk about how the society would be unable to advance should it not imitate all aspects of Western civilisation, whether in ideas, work, values, behavioural patterns, government, or trade and the economy. They stated that this required the complete severance of ties with tradition, liberation from its influence, and the abandonment of its values and customs. Religion was not exempt from all this, for the same applied to its ideas, roots, rules and values. The Arab world witnessed these trends in many forms; they were illustrated by an invasion of minds, influence on the sentiments and the suppression of behavioural patterns, causing a cultural westernisation that affected values and lifestyles. People imitated all aspects of Western civilisation, organising their lives accordingly, for they were completely convinced by its growth and artificial power. They were unable to disassemble, criticise or evaluate it. They became subservient societies, alienated from themselves in terms of politics, ideas, work and economics. They absorbed everything offered to them, whether values, customs or ideas. They had no identity, no cultural independence, no history, no traditions, and no heritage.

Our thinkers adopted one of three stances. Some advocated a blind pursuit of the West that invited society to embrace Western culture in all its aspects. Others clung to the past and ancient traditions, without acknowledging the present reality and having the courage to confront it, and faced complete isolation. Yet others tried to modernise the concepts, values, teachings and laws of Islam that they might be compatible with new ideas and values, and so that their radiance might never fade.

Muṭahharī had observed these trends ever since he devoted himself to studying the relationship between Islam and the present era, and his eyes had been opened to the influences dominating his society. Since he believed that inertia, intolerance and isolation, or distancing oneself from reality, do not solve anything or achieve any results, he opted to confront the trends threatening society and its values, and guard himself against their influence in an attempt to protect his own identity. He also found that the other two positions, mentioned in his criticism of the religious establishment, were just as threatening, and were defects that needed to be eradicated. In order to do so, he would call for people to immerse themselves in awareness, consciousness, logic and knowledge,[284] because he believed that a fervent position would not result in anything, and that a reckless confrontation would only cause disaster.

Muṭahharī attempted this in a courageous, objective and humble manner, with firm knowledge and sound logic, and he set himself three tasks. The first was to confront the comprehensive westernisation of life and its separation from Islam. The Persian national heritage had been redefined according to western nationalistic trends such as Nazism, with a condescending attitude towards ideas that considered Islam an obstacle in the path of progress and the cause of inertia and backwardness. In his book, *Mutual Services of Iran and Islam*,[285] he managed to refute the nationalistic trends, and argued against the notion that Islam obliterated Persian culture, destroyed the progress of its civilisation when it was in its prime, leading Iranians into decline. He presented the benefits Islam had brought for Iran and the Iranian people. He also spoke of the services that Iranians have contributed at all levels to Islamic culture; for they were efficient, innovative and productive (whether in science, knowledge or ideas), and they took part in building its institutions, while playing an active role in guiding it along the path of progress and prosperity. The people of Iran adhered to the Islamic traditions and religious heritage, and their revolution had an irreversible effect in reducing the influence brought upon them by the nationalistic, isolationistic notions that originated in a tyrannical power structure.

His second task was to deal with the constant distortions of the *shari'ah*, whilst re-assessing it so that it would be compatible with the basic needs of life. Muṭahharī work in this context was presented in three books: *The Problem of Veil*, *Woman and her Rights in Islam* and *Sexual Ethics in Islam and in the Western World*, which are collections of his points of view and lectures, articles and activities.

With these books, Muṭahharī intended to reintroduce certain concepts of Islamic jurisprudence, which had been selected because they were considered ancient and applicable only to traditional societies of yesteryear, and were obstacles in the path of progress that needed to be overcome. He was not alone in claiming that Islam allowed us to progress and use our minds to improve the shari'ah so it may be compatible with our circumstances, and may serve our best interests, giving us the freedom to discard the laws, customs, rituals and traditions that do not suit the time we currently live in.

In the second of these books, Muṭahharī analysed the nature of the family system and its position in society, as well as its natural composition of having a man and a woman as its two basic elements. Then he distinguished between them in terms of equality, stating that each of them has a nature that is different from the other, which together affect the nature of the role each of them should play.[286] In order to do so, he explained the sources of the natural intrinsic rights of humankind,[287] while clarifying the differences between them in terms of creation and formation, rather than according to a particular environment or tradition. According to him, we should use nature to discover freedom and equality, as well as recognising our differences. He believed that nature had a purpose in doing so, and that contradicting it led to undesirable and catastrophic consequences. Muṭahharī refuted the Western experiences pertaining to women, for he believed that the tendency towards liberation arose for economic reasons, when women could be used as cheap labour to work in factories and operate machinery at the peak of industrialisation. This freed women from household chores, only to become the slaves of perpetual torture in factories.[288] Even though the earlier miseries came about through the forgetfulness of her human nature, the new miseries of woman are a product of forgetting her femininity, her role, her natural position, her instinctive needs and her capacities.[289]

According to Muṭahharī, the issue pertaining to men and women is not one of deficiencies or privileges. It is an issue of nature, predisposition, capabilities and tendencies; it is these that differentiate men and women. Therefore a woman should perform tasks appropriate to her nature, and a man tasks appropriate to his.[290] The call for the equality of the two genders burdens the woman with unbearable tasks, forcing her to undertake what she has not been created to do, and imposes upon her difficulties that do not comply with her nature.[291] The consequences of this affect both sexes, and ruins the relationship between them, leading to a distortion and the possible termination of family values, which in turn has a negative effect all aspects of society.[292]

Muṭahharī discussed in detail the true Islamic view on woman's status, and emphasised her rights, which are not to be taken away under any circumstances. He also explains the philosophy of Islam pertaining to the differences between the qualities and responsibilities of the two sexes,[293] while strongly denying claims that Islamic laws concerning dowry, expenditure and divorce humiliate and degrade women, taking away her will and freedom.[294]

He considers the early Islamic praxis concerning women to be a prominent example. Islam freed woman when she was enslaved and subdued in pre-Islamic Arabia, and had no value or voice whatsoever. It made her an equal partner in life and in building society in a way that suited her abilities. She could facilitate changes within society, and was an educator who had the power to either reform or corrupt society according to her inclinations. Islam protected her from domination by men and the injustices of society.[295]

Recreating this notion and spreading it amongst the people helps correct our perception of woman and the way we act towards her. It also allows us to recognise the meaninglessness of the so-called equality we all rush towards, which results in weakening the role and status of women, and disintegrating the family unit. The effects on society are disastrous. Even the West is starting to feel the pressure of the consequences.

Muṭahharī assigned his third book to a discussion of sexual relationships from the Islamic perspective. He explained the dangers of having no restraints on the satisfying of lusts as the influence of Western concepts and practices. He believed that Islam respects and values sexual intimacy, and considers it a natural relationship arising from instincts and basic needs. Thus, it has set a number of rules and guidelines for the satisfaction of these desires in a proper manner.[296] This was at a time when many people viewed sexuality with caution, and considered it an evil to be avoided. Others saw it was a sin that corrupted mankind.[297]

The guidelines on sexual behaviour in Islam are a part of general ethics. They consist of everything related to sexual desire. They identify the natural methods that ensure satisfaction, respecting woman and her dignity, and protecting her from the humiliation and degradation brought about by visualising or treating her as an object for fulfilling needs or satisfying lust.[298]

Many Western thinkers have denied the necessity of chastity or honour, for example. This has contributed to the phenomenon – as will appear later on – in which the world becomes a place where the idea of honourable conduct is ignored and extreme attitudes displace deep-rooted values for the benefit of animalistic tendencies, that is, the urge to satisfy sexual desire with no consideration of the consequences.[299]

Muṭahharī wished to address mankind's universal interests, and the tendency to assert one's needs and act upon desires had to be taken into consideration. However, he does not discuss the source of these values, whether they originated from instinct or customs and traditions (discussed in Chapter Four). Instead, he focused on the results.[300]

The question asked here is what form should sexual ethics take in order to achieve the interests of the individual, and preserve the integrity and harmony of relationships within society, in the best and safest way? Does this require us to step outside certain limits and let loose a boundless freedom that stops at nothing to satisfy its needs?

According to Muṭahharī, reason and logic necessitate a realistic way of tackling needs that provides the conditions for satisfaction within the boundaries of the best interests of society. This would be in harmony with its purposes and guidelines, and rid it of the blind and uncontrollable release of desire which would plunge society into chaos.[301]

Those who advocate sexual freedom claim that the restraints imposed in the past were a result of customs, and that the new ethics advocate the freedom of the individual to achieve happiness by satisfying his personal needs, and require that free rein be given to these energies. They stress that the suppression of these energies only causes them to build up, causing the desire to turn into an insatiable urge. The remedy is to allow these energies to be satisfied by acts free of any restraint, removing all obstacles and giving them complete freedom.[302] This idea fascinated many young people, and they started to apply it in their own lives, drowning themselves in their desires, and ruining their potential by devoting all their strength to such claims. Those delving into modern sexual ethics claim that sexual freedom is a different kind of freedom, and has nothing to do with the freedom of the society, since it does not affect the freedom of others or harm them in any way.[303]

However, Muṭahharī believed it was not the instinctive tendencies in the individual that gave him freedom, and obliged others to respect it. Freedom is truly an instinctive predisposition granted to man by life, so that he may progress towards perfection. If the will of the individual is compatible with this predisposition, then it demands respect. However, if this is not the case, then all respect is lost, just as with the will of one who aimlessly wastes his potential or is driven to suicide.[304] For this reason, it is wrong to believe that man's freedom in satisfying his desires is valid as long as it does not affect the freedom of others, because the argument misses the point; this freedom is subject to how well it serves man's best interests. Nature has decreed impulses for a specific purpose, and their indulgence and satisfaction must serve this purpose, and so guidelines are set down, with boundaries to ensure that this purpose is accomplished.[305]

Supporters of this so-called freedom claim that the release of sexual energy generates tranquillity in the individual and stability in society, and believe that its restraint can only lead to disruption and chaos that would harm everyone concerned.[306]

According to Muṭahharī, the last statement is true to an extent, but the first one is incorrect.[307] He believed that nurturing, developing and satisfying the tendencies and dispositions is required to achieve the serenity of both the individual and society. However, a clear structure is required; nurturing only refers to the aid provided to help someone grow and mature. Choosing suitable methods and means, helps avoid being lead to defect, disorder and chaos.[308] Islam does not think poorly of the instinctive predispositions or the human soul, but it believes in the possibility of its corruption,[309] thus will and mind need to it in control, so it is used in a way that serves man's purpose.[310]

If restraint harms man and does not help his aptitude to develop and bloom; costing humanity and causing dangerous complexes;[311] then disregarding all ethical issues and unleashing these desires without any boundaries equally causes disorder that brings about defects greater than that of the former. The results of sexual liberation are catastrophic; the tension and agitation of the individual increases, and his psychological illness and complexes accumulate, and his life becomes even more miserable.[312] Furthermore, it destroys family ties, disturbs the relationship between man and woman, and generates endless troubles and boundless anxieties, since the status of family and security of the future is bound to forming social relationships.[313]

In addition, unleashing sexual lusts does not result is tranquillity, but rather prompts man to become greedy and think of endless new ways to achieve satisfaction, using shocking methods that humiliate man and degrade women.[314]

According to Muṭahharī, if giving these energies free rein helps in achieving balance and peace, then other desires would also help in doing so – as is the case with the desire to possess, control, and so forth – and there will be no need to set rules.[315] Furthermore, since the foundation of the relationship between man and woman is respect, kindness, love, compassion and selflessness, mindless sexual intimacy is selfish and materialist, devoid of love and compassion, and destroys the pure feelings of respect and intimacy that connect a man and a woman.[316]

The first book, *The Issue of the Veil,* falls within this context as well, reifies our perception of the woman and her relationship with the man, and discusses sexual impulses. Muṭahharī has asserted that the veil does not oppress woman by distancing her from life, or dismiss her in terms of her capacities. The veil in Islam represents modesty, whereby the woman protects herself from the gaze of outsiders and conceals her charms, thus preventing desire from arousing and protecting her from unwanted attention.[317]

The third task Muṭahharī worked on was to confront the Western cognitive and intellectual challenges, which had become firmly rooted in the minds of the Iranian people, especially the younger ones, and motivated their actions. This affected society more than the Marxist view, which had spread like wildfire among young people, and more than the philosophical, scientific, materialistic, nihilistic and communal trends adopted by a generation of Iranian intellectuals. This was quite apart from philosophical and ethical outlooks, and the circumstantial and experimental methods for explaining ethics and the cognitive vision of the world, which had completely captivated generations of scientists, scholars and thinkers. In the next chapter, we will discuss these topics.

Notes

1. "The Ailment and Medicine of Muslims," p. 15, copied from the introduction of *Revival of Thought in Islam* by Muṭahharī, translated by Muḥammad Ādharshab, al-Bi'tha Foundation, 1402 AH, p. 9.

2. Al-Maududī, *Renewal and Revival of Religion*, pp. 33-34, copied from op. cit., p. 10.

3. See Muṭahharī's discussion of his basic idea in op. cit., pp. 15-21.

4. "Our Message," taken from *Revival of Thought in Islam*, pp. 8-9.

5. *Revival of Thought in Islam*, op. cit., p. 13.

6. Ibid., op. cit., p. 15.

7. Muḥammad al-Bahi, *Modern Islamic Thinking and its connection to Western Colonialism,* 7th ed., Beirut, Dār al-Fikr, 1991, pp. 421-422.

8. Zaki al-Milād, *Islam and Renewal*, Beirut, Arab Cultural Center, 2008, p. 14.

9. Compare in regards to this: Muḥammad Hossein Fadlallah, "Authenticity and Renewal," *al-Minhaj Magazine,* Issue No. 2, pp. 65 and 69-70, Beirut, Summer 1996; Muḥammad Hossein Fadlallah, "Ijtihād and Renewal Capacities," in Zainab Shorba, *Towards a Modern Understanding of Ijtihād*, Beirut, Dār al-Hādī, 2004, p. 63; Muḥammad Mahdi Shamsddine, *Ijtihād and Renewal*, Beirut, International Foundation for Research and Publishing, 1996, p. 85; Muḥammad Hossein al-Amin, *Modernity and Heritage* (dialogue), Hayat Medical Magazine, Issue No. 5, pp. 16-17 and 19, Winter 2001.

10. Muḥammad Amara, *Islam between Enlightenment and Malpractice*, Beirut, Dār al-Shurūq, 1995.

11. See with regards to several definitions of renewal: ʻAbd al-Jabbār al-Rifāʻī, Muḥammad ʻAbduh, Muḥammad Iqbāl, *Al-Tasamoh Magazine*, Issue No. 15, pp. 224-225, Summer 2006; Zaki al-Milad, *Islam and Renewal*, pp. 242 and 244; Yahya Muḥammad, *Polemics of Rhetoric and Reality*, Beirut, Arab Diffusion Company, 2002, p. 7.

12. Omar Farrukh, *Renewal in Muslims, not Islam*, Beirut, Dār al-Kitāb al-ʻArabī, 1986, pp. 9-23.

13. *Revival of Thought in Islam*, op. cit., pp. 21-22.

14. Op. cit., p. 22.

﴿لِيُنذِرَ مَن كَانَ حَيًّا﴾

﴿أَوَ مَن كَانَ مَيْتًا فَأَحْيَيْنَاهُ وَجَعَلْنَا لَهُ نُورًا يَمْشِي بِهِ فِي النَّاسِ كَمَن مَّثَلُهُ فِي الظُّلُمَاتِ﴾

﴿يَا أَيُّهَا الَّذِينَ آمَنُواْ اسْتَجِيبُواْ لِلّهِ وَلِلرَّسُولِ إِذَا دَعَاكُم لِمَا يُحْيِيكُمْ﴾

15. *Revival of Thought in Islam*, op. cit., pp. 23-28.

﴿وَأَن لَّيْسَ لِلْإِنسَانِ إِلَّا مَا سَعَى﴾

﴿فَمَن يَعْمَلْ مِثْقَالَ ذَرَّةٍ خَيْرًا يَرَهُ* وَمَن يَعْمَلْ مِثْقَالَ ذَرَّةٍ شَرًّا يَرَهُ﴾

16. Ibid., op. cit., pp. 29-31.

17. Ibid., pp. 32-33.

﴿وَلَنَصْبِرَنَّ عَلَى مَا آذَيْتُمُونَا وَعَلَى اللّهِ فَلْيَتَوَكَّلِ الْمُتَوَكِّلُونَ﴾

﴿إِنَّمَا النَّجْوَىٰ مِنَ الشَّيْطَانِ لِيَحْزُنَ الَّذِينَ آمَنُوا وَلَيْسَ بِضَارِّهِمْ شَيْئًا إِلَّا بِإِذْنِ اللَّهِ وَعَلَى اللَّهِ فَلْيَتَوَكَّلِ الْمُؤْمِنُونَ﴾

18. *Revival of Islamic Thought*, op. cit., p. 43.

19. Ibid, pp. 44-45.

20. Ibid, p. 45.

21. Muṭahharī, *Islamic Movement in the Last Century*, pp. 17-18.

22. Ibid, pp. 8-10; *Islam and the Demands of the Era*, pp. 63-64; *Articles about the Islamic Revolution*, pp. 81-103.

23. *Islam and the Demands of the Era*, op. cit., pp. 14-15.

24. See "On putting Revival against the Era," Tahā Jabir al-Alwāni, *Reform of Islamic Thought*, Tehran, Al-Aarāf Company, p. 69.

25. *Islam and the Demands of the Era*, op. cit., p. 65.

26. Ibid., pp. 16-15.

For the transformation of the Arab renaissance movement after 'Abduh and al-Afghānī to a Salafism that hoped to preserve identity instead of leading the renaissance, see: Riḍwān al-Sayyid, *Policies of Contemporary Islam*, p. 7; "Dualisms-Terms-Trends in Contemporary Islamic Thinking," *Contemporary Islamic Issues Magazine*, Issue No. 26, pp. 62-64, Winter 2004; Ḥasan Ḥanafī, "Philosophical Studies" in *Contemporary Islamic Thinking*, Beirut, Dār al-Tanwīr, 1995, pp. 159–162; *'Abd al-Jabbār al-Rifā'ī, Muḥammad 'Abduh and Muḥammad Iqbāl*, p. 230.

27. For a contemporary understanding of *Ijtihād* see: Yūsuf al-Qaraḍāwī, *Ijtihād in Islamic Shar'iah*, Kuwait, Dār al- Kalām, 1996, pp. 114-133.

28. *Ijtihād in Islam*, translated by Ja'far Khalīl, Tehran, al-Bi'tha Foundation, no date, p. 7; compare with 'Abd al-Karīm Surūsh, *Tradition and Secularism*, Tehran, Farhang Sirat Company, 1382 AD, pp. 27-28.

29. *Ijtihād in Islam*, op. cit., p. 11; *Islam and the Demands of the Era*, p. 33.

30. *Ijtihād in Islam*, pp. 20 and 22-23.

﴿إِنَّا وَجَدْنَا آبَاءَنَا عَلَىٰ أُمَّةٍ وَإِنَّا عَلَىٰ آثَارِهِم مُّقْتَدُونَ﴾

31. Ibid., p. 27.

32. Op. cit.

33. Op. cit., p. 28.

34. Op. cit., p. 29.

35. *Ijtihād in Islam*, op. cit., p. 30.

36. Ibid., op. cit., p. 31.

37. Ibid., op. cit., pp. 32–33.

38. See Muḥammad al-Bahi, *Contemporary Islamic Thinking*, p. 4; Omar Farrukh, *Renewal in Muslims*, pp. 12-23; Taha al-Alwani, *Reform of Islamic Thinking*, p. 69.

39. Muḥammad Amara, *Islam between Enlightenment and Malpractice*, several sections.

40. *Muṭahharī and Intellectuals*, Tehran, Sadra, p. 98.

41. *Islamic Movements in the Last Century*, p. 92. They are mentioned in the discussion of the obstacles of revival.

42. Muḥammad Baqir al-Sadr, *Our Economy*, Beirut, Dār al-Ta'āruf, pp. 392-399.

43. See Haidar Huballah, *Renewal in Religion*, a paper presented to a seminar on religious renewal in the Islamic Cultural Centre in Beirut on 10/10/2008, p. 26, (unpublished).

44. *Islam and the Demands of the Era*, op. cit., p. 14.

45. Ibid., op. cit., p. 50.

46. Ibid, p. 50.

47. Op. cit., p. 14.

48. Op. cit.

49. Op. cit., p. 15-16.

50. Op. cit., p. 14-15.

51. *Islam and the Demands of the Era*, op. cit., p. 15.

52. Op. cit., pp. 16-17. See Muṭahharī, *Prophethood*, translated by Jawād 'Alī Kassār, Tehran, Um al-Qurā Company, 1420 AH, pp. 50-51.

53. *Islam and the Demands of the Era*, op. cit., p. 27.

54. Ibid., p. 27.

55. Ibid., pp. 31-32.

56. Ibid.

57. Ibid., p. 33.

58. Ibid., p. 35.

59. Ibid., pp. 36-37.

60. Ibid., pp. 38-39.

61. Ibid., p. 38.

62. Op. cit., p. 40.

63. *Islam and the Demands of the Era*, p. 41.

64. Ibid., p. 81 onwards, p. 57 onwards, and p. 151.

65. Ibid, p. 151.

66. Ibid., p. 151.

67. Ibid., op. cit., p. 152.

68. Ibid.

69. Ibid., p. 153.

70. Ibid., p. 154.

71. Ibid., pp. 154-155 and 156.

72. Ibid., pp. 158-159.

73. Ibid., p. 159.

74. Ibid.

75. Ibid., pp. 160-161 and 166.

76. Ibid., p. 166.

77. Ibid., op. cit., pp. 172-173.

78. Ibid., pp. 174 and 180.

79. See our book, *Ikhitibārāt al-Maqdis,* Beirut, Dār al-Amīr, 2007, Section 2.

80. Muṭahharī, "An Introduction to an Islamic Universal Vision, 2," *Monotheistic Universal Vision*, (*Muqaddame-yi bar Jahānbīnī Islami*, section of *Jahanbini Tawhidi*) translated by Muḥammad al-Khāqāni, Tehran, Islamic Media Organization, 1403 AH, p. 8.

81. *Monotheistic Universal Vision*, op. cit., p. 9.

82. Ibid., p. 11.

83. Ibid., p. 11.

84. Ibid., p. 12.

85. Ibid., pp. 12-13.

86. Ibid., p. 13.

87. Ibid., p. 15.

88. The author refers to Russell's book, *The Universal Vision of Science*, which denies its theoretical benefits. See: *Monotheistic Universal Vision*, p. 16.

89. *Monotheistic Universal Vision*, pp. 16-17.

90. Ibid., p. 17.

91. Ibid., p. 18.

92. Ibid., pp. 18-19.

93. Ibid., p. 19.

94. Ibid., p. 19.

95. Ibid., p. 20.

96. Ibid., p. 21.

97. Ibid., p. 22.

98. Muṭahharī, *The Goal of Life*, Beirut, Dār al-Aḍwā', 1989, pp. 75-77.

99. Ibid., op. cit., pp. 86-88.

100. *Monotheistic Universal Vision*, op. cit., p. 25.

101. Ibid., p. 25.

102. Murtada Muṭahharī, *Man and his Faith*, translated by Muḥammad al-Khafani, Tehran, Islamic Media Organization, 1403 AH, pp. 14-15.

103. *Monotheistic Universal Vision*, p. 15.

104. Ibid., p. 16.

105. *Man and his Faith*, p. 16.

106. Ibid., pp. 16-17.

107. Ibid., p. 17.

108. Ibid., pp. 18-19.

109. Ibid., pp. 20-22.

110. Ibid., p. 23.

111. Ibid., p. 24.

112. *Monotheistic Universal Vision*, op. cit., p. 20.

113. *Monotheistic Vision of the World*, pp. 21-23. Compare with: Muṭahharī, *God and Man*, translated by Ja'far Hishmat Khāh, Tehran, Islamic Media Organization, 1985, the first and second lecture. See also: *Monotheistic Vision of the World*, pp. 41-93.

﴿لَيْسَ كَمِثْلِهِ شَيْءٌ﴾

﴿وَلَمْ يَكُن لَّهُ كُفُوًا أَحَدٌ﴾

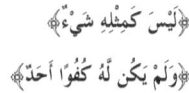

﴿قُلِ اللَّهُ خَالِقُ كُلِّ شَيْءٍ﴾

﴿أَلا إِلَى اللَّهِ تَصِيرُ الأُمُورُ﴾

114. *Monotheistic Vision of the World*, op. cit., pp. 41-44.

115. Ibid., p. 45; *God in Man's Life*, pp. 7-10.

116. *The Goal of Life*, op. cit., p. 17.

117. Ibid., p. 18.

118. Ibid., p. 19.

119. Ibid., op. cit., pp. 17-18.

120. Ibid., pp. 18-25.

121. *Monotheistic Universal Vision*, op. cit., p. 27.

122. Muṭahharī, *Monotheism*, translated by Irfan Muḥammad, Beirut, Dār al-Hawrā', 1324 AH, p. 23.

123. *Monotheistic Universal Vision*, pp. 27-28.

124. Ibid., pp. 30-31.

﴿إِنَّ فِي خَلْقِ السَّمَاوَاتِ وَالأَرْضِ وَاخْتِلافِ اللَّيْلِ وَالنَّهَارِ وَالْفُلْكِ الَّتِي تَجْرِي فِي الْبَحْرِ بِمَا يَنفَعُ النَّاسَ وَمَا أَنزَلَ اللَّهُ مِنَ السَّمَاء مِن مَّاء فَأَحْيَا بِهِ الأَرْضَ بَعْدَ مَوْتِهَا وَبَثَّ فِيهَا مِن كُلِّ دَابَّةٍ وَتَصْرِيفِ الرِّيَاحِ وَالسَّحَابِ الْمُسَخَّرِ بَيْنَ السَّمَاء وَالأَرْضِ لآيَاتٍ لِّقَوْمٍ يَعْقِلُونَ﴾

125. Ibid., p. 31.

126. *The Goal of Life*, op. cit., pp. 86-87.

127. *Man and his Faith*, op. cit., pp. 40-41.

128. *The Goal of Life*, pp. 136-137.

129. *Allah in the Life of Man*, pp. 16-17 and 18.

130. Ibid., pp. 10-11.

﴿لَوْ كَانَ فِيهِمَا آلِهَةٌ إِلاَّ اللَّهُ لَفَسَدَتَا﴾

131. Ibid., pp. 23-24.

132. *Allah in the Life of Man*, pp. 47-62; *Man and his Faith*, p. 45.

133. *Man and his Faith*, op. cit., p. 50.

134. *Monotheistic Universal Vision*, op. cit., pp. 85-93 and 57.

﴿وَمَنْ أَعْرَضَ عَن ذِكْرِي فَإِنَّ لَهُ مَعِيشَةً ضَنكًا﴾

135. *Man and His Faith*, op. cit., pp. 48-49.

136. Ibid., pp. 55-69.

137. Fahmi Jud'ān, *The Foundations of Progress According to Islamic Intellectuals*, Amman, Dar al-Shuruq, 1988, p 191.

138. Ibid., op. cit., p. 192.

139. Ibid., p. 191.

140. Ibid., op. cit., p. 113.

141. Muḥammad Iqbāl, *Renewal of Islamic Thought*, translated by 'Abbas Maḥmūd, Cairo, 1955.

142. Mālik Bin-Nabī, *Trend of the Islamic World*, translated by 'Abd al-Sabūr Shāhīn, Cairo, 1959, p. 55. Compare with: *The Foundation of Progress According to Islamic Intellectuals*, op. cit., pp. 194-195.

143. Jamal-al-Din al-Afgḥani, *Responding to Atheists*, part of his work translated by Muḥammad Amara, Cairo, General Authority for Books, no date, pp. 170-173.

144. Ibid., p. 173.

145. Ibid., p. 172.

146. Jamāl-al-Dīn al-Afghānī, *Theology of Predestination* (part of the full work).

147. *Responding to Atheists*, pp. 184-187.

148. Muḥammad 'Abduh, *Theology of Unity*, Cairo, Dār al- Ma'ārif, 1971, pp. 59 and 125-126.

149. Ibid., pp. 150-155.

150. Muḥammad 'Abduh, *Islam and Christianity in Relation to Science and Civilization*, Cairo, 192, pp. 90-104.

151. Printed in Cairo, no date.

152. Printed in Beirut, 1306 AH.

153. Muṭahharī had utilised much philosophy and logic. He believed that philosophy did not end with Averroes, as many had believed, but rather it had expanded in intellectual circles in many parts of the Islamic world. It was portrayed in encyclopaedic doctrines that used the heritage of the mind and soul as inspiration, i.e. the logical and philosophical Islamic doctrines, and the doctrines of Sufism, Mysticism, and Orientalism, as is the case with Mullā Ṣadra and Shaykh Suhrawardī. He also believed that Islamic philosophy, which used the Greek heritage and its many sources as inspiration, surpassed this heritage after its interaction with it, and added to its content in order to build a prophetic philosophy – or a divine philosophy, to be more accurate – that explores the expanse of religion, as well as its deep moral and spiritual implications. His work expresses his knowledge of this heritage, and his ability to reform it and benefit

from it. For example, see: Muṭahharī, *Islamic Philosophy*, translated by 'Abd al-Jabbār al-Rifā'ī, Tehran, The Islamic Library, 1415 AH.

154. Muṭahharī, *Prophethood*, op. cit., pp. 84-96.

155. *Allah in the Life of Man*, different locations; *Man and His Faith*, p. 41 and onwards; *The Goal of Life*, p. 20 and onwards.

156. See: *Man and His Faith*, op. cit., pp. 26-38.

157. Muṭahharī, *Prophethood,* op. cit., different sections; Muṭahharī, *Judgment Day*, translated by Jawād 'Alī Kassār, Tehran, Umm-ul-Qurā', 1420 AH.

158. *Man and His Faith*, op. cit., pp. 72-79.

159. Ibid., op. cit., pp. 26-27.

160. Ibid., p. 28.

161. Ibid., p. 28.

162. Ibid., op. cit., p. 28.

163. *Monotheistic Universal Vision*, op. cit., p. 15.

164. *Man and His Faith*, op. cit., p. 30.

165. Ibid., p. 34.

166. Ibid., p. 34.

167. Ibid.

168. Ibid., p. 35.

169. Ibid., op. cit., p. 35.

170. Ibid., p. 36.

171. Ibid., op. cit., p. 36.

172. Ibid., p. 37.

173. Ibid.

174. Ibid., p. 31.

175. Durant, *The Pleasures of Philosophy*, recounted from: *Man and His Faith*, p. 32.

176. Ibid., p. 32.

177. Ibid.

178. Russell, *Marriage and Morals*, p. 122, Persian translation, recounted from: *Man and His Faith*, p. 37.

179. George Sarton, *Six Wings*, Persian Translation, p. 305, recounted from: *Man and His Faith*, pp. 37-38.

180. Muṭahharī, *Monotheism*, different locations.

181. Muṭahharī recounts these texts from one of William James' books translated to Persian under the title *Religion and the Soul*. See: *Monotheism*, p. 49. Compare with: Muṭahharī, *The System of Woman's Rights in Islam*, p. 83.

182. *Monotheism*, p. 49.

183. Ibid., pp. 49-50.

184. Ibid., op. cit., p. 52.

185. Ibid., p. 54-55.

186. Ibid., pp. 57-58.

187. Ibid., pp. 58-59.

188. Ibid., p. 65.

189. Ibid., p. 88.

190. Ibid., p. 100.

191. Ibid., op. cit., p. 103.

192. Ibid., p. 104.

193. Ibid., p. 106.

194. Ibid., pp. 128-129.

195. Ibid., p. 133.

196. Ibid., p. 150.

197. Ibid., pp. 190-225, where he recounts ideas from Poincaré, Carlyle, Einstein and other contemporary scientists.

198. Muṭahharī often mentioned the following books by Bāzargān: *The Traversed Road*, *A Lesson in Piousness*, *The Infinite Entity*, and *The Young Islam*. He benefited from them, and discussed their content, objecting to some of the opinions expressed, but he would do so politely and humbly.

199. Muṭahharī, *Judgment Day*, translated by Jawād 'Alī Kassār, Tehran, Umm-ul-Qurā', 1420 AH, pp. 196-210.

200. We should direct the question to Bāzargān himself as regards the source of these words. The ancients did not initially know what "energy" was, although they were well aware of its "effect," whereas matter was, of course, accepted. (A footnote included by Muṭahharī in the original text.)

201. This is a very important consideration. We believe that this point, that the Qur'an does not often mention the third element, but only in certain places, somewhat contradicts the result Bāzargān hoped to achieve. (A footnote included by Muṭahharī in the original text.)

﴿كَذَلِكَ النُّشُورُ﴾

﴿وَكَذَلِكَ تُخْرَجُونَ﴾

﴿إِذَا دَعَاكُمْ دَعْوَةً مِّنَ الأَرْضِ إِذَا أَنتُمْ تَخْرُجُونَ﴾

202. Fathi Milkawi, "Islamic Instillation of the Concept of Values," *Journal of Islamic knowledge*, Washington: International Institute of Islamic Thought, Year 14, Issue no. 54, Autumn 2008, p. 9.

203. ﴿وَعَنَتِ الْوُجُوهُ لِلْحَيِّ الْقَيُّومِ﴾: *All faces will be subservient to The Ever-Living, The All-sustainer* (20:111); ﴿قَائِمٌ عَلَى كُلِّ نَفْسٍ بِمَا كَسَبَتْ﴾: *Sustains every soul in spite of what it earns* (13:33).

204. ﴿فَأَقِمْ وَجْهَكَ لِلدِّينِ الْقَيِّمِ﴾: So stand firm in your devotion to the upright religion (30:43). The Arabic *Qayyim* has the same root as *qiyam*.

205. The Arabic *Mustaqīm* (straight) is another variation of *qiyam*. (Trans.)

206. ﴿فَاسْتَقِمْ كَمَا أُمِرْتَ﴾: So be steadfast as you have been commanded (11:112); ﴿اهدِنَا الصِّرَاطَ الْمُسْتَقِيمَ﴾: Guide us along the straight path (1:6).

207. ﴿إِنَّ هَذَا الْقُرْآنَ يَهْدِي لِلَّتِي هِيَ أَقْوَمُ﴾ (17:9). *Aqwam* (most upright) is also from the same root as *qiyam*. (Trans.)

208. ﴿لَقَدْ خَلَقْنَا الإِنسَانَ فِي أَحْسَنِ تَقْوِيمٍ﴾ (95:4). *Taqwīm* (stature of being) is another variant of the word *qiyam*. (Trans.)

209. ﴿وَالَّذِينَ إِذَا أَنفَقُوا لَمْ يُسْرِفُوا وَلَمْ يَقْتُرُوا وَكَانَ بَيْنَ ذَلِكَ قَوَامًا﴾ (25:67). *Qiwām* (balance between the two) is another variant of *qiyam*. (Trans.)

210. *Islamic Instillation of the Concept of Values*, op. cit., pp. 6-7, adaptation.

﴿أُولَئِكَ الَّذِينَ كَفَرُوا بِآيَاتِ رَبِّهِمْ وَلِقَائِهِ فَحَبِطَتْ أَعْمَالُهُمْ فَلَا نُقِيمُ لَهُمْ يَوْمَ الْقِيَامَةِ وَزْنًا﴾

﴿إِنَّ الْمُتَّقِينَ فِي مَقَامٍ أَمِينٍ﴾

﴿الرِّجَالُ قَوَّامُونَ عَلَى النِّسَاءِ﴾

﴿اللَّهُ لَا إِلَهَ إِلَّا هُوَ الْحَيُّ الْقَيُّومُ﴾

﴿أَفَمَنْ هُوَ قَائِمٌ عَلَىٰ كُلِّ نَفْسٍ بِمَا كَسَبَتْ..﴾

﴿وَأَن لَّوِ اسْتَقَامُوا عَلَى الطَّرِيقَةِ...﴾

211. See: Ziyād Khalīl al-Dgamin, "Building the Universe in the light of the Texts", *Journal of Islamic Knowledge*, op. cit., p. 23 and onwards.

212. Muṭahharī, *Education and Pedagogy in Islam*, translated by al-Huda Committee, Beirut, Dār al-Hādī, 1993, p. 177.

213. "Building the Universe in the light of the Holy Texts," *Journal of Islamic Knowledge*, p. 17.

214. Muṭahharī has benefited considerably from this book; he describes it as a wonderful book and highly recommends it. See: Muṭahharī, *Education in Islam*, p. 194. He finds the same dimensions in the writings of the famous psychologist Jung. See: op. cit., pp. 40-41.

215. *Education in Islam*, pp. 135-140.

216. Ibid, p. 9.

217. *Education and Pedagogy in Islam*, pp. 169 and 170.

218. Ibid, p. 170.

219. Ibid., p. 9.

220. Ibid., pp. 15, 17, 33 and elsewhere.

221. Ibid., pp. 10-11.

222. Ibid., op. cit., p. 50, and pp. 17-18.

223. Ibid.

224. Ibid., pp. 22, 25, 27, 28, 29 and 30.

225. Ibid., 30-31.

226. Ibid., p. 31.

227. Ibid., p. 32.

228. Ibid., pp. 12-13 and 15.

229. Ibid., p. 119.

230. Ibid., p. 124.

231. Ibid., p. 122.

232. Ibid., p. 122.

233. Ibid., pp. 123, 192, 200 and 204.

234. Ibid., pp. 209-218.

235. Ibid., p. 239. Compare with *Revival of Thought in Islam*, pp. 7-11.

236. Ibid., pp. 239-241 and 245.

237. Ibid., p. 245.

238. Ibid., p. 246.

239. Ibid.

240. *Revival of Thought in Islam*, op. cit., p. 30.

241. Ibid., p. 45.

242. Ibid., pp. 8-9.

243. Ibid., op. cit., p. 9.

244. See: Muṭahharī, *Islamic Movements in the Last Century*, various places.

245. *Islam and the Demands of the Era*, op. cit., p. 33.

246. See in detail: Muṭahharī, *Articles on the Islamic Revolution*, pp. 99-101 and 78-93.

247. *Islam and the Demands of the Era*, op. cit., pp. 38-39. He says: "Those who regreted that had to close their mouths and remain silent, at a time when the educational programmes continued to decline and ignore the demands of the era, when publications and production declined, when creativity was almost lost, when appearance and title became increasingly important day by day, when good, open-minded scholars lost the ability or desire to reform even when they were in a position to make a decision."

248. Ibid., p. 38. He says: "The cognitive abilities and interests of this institution have diminished to the point where they no longer taught anything other than jurisprudence, while neglecting all the other branches of Islam."

249. See: *Islam and the Demands of the Era*, pp. 44-47.

250. Ibid., pp. 48-55 and 57-58.

251. Ibid., pp. 63-64. In this book, Muṭahharī discusses in detail the defects of the religious institutions, and reviews the methods by which this could be remedied.

252. See what we have mentioned in Chapter 1 of this book. See also: Muṭahharī, *Articles on the Islamic Revolution*, pp. 87-88.

253. Muṭahharī, *Articles on the Islamic Revolution*, p. 81; *Islamic Movements in the Last Century*, pp. 17-18.

254. *Islamic Movements in the Last Century*, p. 18.

255. Ibid., p. 18.

256. See: 'Alī Davānī, *A Journey in the Life of Martyr Muṭahharī*, op. cit., pp. 60-63 and 70.

257. Muṭahharī, *Articles on the Islamic Revolution*, pp. 88-91, where he lists the practices and the deviations of the authorities in detail.

258. Ibid., p. 93.

259. Ibid., p. 94. Muṭahharī believed that the revolution should be comprehensive.

260. On the freedom of thought, and the importance of confronting ideas with ideas, see: Muṭahharī, *Articles on the Islamic Revolution*, pp. 91-93 and 8-10.

261. Muṭahharī, *Islam and Iran*, translated by Muḥammad Hadi al-Yusufi, Beirut, Dār al-Ta'āruf, no date; *Articles on the Islamic Revolution*, pp. 90-91.

262. Muṭahharī, *The System of Woman's Rights in Islam*, p. 5. This book is the result of a debate between Muṭahharī and an Iranian legal expert in charge of developing the Personal Status Laws.

263. Ibid., pp. 6, 140-141 and 145.

264. Ibid., pp. 10 and 114-116. He discusses the meaning of human rights in the United Nations list of 1948.

265. Ibid., pp. 9-10.

266. Ibid., pp. 11, 129-131 and 140-141.

267. Ibid., pp. 129, 145 and 132-133.

268. Muṭahharī stresses the central role of the family, and that mankind has nothing better to protect its existence: *The System of Woman's Rights in Islam*, pp. 132-136.

269. Ibid., pp. 103-104.

270. Ibid., p. 102.

271. Ibid., pp. 104-106.

272. Muṭahharī, *Sexual Ethics in Islam and in the Western World*, Arabic translation with title *Al-Ḍawābit al-Akhlāqiyyah li al-Sulūk al-Jjinsī*, Beirut, Dār al-Rasūl al-Akram, 1988, pp. 5-6 and 10.

273. Ibid., pp. 7 and 8-10.

274. Ibid., pp. 13-15.

275. Ibid., op. cit., pp. 18-19 and 26-27.

276. Ibid., p. 20.

277. Ibid., p. 22.

278. Ibid., pp. 22-23, 26 and 30-33.

279. Ibid., pp. 37-38.

280. Ibid., p. 39.

281. Ibid., p. 39.

282. Ibid., p. 50.

283. Ibid., pp. 59 and 60.

284. Ibid., p. 60.

285. Ibid., pp. 52-54.

286. Ibid., pp. 56-57.

287. Ibid., p. 60.

288. Ibid., pp. 62-65.

289. Ibid., pp. 44-45.

290. Ibid., p. 67.

291. Ibid., pp. 68-69 and 72.

292. Ibid., pp. 83-94.

293. Muṭahharī, *The Issue of the Veil*, translated by Haidar al-Haidar, Beirut, al-Dar Islamiyah, 1987.

CHAPTER 4

FUNDEMENTAL ISSUES OF INTELLECTUAL CONFRONTATION IN MUṬAHARĪ'S REVOLUTIONARY PLAN

INTRODUCTION

The problem of Western Modernity and its Consequences

It is difficult to determine accurately the time when Western civilisation entered the modern age, with all its cultural, intellectual, scientific and political ramifications, for there are a number of factors whose precursors began at the time of the Renaissance. These many complex and ambiguous factors accumulated, and contributed to what is now known as the modern era. There is no doubt that the results of this, spectacular in many respects, gave Western society a new image. However, there was virtually a total disconnection with the past, and the ideas of earlier times had only a faint echo on the modern landscape, and attempts to restore the traditions amounted to memorisation and empty ritual with little meaning.

One the one hand, in general, modernity is a result of attempts to refine the heritage of western civilisation. On the other hand, the basis for reconstruction on which the new picture of civilisation relied, was a hasty attempt to reconstruct a total conception of the world and man that unleashed the materialistic and experimental capacities of man, and took him away from any theological or metaphysical interpretation.

In fact, the developing stages of modernity cannot be clearly determined. The abandonment of traditional social structures and the authority of the priesthood led to unknown territory and thus the sciences began their experimentation of the natural world to discover the secrets of its laws and a methodological concept of creation. Its influence expanded into an ideal aspired to by society, which was to establish a balanced system that served the people and organised human activity with no overbearing, predestined authority.

Thus, a sense of certainty gradually became clearer and shaped the culture, whereby man was able to run the world he lives in by virtue of reason. Modernity presented itself as something which could be achieved by way of freedom and rationality, which in turn unleashed latent energies on the one hand, and established the idea of the rational interpretation of the world on the other.

Therefore, modernity was a continual process, rather than something that happened at a particular point in time. The overall means were the achievements of science, the development of industry, and changes in the social and economic structure. Other factors were systems of government and political practices based on a revised attitude towards authority deriving its legitimacy from the authorisation of a majority, the crystallisation of a different cognitive perception of man and the world divorced from the inherited traditions, and a comprehensive change of values and behaviour. Manifestations of modernity started to become comprehensive, affecting many aspects of life and the sum of human activity in general. In brief, it was an unrestrained progression in terms of knowledge, art, politics and economics, promising prosperity and luxury, which changed Western civilisation forever.

The onset of modernity precipitated a rush for expansion and containment, which was motivated by a search for primary resources as well as markets, and thus provided a basis for launching two devastating wars motivated by the will to monopolise and influence. The results of both wars affected the whole world. Once these wars over, there was an awareness of what the development of science and technology might lead to. There was also an awareness of where ideas of self-interest might lead to, but placing man in the position of master of the world, and using reason to manipulate it to his own advantage. Notwithstanding this is not the place for a discussion of the development modernity and its results. Much has been written on this comprehensive subject,[1] but what matters to us is the effect modernity has on Muslim society.

Muslims embraced the modern world at the height of their political, economic and intellectual decline. At this time, Islamic nations had been suffering from long years of suppression by local authorities, and a systematic wasting of their capacities. This had been brought about by an arrogant, self-interested authority whose legitimacy depended on the West.

The thrust of modernisation was spurred on by a feeling of uniqueness which justified its behaviour in dealing with other nations as parties serving the centre, offering it resources, tools and raw material, as well as serving as open markets for its own goods, with no competition worthy of mention.

This interaction with the West caused contradictory feelings and gave rise to conflicting situations, as change in different fields of public life was the first thing that drew the attention of the people to the West. The progress, urbanisation and prosperity which Muslims saw in the everyday life of European society caused confused feelings of admiration and grief, and for a while posed vital questions: Why could Muslims not achieve what the West had achieved? And why had the West managed to achieve this at a time when the Muslim world was sunk in degradation, with hardly a hope of getting out?

Although this unhappy feeling prevailed in all those who had had a chance to witness the different aspects of progress and urbanisation, the answer to those questions was unclear. Answers could hardly be found in a context that barely related to the situation. Some of the answers relate to other reasons apart from the backwardness of the Muslim nations, reasons related to the means by which an inevitable progress ensues, or the conditions which guarantee such progress; these are answers we have already referred to earlier.

During this period, our societies became familiar with many Western values, ideas and etiquettes. This influenced them, and they began to look for ways to benefit from these advantages, and ways escape from the inertia they found themselves in. These factors had a deep influence on everyday life and awareness, and in establishing new organisations. New movements and schools of thought emerged in sociology, philosophy and ethics, as well as the approach taken towards literature, history and theories of civilisation. Our societies were inspired and influenced by these western teachings. This caused much confusion between the traditional belief system and the new ideas. These were foreign ideas in a different environment; they were introduced to the Islamic world without a foundation of appropriate rules to make them synchronise with the ideological and intellectual environment, and the consequences were difficult to remove. This caused many problems and we were embroiled in an endless spiral of doubt, failure and defeat. This took us from one downward step to another, from inertia to stagnation and an eventual subordination, with no light at the end of the tunnel or any inspiration to explain our downfall or provide a clear vision of how to achieve the conditions for prosperity. Thus, a fascination with the new suppressed us, and caused a rush towards imitation, without even knowing how to construct a purposeful model for its utilisation or establish a sensible behavioural practice.

This spiral was the result of the hurry towards the different world of the West, and the desire to be free of a burdensome and hindering heritage. In the midst of addressing these issues, Muṭahharī realised that they had no inner cohesion, and had failed to prove themselves in the history of Western society; they had presented the world with overwhelming dilemmas, along with shattering experiences such as Marxism and Fascism. They brought us calamities bigger than some they had already caused, and left us in the unknown, cut off from our heritage and cultural values.

Alongside Muṭahharī, we will address three of these spirals, which appeared through processes of the modern West affecting different aspects of our life. The first is related to the Marxist view of society and history, the second to philosophical, scientific and materialistic trends, and the third to ethics and moral theory. These themes not only had a negative effect in the context in which they originated, but also on Islamic civilisation, and thus hindered any attempt to progress due to our precipitate response to them, and the cognitive problems that were expressed through them.

1

AN ISLAMIC ANALYSIS OF SOCIETY AND A HISTORICAL CRITIQUE OF MATERIALISM

1. The nature of society and its tools

According to Muṭahharī, the human being has a special feature which is absent in other creatures. Only man is able to establish a society with clearly defined characteristics, organised by tradition, customs, systems and ideas, which together unify society. There are two aspects to this: the first is an organised division of functions to distribute benefits and cater to needs, the second is the sum of the ideas, beliefs and values which directs the mechanism. Therefore, society as defined according to this paradigm is a community living in a unified social framework that serves the interests and needs of the people, and is directed by unified viewpoints, traditions and collective beliefs.

We should not think that this is necessitated by external factors, for people gravitate to it due to an instinct to engage in unified communities. This might also be due to an intuitive realisation that man's needs are better served by cooperation within a unified collective. According to Muṭahharī, the Qur'an teaches us that urbanisation is intuitive, for Almighty Allah says:

> *O mankind! Indeed We created you from a male and a female, and made you nations and tribes that you may identify yourselves with one another. Indeed the noblest of you in the sight of Allah is the most pious among you* (49:13).[2]

This verse indicates that man is created with an intuition that causes him to live within a group. This is also evident when Allah says:

> *And He is The One Who created the human being from water, then invested him with ties of blood and marriage* (25:54),[3]
>
> and: *Are they the ones who dispense the mercy of your Lord? We are the ones who have dispensed among them their livelihood in the present life, and raised some of them above others in rank, so that some may take others into service* (43:32).[4]

The first of these verses states that man is created with this intuitive need of cooperation because of a common natural purpose. The second verse refers to the differences in gifts and abilities among the people, in a way that distinguishes them from each other, and in turn necessitates a need for interdependence; a synergy through which they may help each other according to that which distinguishes one from the other, and thus secure their interests through cooperation. Had the people had equal abilities, there would have been no need for them to live in a group, and such a thing would not have existed. In Muṭahharī's view, according to this need, social life, and hence urbanisation, is a naturally intuitive matter.

Muṭahharī's attention was drawn to a recent debate on the truth behind human society, as to whether it is unique and has a self-regulating law, or a mere happenstance? In other words, is it simply a number of people coming together with no realistic conditions and laws, apart from those which govern the individual?

In this context, Muṭahharī considers four theories:

The first theory perceives society as a corporate entity whose individuals have their own characteristics. The second perceives society as an invented compound of individuals who have their own characteristics, and lose nothing of them in the midst of their involvement in society, which also has its own special characteristics, and rules which govern it. The third theory supposes that the society is a compound of the emotions, desires and wills of the individuals, because the individual enters society with his own personal identity, gifts and abilities, which intermingle to produce a new compound. It is a compound because each part of it directly influences the others, and necessitates a corresponding change in all the elements forming it, and thus the compound acquires a new identity different from the identities of the individuals. Muṭahharī calls this the real compound, because the interaction of its parts never stops, which changes the individual perspective into a group perspective without changing the group into individuals or dissolving the individuals into a group.

The fourth theory perceives society as a real compound of a different order; and it is not possible to define the human being outside a social entity. Before this assimilation, the human being is a mere faculty that is manifest in the external world, and a reality inspired by the social spirit. One's preferences, emotions, thought and the sum of one's energies do not emerge or disappear unless based within society, its profundities and changes.[5]

The first theory consequently asserts the validity of the individual's fundamental nature. It affirms that the individual is "real," and that the very same law that governs human society governs the individual, and that the effects of society are merely the effects of the individual and his action. Thus, there is no norm for society beyond this concept, and there is no separate law that governs and directs it.

The second theory comes to the same conclusion, but with an additional factor; namely, that the relationship between individuals within a unified society is similar to the physical connections between different parts of physical composites. Hence, the resulting aggregate of the collective deeds of individuals is its cause, and thus leads to a unified and common destiny. As a result, society acquires a seemingly real existence, based on the existence of this powerful organic relationship between its members.[6]

On the other hand, the third theory affirms the fundament nature of both the individual and the society, since this theory rejects the absorption of the individual into society as a whole which results in the loss of the individual's identity and characteristics. It also rejects the attribution of an independent existence to the society, but rather considers that society acquires a new identity generated by the relationship of the emotions and activities of those within it.[7]

The fourth theory assigns a fundament nature of society as an entity in itself, and affirms that what is found in human society is nothing but the social spirit – its own conscience, will and feeling – whereas the individual feeling, conscience and will are simply manifestations of the collective perception.[8]

Having reviewed these four theories, Muṭahharī suggests that Islam confirms the third theory. According to his perspective, the Qur'an establishes that the consequences of any human society exceed beyond the life of the individual – his movement, experience personal feelings and will.[9] As a result, society has a destiny that is distinct from that of its members; its collective activities and general sense of perception, steadfastness or deviation, are independent of those of the individual. For instance, the Almighty says:[10]

> *There is a [preordained] time for every nation: when their time comes, they shall not defer it by a single hour nor shall they advance it* (7:34).[11]

Thus, a society has its own distinct destiny and pre-ordained time – which indicates that there is a disintegration, decline and extinction – distinct from the lives and destinies of its members. This happens in such a way that the loss of a society's cohesion, the erosion of its institutions and its decline does not necessarily imply the end of the lives, or the extinction, of the members that form the society.

Allah also says:

> *Every nation attempted to lay hands on their apostle, and disputed erroneously to refute the truth. Then I seized them; so how was My retribution?* (40:5).[12]

Since this verse speaks about a collective ill will embodied in a failed attempt to oppose the truth, the outcome was a general punishment. Therefore, there are certain actions not undertaken by individuals, but rather by entire nations and societies. Such actions leave general effects on the society as a whole in the form of a general punishment, which leads to a breakdown of the cohesion of society, and ultimately leads to perdition.[13]

There are many verses in the Qur'an that attribute the actions of an individual to a nation as a whole, and similarly, the actions of a society attributed to subsequent generations. These verses seem to underline the existence of a collective essence, as well as a collective perception and outlook that directs the behaviour of its members in a manner that renders the actions of a society attributable to its individual members, since the individual is seen to be part of the collective essence – in one's thought, perception, goals, will and choices. Conversely, the actions of an individual are attributed to the group – its thought, values and will – for the individual's experience is a reflection of the social essence, mind and conscience[14] (2:79; and 3:112).[15]

Habits, traditions, customs, culture, collective perceptions and general goals form the group's essence, which directs the lives of its members, determines their choices, provides them with an identity, regulates their behaviour, draws up a vision of their future and entrenches these through universal traditions. As a result, individuals exist within a unified entity in this context. Due to this, Muṭahharī deemed that the society as a whole carries some of the experiences of earlier generations in spite of being composed of different members. Consequently, the deeds of earlier generations are attributable to the society, and it shoulders this responsibility because it constitutes a continuum of the collective essence and general conception that stems from experiences.[16]

This theory necessitates the existence of particular rules and norms for human society that do not cancel or repeal the laws that govern individuals and direct their lives. Thus, in every human society there are two sets of laws that direct the society as a whole; two sets of norms that order and administer society, are impressed upon its members and reflect on their own unique experiences. In addition, they assist in ordering the personal lives of individuals, determine their behaviour, govern their actions and organise their capacities. Muṭahharī refers to the first set of these norms as social norms, and the second as rational norms.[17]

According to Muṭahharī, the Qur'an has alluded to this viewpoint in several verses, especially when it outlines the governance of general phenomena – progress and retrogression, prosperity and decline, subsistence and extinction – by norms, laws and conditions. Had it not been for these norms, a common destiny for the members of human society would not exist.

The Almighty has pointed out this reality in the verse:

> *We revealed to the Children of Israel in the Book: "Twice you will cause corruption on the earth, and you will perpetrate great tyranny." So when the first occasion of the two [prophecies] came, We aroused against you Our servants possessing great might, and they ransacked [your] habitations, and the promise was bound to be fulfilled* (17:4-5).[18]

The main theme in these verses is that the collapse of societies is a direct corollary of corruption on earth, and conversely, the rise and prosperity of a society is a result of the qualities of steadfastness and integrity.[19]

2. The Reality of Society and Individual Freedom

Belief in the reality of human society and its real existence by no means abrogates individual freedom, and does not relieve the individual from shouldering a responsibility for his own deeds. According to the viewpoint of Muṭahharī, however, this freedom is not absolute. This is due to the fact that the sum of the factors that form human society – habits, traditions, customs, culture, the social system and common goals, and so on – have an effect – either directly or indirectly – on the choices that are available to its members.[20] These factors also contribute to the formation of the outlook on whose basis the individual's freedom and behaviour is determined and manifested. These factors subject the individual, even indirectly, and lead him to courses of action that go beyond his personal will. However, according to Muṭahharī, this is not fatalism, since the human being exercises his freedom within the conditions of history and the circumstances of society. In other words, the freedom of the individual is not determined in a vacuum. There are individual and social factors, such as talents, desires, inclinations, instincts, education, environment, culture, traditions, outlooks and beliefs, that mark out the path of freedom. They also contribute to the nature of the choices that the individual selects in consonance with his freedom.[21]

Therefore, the human being is neither obliged to do what is expected of him by the community in a manner that abrogates his freedom and relieves him of personal responsibility, nor does he enjoy an absolute freedom that is unconditioned by circumstances that prevail in the wider community. He is rather betwixt and between – that is to say, the human being is free to make his own decisions and determine his choices. His freedom alone leads him to choose one course of action or one behavioural pattern amongst many others. He makes one choice rather than another. Nevertheless, his freedom is not a principle, or starting point for action, except in light of real conditions and circumstances, since freedom correlates with belonging to a human society and the association of its individuals, as much as it is also an outcome of the aggregate rational formation.[22]

In this context, Muṭahharī criticises Durkheim for his belief that human choices are an outcome of society, that the inclinations of the individual are not a real choice, and that his role is merely to take and accept; and consequently, the human being acts in accordance with what is prevalent in society in terms of patterns of behaviour, and behaves within the context of the range of customs and habits established in the society prior to the existence of the individual. The individual acquires them through education, practice and familiarity, and he abides by them without the slightest freedom to disavow himself of these norms and their respective effects. If all individuals are fully subject to these factors, then their choices will be general and comprehensive, stemming from the society's choices and comprehensive inspiration.[23]

In Muṭahharī's view, this doctrine removes responsibility from the individual and negates any commitment and sense of duty towards his fellow human beings. Consequently, reward or punishment are effaced and rendered meaningless. In addition, the law itself cancels itself out by becoming useless and meaningless. According to Muṭahharī, although the Qur'an gives the society an actual existence and identity independent from the existence of individuals, it supports the free will of the individual to react to social influences. The Qur'an considers instinct to be the reason behind this matter, since it distinguishes between the good and bad, and what is useful and what is not. It also shows the individual the way amidst the pressures of the society, and helps him make the right decisions to bring him goodness and happiness when he is unsure.[24]

According to the Qur'anic conception, one cannot excuse oneself for not shouldering the responsibility for doing something one should not do, but which is nonetheless sanctioned by society, due to an inability to go against the traditions, habits and culture of society or acting contrary to its will. One cannot vindicate oneself on the pretext of being coerced by the general orientation of the society. Such a justification is not acceptable from the Qur'anic perspective. If an individual is unable to change the course of the society in which he lives, he is nevertheless able to abandon a corrupt society for a righteous one – or at least one that is less corrupt. Thus, the concept of migration (*hijra*) acquires an edifying connotation, and constitutes a social position. This is because it embodies the individual's feelings about himself with respect to the scale of the pressures of the society; through migration, the individual expresses a rational assertion of his free will (4:97).[25]

Generally speaking, according to Muṭahharī, the Qur'anic teachings are underpinned by an emphasis on individual responsibility, which would include the ability of the individual to exercise his free will to effect change in a base society in the face of social pressure to the contrary. The human being enjoys the faculties of perception, rationality and understanding, and possesses a free will, each of which are cornerstones of the primordial human nature, irrespective of any connection with a social entity.

With these faculties the individual is able to make personal choices in contradistinction to those of society. Certainly there would be overarching influence and pressure from the habits and customs of society for him to do otherwise, and these might cause him to refrain from acting in accordance with his own choice. However, this does not extirpate his perception of his own freedom, or suspend his innate ability to act according to his beliefs. If he finds an opportunity to release himself from the established practices, he would take it, so he may thereby act in accordance with his beliefs.[26]

3. Unity and Plurality within Human Society

According to Muṭahharī, all human societies are similar in essence, and differ only in outward appearance, because all human beings are the same in nature. Since the human being tends to socialise because of an natural innate imperative, all of humanity is alike in this respect; they form societies to realise their needs and aspirations. Human beings determine the features of their society based on their nature as well as the goals they set themselves.[27]

Every human society serves the aspirations of the primordial nature. Since people are the same in essence, human societies are also basically the same. Although a society may deviate from its ideal course, this is similar to when an individual from his natural propensities, but this does not imply a change in the essence of the society.

Societies form according to general and comprehensive patterns; they do not differ, and nothing is left out. Essential elements such as arts, religion, customs and traditions are found in every society without exception. These elements qualified by perpetuity, regardless of how large a part they play in a given society, or how advanced they appear. According to Muṭahharī, Islam considers societies similar in form, when it emphasises the unity of religions, which is nothing other than an integrated system for the individual and society. Had societies been diverse and multiple in their essence, their ultimate objectives would have varied, and the paths to attain these would have been numerous; this would consequently necessitate a multiplicity of completely unrelated religions. The Qur'an points out that religion is essentially for all societies throughout all the ages, and that all the divine prophets preached the same basic message. The multiplicity of religions enjoin man to not deviate from primordial human nature and universal norms:[28]

> *He has prescribed for you the religion which He had enjoined upon Noah and which We have [also] revealed to you, and which We had enjoined upon Abraham, Moses and Jesus, declaring, "Maintain the religion, and do not be divided in it"* (42:13).[29]

According to Muṭahharī, this form of unity does not prevent human diversity in expression, since this is evident in the diversity of cultures and traditions, and so on. Nevertheless, all these factors will eventually form a comprehensive unified civilisation, where all distinctions disappear.[30]

At this point, Muṭahharī focuses on the same principle that governs his perspective on human society, which is based on the premise that as long as the social spirit is in accord with the primordial human nature – by which it reaches its final perfection – then all civilisations must eventually arrive reach a common end. As a result, human society, in all its diversity, climaxes in a comprehensive global society, in which all human capacities reach their zenith, and mankind reaches true perfection.

Muṭahharī disagreed with the notions of those who believed that Islam does not support the unity of cultures and human societies. The basis of his argument is the assumption that the identity of each nation is found in its culture and the social essence that gives it a unique history. It is also the identity and real character of the individual. Nevertheless, a nation may adopt certain qualities from another over time in accordance with complex historical conditions, as well as a variety of other factors; all these considerations serve to distinguish one given society from another. He similarly disagreed with those who assert that religion is a kind of ideology that imposes determined behaviours, as well as with those who claim that nationality is an exceptional qualification that gives rise to a common essence amongst individuals, and unites them with a common destiny.

He also discusses the notion of those who believed that Islam prevents racial discrimination and national superiority, but does not prevent the existence of national diversity. It rather recognises its existence, admits its reality and deals with it as a factor actualised in history, as the Almighty states:

> *O mankind! Indeed We created you from a male and a female, and made you nations and tribes that you may identify yourselves with one another. Indeed the noblest of you in the sight of Allah is the most pious among you* (49:13).[31]

This verse affirms the initial division of humanity on the basis of gender into male and female, and then into nations and tribes; this implies that divisions and the formation of nations is a natural phenomenon, which ought to be governed by mutual knowledge and understanding in a manner that reveals the characteristics of every nation in juxtaposition to others.[32]

Muṭahharī found that all these claims were founded on two erroneous theories: the first relating to the human being, and the second relating to the origins of human culture. The first assumes that the human essence has no internal guide to direct his outlook of the world, by enlightening him and showing him the path to his ultimate aspirations; the individual is merely an empty vessel, and acquires his character by imitating his surroundings, and thereby he determines his destiny. Muṭahharī says that this is false not only from an Islamic perspective, but also from a philosophical point of view.[33] As a result of the necessary implications of his unique individual qualities, a human being possesses a definite character and a means of perceiving both this and his objectives through his primordial nature. The cultural environment of one's upbringing may clash with the imperatives the individual's primordial nature, or those of another milieu. Then, how can an individual's character be the result of his culture or other environmental factors?

The second theory presupposes that the elements of human culture are like raw materials, with no definite form or direction, and that history alone generates culture. Consequently, the individual's identity forms in lieu of the deep-seated reality within the person, plus other factors generated by history.[34]

According to Muṭahharī, this viewpoint leads one to believe in the relativity of knowledge and culture. However, this relativity is only found in extrinsic matters, which differ amongst nations, conditions, times and places, and points toward an underlying exterior reality that acts as a yardstick. On the other hand, universal precepts and knowledge are immutable, absolute and definite principles that the primordial human nature deduces and which young minds can perceive. What history or experience does with respect to culture is to mobilise it, manifest results and churn out its contents, but it does not create or originate it as a concomitant of its movement.[35]

Moreover, in the view of Muṭahharī, religion came to provide an overall outlook of the universe based on firm and authentic knowledge of the broad spectrum that is established on monotheism (*tawḥīd*). Religion also came to cultivate the human in accordance with this precept, which necessitates the construction of a comprehensive outlook towards the human being, and a way of life that is universal and general rather than a series of narrow cultures based on the multiplicity of races, nations and communities. Since the Islamic promulgation is general and comprehensive in terms of the outlook it offers, its laws and principles necessarily transcend the limits of nations and races, and sublimates them from any idiosyncratic dilemma.[36]

The Qur'anic verse that includes the phrase *Indeed We created you from a male and a female* does not mean that God created mankind as two distinct entities, but rather as spouses or partners – husband and wife – because the verse is in the context of human procreation from a male and a female which is uninterrupted through time. As for membership of a particular group or nation, its goal is one; namely, that people may know each other by referring to their different lineages. However, this does not imply that racial and national differences lead to irreconcilably different implications and outcomes.

4. The Islamic Interpretation of History and the Criticism of Historical Materialism

A. The Meaning of History and Historical Inevitability

According to Muṭahharī, the term "history" has three interconnected meanings. The first distinguishes between events that happened in the past and those that occur in the present or will occur in the future. The science of history thus studies past events.

The second refers to the rules and conditions that control human life and society, and have directed events throughout the past. These rules and conditions may be deduced by examining the experiences of past generations. The science concerned with this study he calls "scientific history," and resembles any other science that is concerned with the study of facts and details with the aim of deducing universal rules and generalised norms, which can be then be used to interpret and predict.[37] However, it differs from the natural sciences in that it studies events that no longer exist, but whose details are examined through documents, evidences, notes, witnesses, and so on, to be later processed through a rational, rather than experimental, method of analysis.[38] By this Muṭahharī means that the historical method is based on a critique of documents, and not conducted through direct experimentation by recreating events in a laboratory setting. It is for this reason that the mind plays a central role in this regard, in terms of analysis, deconstruction, comparison and reasoning.

The third meaning refers to the patterns which direct societies, govern their rise and fall, and determine their prosperity or ruin. This method is the "philosophy of history." The philosophy of history is the science of the development and transformation of societies. In fact, every society has two types of laws: the laws of social life, and the laws of evolution and perfection. Laws related to the reasons for the existence of societies, cause their decline and collapse, and which dominate the conditions of social life, he refers to as the "laws of the universe" (that is to say, the laws of existence). The "laws of evolution" are those related to the causes of progress, perfection and transformation. According to Muṭahharī, these two subdivisions are usually blurred, and countless mistakes have resulted from this confusion.[39]

Historical research of any type – with view to any of the definitions of history – is useful and beneficial. However, the construction of a universal conception of history and a comprehensive view of its events is contingent upon "scientific history" and the "philosophy of history," which together embellish the partial narrated history in the raw materials which are used for interpretation and deduction.[40]

Muṭahharī thought that in this connection there are two things that need evaluating. Firstly, to what degree can we trust the recorded narration of past events? Do the records reveal historical events fairly and impartially, and the precise manner in which they occurred, or are there tendencies and purposes that interfere with the narration of history by pruning and distorting it? Taking into account all the records of events that we have, how can we deduce whether or not what has reached our hands through different media has been manipulated? This has to affect how we attempt to deduce the sum of the universal laws governing history, which apply to the rise and decline of different communities, and whatever may lead towards development, perfection and continuity.[41]

Muṭahharī thought positively of historical narrations and records, not because he considered the narrators innocent of distortion, but rather because people have developed tools for examination and evaluation, which allow them to thoroughly review the historical records both objectively and subjectively. The syllabus of history has now reached a level of profundity that has equipped the science with the ability to reveal past events in a more or less definitive fashion.[42]

If we put this aside and believe in the possibility of arriving at the truth of the past through the historical record, how then can we deduce general and universal laws from a collection of partial incidents? Does this not mean that there is some form of causality in history, governing its events and connecting them in a determinative manner, which constantly recurs throughout time? If this is true, then what is the role of human free will in the course of history; and to what extent can we believe in the freedom of the individual and the effect of human choice, so long as historical determinism is a law, on the basis of which society moves and the march of history unfolds?[43]

Muṭahharī found that those who are occupied with these questions are faced with two contradictory propositions. Those who believe in historical determinism implicitly reject the efficacy of human will in directing history, and consider individual freedom as a mere disparity, whose role it is to uncover this determinism and utilise it to realise specific objectives – as in the case of Marxism – and this is not simply limited to external events, but also has personal and psychological implications.[44] Those who believed in the freedom of the individual in directing history rejected the inevitability of historical determinism.

Later, we will come to Muṭahharī's criticism of the second viewpoint, that is, the belief that there is no historical determinism. But what concerns us at this point however, is the Marxist view of human freedom, which it perceives as a mere "knowledge" that directs the events and laws of history. In this context, Muṭahharī rejects both these perspectives of freedom and determinism. He postulates that questions about the influence of freedom remain, even if we assume a determinism which leads the individual along his path. Thus it may be asked: "Can the human being confront the movement of history with his freedom, so that he influences its course, in such a way that his freedom becomes part of the laws and norms of history, as one factor amongst others, or can he not?"[45]

According to Muṭahharī, the Marxist view of freedom in this context leads us to select the first alternative. Thus, if the laws of society direct history – including human beings – what influence or effect will the freedom of the individual have on the changes in history? In this case, attaining knowledge of these changes is of no avail. This is because the knowledge of one who is thrown from the summit of a mountain – who is aware of what is about to happen to him when he falls – does not change anything with respect to the chain of events or the final outcome.

Muṭahharī believed that the freedom of the individual cannot be apprehended except when coupled with a belief in the existence of the primordial human nature. Thus it is said: "In the movement of the world, the human being is born with an extra dimension that is the basis of his character, which then grows and perfects in accordance with the implications of the environment and society." This extra dimension in the human being allows him to interfere in history and to change its course. Since the human being is part of this movement and directly connects to its laws, he contributes in shaping events in a similar way to other factors. Any human action – no matter how small – that emanates from the will effectively contributes to the generation of events and realities, which in turn influence the movement and changes of history.[46]

Using his freedom and will, the individual being is a part of the norms and laws of history – and influences its events – without undermining historical determinism. This is because the historical causes directing events are formed as part of a larger collection of factors amongst which human action – originating in free will – is one of the most important and effective factors.

B. Material and incorporeal Factors of History

The background to history is made up of a variety of material and immaterial factors, and sets out certain limits to freedom and the will of the individual. And so, which ones are prior and essential? Further, which of these factors generates the real and authentic spirit of history, such that it constitutes the central factor upon which all the others are dependent?[47]

From this viewpoint in particular, Muṭahharī argues thoroughly against historical materialism. This theory asserts that the primary moving force of history is the economic factor, embodied in the means of production and commerce. As a result, it renders all other factors and activities secondary manifestations of this central factor, which basically defines the direction of history. Hence, production and its related activities emerge as the principal cause of all moral and sentimental phenomena such as art, ethics, philosophy, religion, law, and so forth, and surfaces as the factor that governs them and determines their direction.

C. The Principles of Historical Materialism

Historical materialism believes in the priority of matter and ranks it higher than the soul, that is, all the moral aspects of human society are nothing but a natural reflection of the world's material factors and conditions. Thus, there is no relation between the moral factors and the movement of history; they do not influence it or direct it in any way. The priority of matter, according to Marxism, does not mean that the individual first satisfies his material needs and then his moral obligations, but rather, that the latter is the result of the former and one of its aspects, because the human being is created with one type of need, which is the material one. His moral duties emerged once his means of production were developed in a way that imposed upon him the need for a hypothesis that would suit them, and is connected to or embodied in art, literature, philosophy and laws, and which follows up and forms material life.[48] Since the level of the means of production imposes a set of teachings, arts, ideas and so on, it then imposes regulation upon society's institutions in a particular way that suits it. Therefore, the whole material and psychological social structure is the result of the development of means of production.[49]

As mentioned earlier, Muṭahharī supposed Marxism to be a philosophy that ranks society above the individual, and gives it the priority to impose its rules on the will and freedom of the human being, whose knowledge of such rules as they appear may be exploited, so that he uses them to his advantage for achieving his goals.[50]

Nevertheless, the means of production develop continuously, integrate in a self-contained way and impose a particular pattern of relationships with production, which in turn directs the nature of the social relationships of the people. As the means of production change, the sum of the consequent relationships also changes. Thus, the economy becomes the basis of all the systems of relationships, such as customs, traditions, judicial and political systems and religious beliefs.

Since Marxism ranks the means of production above other social factors, it also ranks labour above thought at the level of the individual, so that the assessment of humanity is not by the thought it generates but by the labour it accomplishes.[51] In its movement, thought is a result of this structure, on the basis of labour. The economic factor, as seen here, includes two other factors: means of production, which is the result of the human-nature relationship, and production relationships, which is the result of the human-human relationship. The connection between means of production and production relationships is dialectic. As long as the means are expanding and integrating, they need new suitable relationships, and thus the society's structure changes at all levels.[52]

Muṭahharī deduces many consequences of this theoretical construction of historical materialism, which can be summarised as follows:

1. The way to comprehend events is to understand the economic and material factors that control them, because the movement of history is nothing but the result of the development of means of production and their subsequent relationships. For all the major changes and revolutions affecting the superstructure of society, in terms of habits, traditions, religion and culture, are rooted in the economic factor.[53]

2. The laws of history are inevitable, and far exceed the wilful choices of the individual, because society is controlled and moved according to a set of comprehensive, collective and controlling norms exactly the same as the laws of nature. Society is composed of prior and secondary factors. The prior factors are the means of production and their relationships integrated according to a series of necessary natural laws. These change from one form to another in light of these norms, and as a consequence require the secondary factors to change. With his knowledge, which is also his freedom, the human being tries to include himself in the process of these laws in order to utilise and take advantage of them.

Marxism introduces its viewpoint as a scientific theory of society, while this theory only presents the mechanics of historical law, which can be taken advantage of at each stage of change.[54] Knowledge of these laws is useful for both interpretation and prediction.

3. The stages that societies go through differ, and shift gradually from one type to another. However, each stage has its own laws, and the laws of one stage do not apply to one that follows; hence there are no permanent or eternal laws.

4. The development of means of production was the reason behind the establishment of the system of private property at the dawn of history. This system divided society into two classes: the bourgeoisie and the workers. These two classes are still central in present day society, and have been in continual conflict ever since they evolved. Other classes have appeared from time to time, but these two have been the most influential throughout history. However, it is impossible for society to be divided into classes if it is solely based on the means of production; therefore every division within a society has occurred because of a variation in its means of production, which has necessitated a variation in its superstructure. Generally, the bourgeoisie in such societies imposes its viewpoint because it is the most powerful, and imposes its own, ideology, religion and traditions. This explains why it maintains traditions and legacies, while the working class has a tendency to become revolutionary and progressive. This division is a necessary condition for change to take place, because the working class requires a system based on the non-ownership of the means of production, labour and property. When the division of the classes disappears through revolution, the earlier ideology also disappears.

5. The role of an ideology of social classes is weak. As is the case with any ideology, one can suppose that education is the guiding principle. However, Marxism considers that it is only the class situation that paves the way for an ideology whose role is primarily to make the disadvantaged class aware of the paradoxical position it has in the existing society, and hence an awareness of its exploitation, while other matters, which are commonly supposed to be general human characteristics, such as demanding freedom and consideration, do not have any role in such a society. An

ideological motivation is influential in achieving their interests, but it is still only a mere reflection of the socialist position regarding the means of production.[55] Yet when the situation of the proletariat is resolved by a change in the means of production, the classes cease to exist, and the individual rediscovers his real self, which had been torn apart by the property system.

6. All revolutionaries and progressive leaders spring from the working class, which can be divided into two parts according to the work performed. There are thinkers who make decisions and others who perform manual tasks. However, the job of the decision makers is not a doubtful theorising on the nature the working class as a class working for itself, but the result of support for their awareness and their position from the proletariat as a whole and the economic struggle itself.

Neither political parties nor those who present hypotheses outside the scale of the labour movement are capable of change. For this reason, Marx reproached those unlikely socialists, described as proletariat, but who nonetheless do not realise the historical self- emanation of their class and its special significance, and attempt to replace the naturally evolving system stemming from the proletariat as a class with their own fantasies.[58]

In Muṭahharī's interpretation, these are the basic dynamics which determine the course of history according to historical materialism.

D. The Incoherence and Inner Contradictions of Historical Materialism

Muṭahharī intended to present a systematic criticism of historical materialism. He reviewed its structure, ideas and fundamental principles, before attempting to refute it according to reason and the sum of experience, stressing that its overall perception of society and history did not accord with Islam. In the first part of his criticism, he showed how historical materialism in itself was disqualified from interpreting the movement of society and history, since the arguments concerning these factors were incomplete. In the second part, he intended to disprove what was being alleged and circulated about the principles of historical materialism being found in the cognitive system of Islam, according to some Qur'anic verses that seemingly suggest this, and which were taken out of context. Nonetheless, Muṭahharī submitted six arguments in the first part of his criticism, which he considered enough to demonstrate the incoherence of what he had already mentioned regarding the principles of Marxism.

The first argument: Historical materialism is a hypothesis that lacks evidence, because every philosophy of history should either be founded on historical and present-day experiences and events, from which general laws are deduced, or founded on past events which are generalised to include the present and the future, according to a coherent and convincing system.

Historical materialism has no firm basis as such.[57] Having attempted to apply their theory to actual events, Marxists themselves have admitted their surprise at finding events that neither stressed nor even suggested the priority of an economic factor. Consequently, the principles of Marxist theory essentially derogate the importance and effectiveness of the other elements making up the movement of history and developments within society.[58]

Moreover, there is evidence in the Marxist experience itself, which proves the invalidity of the principle of inevitability in which Marxists believed and upon which its vision was in many ways formulated. For the Chinese revolution was against a feudal society controlled by determined production relationships and indistinct methods of production. According to this Marxist inconsistency, it is supposed that historical development requires society to change its internal mechanisms in order to become an industrial society within which the powers of production and their relationships automatically develop. The society then evolves radically, due to the class distinctions within it, into a socialist society in which the proletariat prevails and all class disparity disappears. Despite the Chinese Revolution having shifted towards a socialist society, what happened next? In one of its stages of development, the society moved to a higher level, beyond the main intermediate levels, to integrate the basic principles necessary for the change, that is, the powers of production and its relationships. What is learned from the Chinese Revolution is that the sum of what formed the superstructure of society, according to historical materialism – such as culture, ideology and propaganda – can be affected by social sentiment and a tendency towards revolution, which can change the relationships of production and the traditional basis on which the distribution of the means of production are based.

Experience reveals another inconsistency of materialism. Marx supposed that the revolutionary class cannot be made up of the peasant class, in the form of a proletariat with no revolutionary inclination, for it lacks the means of change which inevitably lead to socialism; it is a self-nullifying factor. The class that plays this role is not the proletariat, but rather the bourgeoisie itself.

The Chinese experience proves these two hypotheses wrong. This same proletariat, which Marx supposed as null and void, and Engels considered retroactive and vile, Mao Tse-Tung was able to accommodate in two stages of the inevitable historical stages of Marxism, and shifted society from feudalism to the socialist stage with the peasantry as the Revolution's driving force. In addition, the same is observed in Russia, where Lenin changed a semi-industrial society to a socialist state by influencing the superstructure from below. More precisely, it is the ideology, culture and tendency to revolution which had an effect; it was not through the integration of the means of production and its relationships, but by partisan propaganda and the revolutionary power of the proletariat.[59]

It was probably because of these contradictions in the theoretical basis of materialism, that Lenin stated that there is a mutual influence between a variety of social factors in the movement of society.[60]

The second argument: According to Muṭahharī, there are many discrepancies in the Marxist viewpoint regarding the main factors influencing the movement of history. Some of them focus on the economics as the only factor, while others assume an opposing relationship between what forms the basis and what forms the superstructure in Marxism, which requires a hypothesis of mutual influences with no priority of one over the other. For example, according to Engels, the political content of the class conflict, such as the issue of rights and reactions that appear in the form of ideology, art, literature, religion and so on, have a fundamental influence on the development of the historical conflict and the stages of social change. It may even determine the outcome in a radical way, while the economic factors follow a predictable course through an indefinite number of inconsistencies.[61]

In addition, Lenin states that when superstructures such as literature, policy, religion and so on prevent the development of economic factors, political development acquires a crucial role. This is because even if we admit that material factors affect moral factors, and that the social entity affects the social essence, we also have to admit that there is a mutual influence on the essence and the material, social feeling and social existence and superstructure and the economic factor.[62]

If what the Marxists say is true, then the basis for historical materialism would collapse, due to the change in production relationships before the change on production control. This establishes a revolutionary hypothesis before the actual revolution, and regards the secondary factors as primary, reflecting the priority of thought over labour and material. This also means that political and cultural factors are dependent on the economic factor which equalises the superstructure and is the property which fundamentally influences history.

The third argument: a criticism of the essential typicality of the basis and superstructure: Historical materialism supposes that knowledge of the superstructure typically requires the knowledge of the basis, which are the production relationships, because the methods of production control the relationships which lead the way to a revolutionary change within society. According to Muṭahharī, this does not take place in any capitalist industrial society, since the producing powers control all the relationships, and there is no change in the superstructure. This enabled some industrial societies to reach the top of the capitalist hierarchy; but in contradiction to what Marx predicted, no workers' revolutions took place; there was no socialist regime established if there were no change in the political system, religion, and the sum of artistic, literary and scientific activity. We also find many societies that are similar in what is supposed to be the basic factor of historical development, but differ in their superstructure. The most prominent examples of this are America, Russia and Japan, since America and Japan are very similar in their economic systems. However they differ in their superstructure, that is, religion, culture, traditions, ethics, political system, and so forth, while America and Russia differ radically in their economic systems but are similar in the case of most of their values, traditions, customs and religion.[63]

Thus, historical change denies the necessity of a typical basis for the superstructure in the historical movement of societies.

The fourth argument: There are no typical class and ideological positions. "Historical materialism considers that the superstructure of society – thought, culture, religion, and so on – come second to the basic economic factor, and every superstructure is related to this factor in each stage of development." Hence, it is an inevitable result of the requirements of the age in which it occurs, which is why it does not suit other ages or stages in which the economic factor in different, since the development of the basis necessarily influences the superstructure.

But Muṭahharī found that experience proves the opposite, since many systems, beliefs, philosophies and arts continued to exist even after a change in the economic factor, and continued to influence different levels of society.[64]

The fifth argument: Historical materialism states that the cultural factor does not develop in isolation from the economic factor. However, experience demonstrates the opposite of this, and has shown that means of production do not develop on their own, but rather through the influence of human factors; since the individual makes discoveries through experience and experimentation, the main source of his knowledge of himself and the world with its laws and relationships, which he uses to develop his talents and abilities. Thus, the integration and development of the individual occurs before the development of the means of production. Other types of knowledge, such as the arts and literature, also relate to the economic factor and affected it a similar way.[65]

The sixth argument: Marxism considers all the ideas, systems and values relative, and therefore not liable to continuity or permanence. This is because they are consequents of the inevitable development of the economic factor, which means that historical materialism as a theory – that changes are based on economic conditions – is itself not liable to continuity. If economic conditions improve, which they invariably do, the theory becomes of no avail, and loses its value by the change in the level of its cause, because it is a part of the superstructure of society which has changed according to the change in its basis.

Thus, according to Muṭahharī, the philosophical basis of historical materialism collapses due to an internal contradiction.

E. Islam and Historical Materialism

Muṭahharī exercises a great deal of caution against those who sought to reconcile the social concepts of Islam with the historical philosophy of Marxism, since this served to legitimize an alien social ideology. The basis of concepts of this ideology have a powerful attraction when there is excessive class inequality, political dictatorship and economic exploitation, and it was widespread amongst young people who were aspiring for revolutionary change.

Muṭahharī realised that his position put him in clear opposition to a powerful trend, which had widespread publicity coming mainly from a steadfast opposition to the regime. Nevertheless, he clearly and openly expressed his position, by explaining the negative effects of applying social Marxist concepts to Islam, and trying to deduce them from Qur'anic verses taken out of context, and away from the general cognitive methodology of the Qur'an. He examined the manner of this attempt at reconciliation, and logically refuted it by taking the Qur'anic verses in question and explaining the contexts in which they were to be understood. Various aspects of the argument are given below, followed by the corresponding refutation.

1. The first evidence they employed is that certain verses of Qur'an, in referring to society, support the division of society into two parts on the basis of economy, that is to say, the rich and the poor. When referring to the first of these, the Qur'an used such terms as "the élite," "the arrogant" and "the affluent," and the others are referred to as "the abased," "the people," "the progeny" and "the simpleminded." The Qur'an uses those two categories in contrast to one another.[66]

There are also verses which divide people into two classes on a moral basis. One such class consists of "the disbelievers," "the polytheists," "the hypocrites," "the transgressors" and "the wrongdoers," Whereas the other class consists of "the believers," "the monotheists," "the pious," "those striving for the cause of Allah" and "the martyrs." The whole of the first category is included amongst the wealthy, while the second category is included amongst the poor and the needy, without no exception. The general rule tends to be that wealth begets disbelief and so forth, while poverty begets belief, piety and righteousness. Thus, it becomes clear that the economic factor is the basis for any movement or change in the superstructure of society.

(7:59-137) (that is, 79 verses) reviews the lives of the prophets and illustrates the humility of their followers and the arrogance of those who opposed them:[67]

We did not send a warner to any town without its affluent ones saying, "We indeed disbelieve in what you have been sent with" (34:34).[68]

The class divisions inherent in historical materialism explains this concurrence.

The Qur'an has stated that wealth and ownership are the cause of oppression and rebellion, and are in contradistinction to the humility and peace enjoined by the prophets (96:6-7).[69] The story of Korah shows the bad influence that wealth has on its possessor, and how it leads to rebellion and obstinacy (28:76).[70]

2. The second evidence they used is that the Qur'an addresses those to whom it speaks as "people," meaning the abased and deprived masses. This illustrates class-consciousness, and states that this is the class suitable for accepting the call. As a result, this means that economy directs history in the sight of Islam, and that history has a material identity.[71]
3. The Qur'an has declared that all prophets, leaders, reformers and inspirers come from this lower class (62:2).[72] This necessarily proves the coincidence between the social ideological position and the economic position. The material identity of history is what makes such a coincidence understandable.
4. The approach taken by the prophets in the Qur'an helps us deduce that the aim was to establish justice and equality, and remove class barriers. In addition, the prophets started from the basis, that is, the economic factor, and moved on to the superstructure. Thus, righteousness, belief and doctrine is the secondary aim of the prophets, after establishing justice and equality and removing class barriers.[73]
5. The position of the opponents of the prophets was one of narrow-mindedness, keeping to the present position, and protecting the norms. However, the position of the prophets clearly opposed this. The first position in a class society is that of the exploiters and opportunists, and the position of the prophets is a revolutionary one; these are two opposing positions, as the Qur'an expresses in number of verses: (43:40-50), (40:23-44), (20:49-71), (26:16-49) and (28: 36-39). These verses clearly state that keeping to the existing norms is the position of opportunists and conservatives, who do not want to change the status quo on the pretext of following in the steps of their forefathers and an exaltation of the past. The verses also clearly state the prophets call for understanding, reasoning and reflection, which is according to the logic of revolutionaries.[74]

6. The end of the conflict, according to the Qur'an, is the victory of the abased, which is just as historical materialism predicts. The Qur'an confirms, along with historical materialism, the inevitable movement of history, and that it is "the abased ones" who have a revolutionary (7:137; 28:5).[75]

According to all the above, the Qur'an therefore corresponds with and confirms the essential thesis of historical materialism.

Muṭahharī mentions these arguments in order to discuss them systematically and thence refute them, by examining each one and highlighting its contradictions, and goes on to explain how they are based on arguments taken out of context from the quoted Qur'anic verses, and a misunderstanding of the meanings.

1) To say that the Qur'an has categorised people into two opposing classes and that the basis of a confrontation is an economic factor is not true. Since the Qur'an mentions many human experiences affirming that from the class of the rich there appeared believers who rose against that class as the Believer of Pharaoh's house and Pharaoh's wife (66:11). The Qur'an has told us about the magicians of Pharaoh and how the natural human essence revolts in favour of justice, and how it frees itself of personal interest and pays no heed to threats;[76]

   Surely I will cut off your hands and feet from opposite sides (20: 71).[77]

   The revolt of Moses (a) is the best example of the contradiction between Qur'anic logic and historical materialism. He lived under the protection of Pharaoh, was raised in his house, and then revolted against him and left to work as a shepherd in Madian. Then he engaged in a conflict with Pharaoh and his followers. Many of Moses' followers were from the class of the rich. Muḥammad (ṣ) married Khadijah, a wealthy woman of high status. Regardless of the wealth that came into his possession, Muḥammad (ṣ) continued to live in piety and humility. According to historical materialism, Muḥammad (ṣ) would be a conservative defender of the status quo, and not a revolutionary. However, he was totally the opposite.[78]

   On the other hand, throughout history, tyrants have relied on subjugated people to protect their dominion. The Qur'an gives us examples of deprived peoples who provided tyrants with the apparatus of their tyranny and followed them, as in 4:97; 14:21; and 34:31-37.

Indeed, the majority of the followers of the prophets were poor abused people, undefiled by wealth, with natural instincts uncorrupted. They considered change a means to regain their rights and their lost dignity, and not according to a law of history that inevitably led them to revolution, as claimed by historical materialism.[79]

According to the Qur'an, the principles that lead to change in history are not only materialistic, but also moral. This is why the call of the prophets included everyone including tyrants, to free their consciousness, activate their human nature, and remove the dregs from their internal instincts. Almighty Allah therefore ordered Moses to declare the truth before Pharaoh, so that he may remember and fear:

Go to Fir'awn (Pharaoh); for indeed he has rebelled. Then say (to him), is that (possible) for you to be purified? And I guide you to your Lord, then you may fear [Him] (79: 17-19;[80] 20:44-45 and 20:15).

The Qur'an emphasises the value of admonition, which can change man, and hence change the nature of society.

2) According to Muṭahharī, "people" in the Qur'an does not refer to the deprived masses, but rather to all mankind. There is no difference between the rich and the poor, the superior and the inferior, the elevated and the lowly.

3) Neither prophets nor reformers come only from the class of subjugated people, and there is no evidence in the Qur'an to indicate this.

4) The purpose of sending prophets is comprehensive reform. Therefore, the first step is to amend the beliefs and the basic teachings of religion which had been distorted. This is what the Qur'anic verses focused on in the context of determining the purpose of the prophets' vocation. Indeed, reformation sometimes also required a direct confrontation of the social reality, however, through the application of reformation.[81]

5) As mentioned earlier, it would be correct to say that the logic of those opposing the prophets is the same logic of the conservatives,

and it is natural for there to be a group seeking to preserve their interests. It is also true that the logic of the prophets was the logic of change, but this was not because of deprivation and class injustice or a compulsive reaction to subjugation. Rather, the reason was that they reached a state of human perfection, which weakened their relationship with the established social order and false behaviour, and aspired to independence.[82]

6) The meaning of the Qur'an when it speaks of victory does not refer to any economic logic, that is, it does not state that those victorious in the struggle between the right and the wrong are the poor subjugated people, while the defeated are the rich leaders. The victory is that of faith over disbelief, right over wrong, and light over darkness:[83]

   Allah has promised those of you who have faith and do righteous deeds that He will surely make them successors in the earth (24:55).[84]

   This verse promises an ideological attribute and practice, that is, it attributes victory to belief and right action, and is nothing to do with rulership and subjugation, or wealth and poverty.

   And the outcome will be in favour of the pious (7:128);[85]

   And indeed We have recorded in the Zabūr (Psalms), after the Remembrance, that the earth will be inherited by My righteous servants (21:105).[86]

   The struggle in this context is not for material benefit but for values. The key factor in this conflict is not class inequality, but the natural inclination towards justice and knowledge, and the search for the truth.[87]

Thus, the verse of subjugation is an instance of the inheritance verse. Almighty Allah wants to confirm through these verses that the oppressed companions of Moses and the believers of his message will inherit the earth, not because of being oppressed, but because they are believers.[88]

Muṭahharī sees many reasons for the tendency among some Muslim thinkers to try to reconcile historical materialism with the Qur'an. One such reason is that if it be supposed that Islamic culture is revolutionary, then pushing such a culture to the maximum limit of change cannot be done except through deprived people, and that can only be accomplished by sustenance, which is the focus of the conflict.[89] Another is that the

Qur'an takes a position in favour of the oppressed and poor people. It is deduced from this that the Qur'an considers the basis for revolution to be the oppressed class. However, the truth is that the Qur'an stresses the primordiality of human nature. It does not attach importance to an alleged social idea or social status. Islam's support of the abased stems from a fundamental principle, since they lack certain rights and have no power. This is not merely support for the oppressed, but for human dignity, and above all freedom.

2

EMPHASIS ON THE MORAL DIMENSION OF THE HUMAN BEING, AND A CRITICISM OF MATERIALISTIC TENDENCIES AND NIHILISM

Muṭahharī addresses, within his epistemological concerns of the westernernised intellectual trends, the problem of the dominance of materialism in human life and its transformation into an ideology, which has its own principles, conceptions and philosophy. In addition, its tangible impact on many societies and its penetration into subtle points of our thought and the way in which we understand man and the world in which he lives.

We are going to summarise his most important thoughts in this area in an effort to highlight his emphasis on the moral aspect of the human personality; the devastating effects of the materialistic notion of "nihilism" on the individual and society in terms of the belief in existential nihilism, futility and emptiness.

However, Muṭahharī did not mean that materialism in this context is a belief in an objective reality with its own character, because this is something that theists and materialists have in common. Rather he means takes materialism as the negation of non-material existence; the belief that everything in this world is subject only to material laws within a framework of time and space and perceptible to the senses, and that anything else is nothing but illusion.[90]

Such a tendency, according to Muṭahharī, is not new, and not simply related to the development of scientific knowledge. It is as old as human thought, as it may be found in the works of some of the Greek philosophers before Socrates. It is also found elsewhere, in some Arab and Persian cultures among others.[91] The Qur'an describes a similar scene, for example,

> *They say, "There is nothing but the life of this world: we live and we die, and nothing but time destroys us"* (45:24).[92]

Muṭahharī's main endeavour regarding this issue is based on an investigation of the motivation behind it, especially in the recent times during which it has developed into a doctrine with its own advocates, followers and philosophy. Muṭahharī's investigation of these incentives supposes that human nature remains the same, with monotheism as its basis, and materialism something secondary which corrupts its essential nature. Henceforth, the question is about the reason for this deviation.[93]

If knowledge and certainty are the foundations of human nature, materialism is a tendency towards scepticism. We may find a similar sceptical tendency within the sphere of religious faith if we delve into the details. Fundamental questions arise which need satisfactory answers. The main different between these two kinds of uncertainty is that sceptical questioning within the sphere of religion leads to faith, certainty and tranquillity – the natural state of the human soul when it contemplates its concepts, visions and beliefs. However, materialism as a philosophy embodies scepticism itself; it opts for it as a reasonable methodology. It is fundamentally an inherent doubt, which becomes an overwhelming obsession.

Nevertheless, materialism has grown from a position regarding certain epistemological beliefs into an independent school. Many people have attributed it to the development of knowledge, culture, and the natural sciences, since this was the position of those who investigated using empirical experimentation and led the way to an unprecedented advance in knowledge. But for Muṭahharī this was not the case. He saw it as unrelated to knowledge and development, because he claimed that we could find deep religious tendencies within societies that have developed greatly in the scientific field, as it is the case with our own societies. We also find well-established religious beliefs in societies that hardly have any scientific development. A good example of this case is the English materialist philosopher Russell, or the deep faith adopted by Einstein.[94]

In fact, the first materialistic tendency is found with the inadequate religious concepts established as facts over the centuries in churches. A second tendency stems from a distorted church experience. Both of these factors have led Western society towards materialism, and consequently affected many other people who have never adopted Christianity or had the same historical experience. This apparent inadequacy is manifest in childish and immature theological concepts, as Muṭahharī likes to call them,[95] of God and his relationship to the world, the role of the Church, the question of mind and faith, and so on. The impact of these concepts are clearly reflected in the works of Auguste Comte who thought that knowledge has cut the father of knowledge (that is, God) off from his work, and placed Him far away in isolation after having appreciated His services and elevated Him to a supreme height. Undoubtedly, Comte is trying to say that previously God was involved in world events and everything was attributed to Him. However, with the development of knowledge, which discovered the real reasons behind these events, the mind has come to realise that God is nothing but an imaginary actor in the events of the world. It was the need for a hidden interpretation of world events that led to the creation and existence of God. According to Comte, humanity has gone through three stages of development: theism, philosophy and knowledge. In the first stage, man would see a supreme metaphysical power behind events. Then his mind developed and could interpret the events by referring them to comprehensive natural laws. And later, he realised in detail the real reasons behind events, and discovered the essence of natural phenomena through experimentation. Despite of the inadequacy of this theory, it came as a response to an ineffective conception of the nature of God and His relationship to the world.[96]

Another reason, related to the first, is the violence practised by the Church throughout history. It stirred strong feelings of hatred towards religion, and the desire to revolt against it and restore the freedom that had been suppressed, bring light to a gloomy future, and nourish the mind whose capacities and creativity had been stunted. It was the desire to live in a society free of coercion.[97]

A third reason behind materialism, according to Muṭahharī, was the inadequacy of certain philosophical concepts. He disapproves of many philosophical conclusions which are well-established in the West. Such conclusions are nothing but an inadequate and superficial treatment of very deep and complicated concerns. He used as an example of this what ancient and traditional philosophy has defined as the First Cause. Hegel thought that the basis of our belief in a First Cause is an indirect proof, because disbelief in it would lead to a hierarchy. Therefore, belief in it is not as a supporting proof from within it, but for as a proof against admitting its non-existence. It is worthwhile mentioning that such a proof is necessary for the mind, but it cannot at all be certain. In Muṭahharī's opinion, the proof given by Hegel is incomplete, since it only differentiates the First Cause from other causes. One might wonder why the First Cause does not require a cause, while other causes do. In other words, why is the First Cause the first?

According to Muṭahharī, the works of great philosophers from Comte to Spencer contain such statements, that the problem regarding the principle of causality is that the mind requires a cause for everything. In other words, a sequence or hierarchy is not acceptable. Moreover, it cannot discover or understand a cause that does not require another cause.[98]

Sartre's statements only differ in form, for he assumes that it is contradictory for an existent to be the cause of itself, because this requires it to exist in order to bring itself into existence. Muṭahharī believed it imperative to know how to apprehend correctly the Principle of Causality. Does it rest on the self-justification that underlines the impossibility of a thing bringing itself into existence, as expressed by Sartre? Is it inevitable, with the exception of the First Cause, to escape the dilemma of an infinite regress as indicated by Hegel and Spencer? Does the negation of infinite regress necessitate the belief that every cause is a self-existent being in itself, or the belief in a First Cause in order to escape from impossibility?

According to Muṭahharī, the hesitation that arises concerning the principle of causality and the First Cause results from a philosophical problem that has remained unresolved in Western philosophy, namely the fundamental nature of existence. Muslim philosophers have thoroughly explored this subject, and concluded that existence is fundamental and truly "real," whereas the mental concepts reflected in our minds are merely extrinsic mental considerations, which exist accidentally rather than essentially. Accordingly, the existents are in need of pure existence in order to actualise; something that invests the existents with reality. In other words, the true being of existents is their very actualisation and their share of existentiation. Hence, an existent is not in need of existentiation until granted reality from pure existence, or in other words, the real entities are self-realising and self-sufficiently existenting. Consequently, if a cause were to add anything of any description to an existent, it would be to the existentiation and not to the real being or reality, that is, its essence and form. Thus, Islamic philosophy believes that the reality of existence necessitates "need" and "ontological poverty" at some level – rather it is this real need and ontological poverty that connects with other levels of reality. However, ontological poverty, as far as existence is concerned, indicates a posteriority amongst the ontological levels, and therefore a dependence on other levels which are prior and more superior. Hence, if we look at existence in its generality – disregarding the gradation of its levels – we find that it is free of "need." This is because "need" arises from an extrinsic consideration; an observation of priority or posteriority in the levels of existence.

Consequently, it is meaningless to state either with Sartre that the assumption of a First Cause involves a contradiction on the evidence that an existent cannot cause itself, or with Hegel that a First Cause is an exception to the problem of "sequence."[99]

In this connection, Muṭahharī discusses the principle of causality in detail. He considers it a fundamental idea governing phenomena, and the foundation of all human sciences. He later raised the matter of why every effect requires a particular cause as articulated by Muslim philosophers and theologians – a point which is not a central concern of this concise review.[100]

One of the philosophical dilemmas that reveal the limitations of certain ideas in Western philosophy is the perceived contradiction between the principle of creation and the principle of evolution, which arises from the belief that the principle of creation necessarily implies that existents are fixed, immutable and can never change. However, experience shows that existents are constantly evolving. As a result, biology and other natural sciences stress the nullity of the principle of creation, and adopt an opposing view to that of theology.[101] The French biologist Lamarck advocated this theory before Darwin;[102] he believed that it negated the theory of creation and faith. Later, Darwin developed Lamarck's theory and corrected many of his mistakes.

Muṭahharī regarded what Lamarck and Darwin presented on evolution as having insufficient reasoning and being an extrapolated hypothesis. He questioned what was stopping us from accepting a theory of evolution of two kinds – a sudden evolution that involves the reality of the living thing, and another occurring either rapidly or slowly, with the evolution of man occurring rapidly through divine intervention? What is it that prevents us from assuming that science has definitive proofs on the theory of evolution, and that it is not possible to provide all the conditions and circumstances needed for a substance to evolve over a long period, and that man's ancestors were animals?[103] It is possible to use texts from the Qur'an concerning Adam in a manner that underscores the dignity of the human being and his position, without contradicting the theory of evolution.[104] Even if we could not use them in this way, what does the principle of evolution have to do with denying the existence of a divine role in creation? Furthermore, how does it come to be a factor of materialism?[105]

Muṭahharī found reasons for the conflict between the theory of evolution and the existence of God, which he summarised in two groups as follows:

1. With the growing acceptance of the theory of evolution theologians lost one of the most important proofs for the existence of God, namely the argument of design – the perfection in the ordering of the universe clearly visible in living creatures. The basis of this argument is the notion that it is not at all reasonable for a living being, created perfectly, not to have a wise and supreme power behind it.[106]

   Hence, the claim that all living beings, with all their characteristics and wonders, have evolved by themselves over millions of years under particular conditions, and existing for the first time without a cause or previous planning, would mean that there is no need to suppose the existence of a wise and supreme power to create them. Moreover, it would be possible to assume a necessary adaptation to circumstances and coincidence are responsible to for the perfection and ordering that we see today.[107] Nevertheless, Muṭahharī poses some objections to this:

   i. The "design" argument is not the only evidence for the existence of Allah.

   ii. The order of creation is not limited to the formation of systems of living organisms.

   iii. The gradual appearance of living organisms and pure coincidence cannot explain the perfection and precision found in these organisms, since arbitrary changes that result from coincidence are random and unorganised. In addition, an arbitrary interpretation of all the organs of the living creatures is not possible, as in the case of a goose's leg, for example.[108] However, there is a marvellous harmony and relationship between the organs of each creature.[109] These organs work perfectly as an integrated unit free of defect, which, when looked upon in its entirety, constitutes a marvellous and perplexing system.[110]

More than at any time before, the principle of evolution according to Muṭahharī proves the existence of a sustaining and guiding power behind the existence of living organisms, and clearly explains "purposefulness" in creation. When Darwin spoke about the principle of adaptation to the environment, he inadvertently made this principle a metaphysical one, because the motivating force behind adaptation to the conditions of the environment is unknown and immaterial. Rather than being a blind force, it is a force which guides creation and provides it with a sense of purpose.[111]

The significance of an evolution-based proof for the existence of a hidden, executive power is no less important than any other. Darwin's principle of natural selection, the struggle for survival and evolutionary genetics are not just arbitrary, blind natural reactions to the requirements of the environment, for if they were, they do not explain for us the many differences and variations that exists among living organisms.

The argument based on a conflict between the principle of purposeful creation and the principle of evolution reveals, according to Muṭahharī, a weakness in the methodology of divine philosophy in the West, for it considered the theory of evolution as a an oppositional and destructive theory works that stood against purposeful creation rather than in support.

2. The presumption that if there was a purposeful creation, then this would have been realised in accordance with a preordained destiny, a perfect plan designed by a supreme divine will.[112] A preordained destiny negates the possibility of life existing by chance, yet we know that chance plays a remarkable role in the life of living organisms and their transformations. The existence of chance or coincidence thus negates any prior divine intention for the world, and consequently invalidates the notion of creation in the first

place. For if things exist due to a divine plan, then they must have been created complete, because the supreme divine will is free of any restrictions or limitations; therefore the world would be created perfect in terms of its design and capabilities from the very outset.[113]

However, Muṭahharī considers that eternal knowledge and divine will do not necessitate a sudden or instantaneous coming into existence, and that all religions believe creation reaches perfection gradually. Coincidence has no role in this existential evolution or the process of perfecting, since that would imply either that the creation of a thing has no definite cause or it results from another thing, which does itself has no definite cause. Naturally, the materialists reject both these arguments.[114] What appears to be a coincidence is a result of ignorance of the cause that generated it. Therefore, there is no coincidence, and mere chance is not the cause of anything. Of course, we can believe that the actuality of the existence of things is through gradual perfection, since both existence and capacities are connected with real conditions. When viewed within the context of their respective sets of conditional factors, one notices that the actualisation of the existence of things is not possible in the absence of conditions. Hence, if Allah wills to create an existent instantaneously, He does so; likewise, if He wills to create it gradually, He does so – His absolute will has no limitations. In fact, the matter has to do with the nature of the existents, and not the will. Theistic philosophers have resolved the actualisation of existence through gradual movement, since there is no immutability or stillness in nature, and Almighty Allah has created things with the qualities of movement, progression and self-perfection in their very nature.[115]

Consequently, purposeful creation does not disqualify the evolution of the world, the integration of its powers and capacities, its purposeful and flowing movement, or its continuous self-development. However, "the tendency towards change should be the vital element whose efficacy is influenced by an unknown factor" as Darwin stated, according to a quotation cited by Muṭahharī at the end of his discussion.

3. One example of the shortcomings in Western philosophy is the contradiction between the belief in the eternity of matter and the divinity of Allah, whereas there is no correlation between the two.

For it is quite possible to believe in the eternity of matter as well as the existence of Allah; many Muslim philosophers have accepted this without seeing any contradiction between the two concepts.[116]

Another example is the presumed conflict between the Divine and the freedom of the human being, based on the premise that the existence of a supreme Will governing the affairs of the world negates any sort of freedom for the individual. Sartre said in this regard,

> "Since I believe in my freedom, I cannot believe in God; because if I believe in God, I have to believe in fate and destiny, and if I believe in fate and destiny, I cannot choose individual freedom. Hence, since I desire to choose freedom and to believe in it, therefore, I am not a believer in God."[117]

Meanwhile, Muṭahharī does not believe there is any conflict between freedom and divine Will; rather, the opposite is true. According to Islam, belief in Allah requires belief in the freedom of the individual, and there is no meaning to one's freedom outside this context. According to Muṭahharī, the Qur'an affirms Allah's greatness and His supreme dominion. Nevertheless, it insists on affirming the freedom of humanity and defends it (76:1-3 and 17:18-20). In Muṭahharī's view, philosophers in the West thought that the human being can only be free when he rejects belief in Allah, and chooses his own fate and destiny. Whereas the truth is that turning away from Allah and purposefulness, undermines human freedom and leaves it prone to futility, anarchy and scepticism. This freedom leads towards emptiness and nihilism, and fetters it unlimited anxiety, disorder and nausea. This is the result of the words of Sartre and his contemporaries, who believed that the freedom of the human being contradicts the existence of a divine being. Indeed, they fell into a dangerous trap that led them into the unknown.[118]

4. The tendency towards materialism is encouraged by shortcomings in social and political concepts in the West. Political despotism was deeply entrenched in Western society over an extended period, based on the claim that the ruler was solely responsible before Allah; therefore the sovereign's will was supreme, and no other human authority could go against it. Consequently, the hope and freedom of the people were dashed. As a result, people could not

make a distinction between political despotism and the notion of the divine duty. They inclined to believe that accepting the absolute will of Allah necessitates submitting to a despotic authority, which the people had right to oppose or dare to criticise.[119]

The Arab and Muslim world has also been acquainted with such a notion for a long time now; it has affected our societies, brought huge losses, and bound them in weakness and servitude. Whereas the truth is that Islam does not recognise the legitimacy of despotism or forceful authoritarian power, regardless of whether such an authority exercises its rule in the name of Allah or not.[120]

This misconceived relationship in the West, between divine right and political despotism, impelled the masses to disavow religion. It generated a hatred for its principles and the rejection of its beliefs. The driving motivation was the aspiration to be free from a despotic authority that wielded power in the name of Allah.[121]

5. Religious practices also motivated the tendency towards materialism in Muṭahharī's view, but he acknowledged that this factor exists in the Muslim world too. Many individuals express their own opinions in the name of religion, the act in deviant ways, exploit a façade of piety, and make erroneous decisions which they claim are based on religious teachings and principles. As a result, they have damaged the image of religion in the minds of the masses, and caused them to turn away from it. According to Muṭahharī, Islam has been plagued by groups who attempted to defend religion using weak arguments and false beliefs, which the people have mistaken for true Islam. There have been confusing issues regarding divine justice, determinism and free will (*al-Jabr wa al-Ikhtiyār*), divine wisdom and the divine will. Accordingly, this undermined the status of religion in the hearts of the people, and many false ideas seeped into the faith. And even more seriously, it made it easier for its enemies to attack it and belittle its values and principles.[122]

In West, many of these problems have deeply affected religion. A prominent example is the equating of monasticism with religion, and regarding piety as living a secluded life. This also involves the confusing of virtue with the suppression of one's desires, energies and natural inclinations, despite the fact that one can never disown the tendencies and desires embedded deep within one's very nature.

Advocates of religion in the West undermined the value of these tendencies and urged for their suppression. For instance, they considered ignorance a prerequisite for salvation,[123] knowledge a cause of deviation, wealth a result of greed, sexual pleasure a Satanic vice, and the enjoyment of worldly pleasures the gateway to self-defeat and spiritual dejection. This was all done in an extremely exaggerated manner, causing the followers of religion to believe there was a strict division between religion and human nature. This division gave man two choices: either follow the call to religion or accede to nature. It is understandable that such a society, which combats human instincts in the name of religion and draws an intractable division between worldly pleasure and spiritual worship, should slide into materialism in search for immediate worldly gratification. Russell states:

"The teaching of the Church faces humanity with two kinds of misfortune: the worldly misfortune of being deprived of its boons or the misfortune of the next world."

One could never prosper in both worlds. This understanding instigated a bifurcating notion established in the name of religion, even though the role of religion is to ensure happiness in both this world and the next, in addition to showing the individual the best and shortest routes for attaining this happiness. This would enable man to realise happiness in this world, by enjoying what has been ordained for him through lawful means, as well as in the next (2:45 and 2:183).[124]

6. The sixth cause behind materialism, according to Muṭahharī, is the ethical and social infrastructure an individual is born into and has developed, since it may either provide man with fertile ground for the realisation of his goals, or lead him on a path to deviation, vice and corruption. Moreover, it can disorientate his faculty of reason and induce anxiety and scepticism regarding the choices he makes for his needs and objectives. In its teachings, Islam emphasises the vital role of rearing children, as well as the import part the intellectual and social environment plays in cultivating human capacities, thought and attitudes within society. This system ensures equilibrium in all spheres of the individual's personality.[125]

While discussing this topic in particular, Muṭahharī highlighted an issue that pertains to the present situation of Muslims, and

> contributes to pushing people towards materialism and the abandonment of religion. Many of those who speak in the name of Islam advocate inertia and submission in order to attain peace and tranquillity. As a result, many have come to believe that Islam legitimises the quelling of free will, and thus promotes weakness. Since the aspiration for liberation from hegemony and imperialism cannot be attained other than by revolution, and since religion – in this sense – rejects it, hence the path to freedom cannot be reached other than through materialism and the discarding of the inflexibility of religion.[126]

The question that emerges is how did this notion spread amongst Muslims and find its way into their minds. The answer is that experience has shown that those who spoke in the name of religion were generally in a position of inertia and submission. Moreover, the sparks of revolution were usually lit by materialists who advocated liberation from the authority of religion. Muṭahharī felt that this observation had a large element of truth to it, since the majority of the leading figures in revolution were materialists. Nevertheless, such an attitude has superimposed certain false attributes on religion, because the reality of religion is the exact opposite: it calls for change, the unleashing of the latent potentials within society, the revolt against injustice, despotism and tyranny, whatever the costs may be. Religion takes the side of the oppressed who have been scarred by the chains of oppression (The Qur'an, 28:5-17; 3:149; 22:41; 32:24; 4:95).

However, those whose speak in the name of religion have limited its role and curtailed its efficacy in this respect, and have sought peace and security by safeguarding their interests and positions. In this respect, there has been no difference between Muslims and non-Muslims.[127]

3

THE ISSUE OF ETHICS

Introduction

Muslims did not confront modernity simply in terms of the technological and scientific challenges it represents, which include philosophical, political and social doctrines, innovation and urbanisation. They also had to reflect upon what modernity represented as far as values and ethics were concerned. Modernity had forced Western society into a comprehensive process of change, which influenced the sum of the philosophical foundations that had directed it throughout the ages. Moreover, it impressed upon the superstructure of civilisation – that is, literature, the arts, traditions, customs, ethical values and laws – its perception of man, nature and the universe. Hence, the issue of ethical values was not excluded from the radical changes that swept through society.

In confronting this new challenge, Muslims were unable to define a precise position for themselves. The enticing lure of progress stimulated a rush to join in, on the assumption that Western civilisation was a complete, indivisible entity. Progress and prosperity were seen as inseparable outcomes that enveloped all aspects of life. This attitude made some Muslim thinkers hesitate: whether to immerse completely in a westernised civilisation or reject it completely. This uncertainty led to a debate that lasted for nearly a century. This contention regarding Western civilisation is visible to the present day. Nevertheless, the debate did not prevent some people from rushing to make a compromise. There was the possibility of benefiting from Western civilisation in terms of what would be to our advantage and was in harmony with our beliefs, and rejecting all the rest. This would preserve the core of our identity, which would outline what would be necessary for the desired progress and growth.

In general, these proposals, and the subsequent debate on the matter, were unable to prevent the accelerating influence of Western ethical values and behavioural patterns from overwhelming the Muslim world. Muslim society followed a path of unconditional imitation, such that the behavioural influence of Western civilisation was larger than any other, such as the intellectual, political, economic or developmental models. This had a corrupting influence on educational and society that was impossible to contain.

From this point, Muṭahharī found it necessary to occupy himself with the problem of values – their philosophical significance, as well as in practice – by reviewing the principles of Western values. Then he turned to delineating their shortcomings and negative results, and later compared this system with that of Islam.

1. The Nature of the Moral Act According to Muṭahharī

To Muṭahharī, undoubtedly, some of our actions may be described as natural, and have nothing to do with morals and values; for example, sitting at the table to eat. Our nature requires such actions, and they become entrenched by habit. However, some actions are different, and require ethical evaluation. However, what is the measure by which we can differentiate between one kind action and another, that is, between a moral act and a natural act? [128]

According to Muṭahharī, there are a number of theories on this. One such theory is that the standard of moral action is love for others, because voluntary human action cannot be without purpose. At times, however, the purpose is personal gain or to prevent harm to oneself. Such an action does not constitute a moral action, since every human being naturally seeks out that which secures his interests and prevents him from harm. However, when the human action transcends the limits of the self or ego, and becomes an act for the benefit of others, only then can it be described as moral action.

However, Muṭahharī regarded some philanthropic actions for others also as instinctive and natural. Thus, these actions do not meet the criterion of moral actions, for instance, a mother's love for her child which motivates her to safeguard his welfare and protect him from harm.[129] Thus, not every action motivated by altruism is necessarily a moral action. According to Muṭahharī, some thinkers believe the criterion for moral action is for the action to be good; reason easily comprehends the goodness of a good action and the badness of a bad one, and thus encourages the former and discourages the latter.[130]

Kant believed that the moral action is an unqualified act performed without a motive, and done only for the sake of the action itself, and according to the sense of duty that emanates from one's conscience; for the conscience dictates to the individual a series of actions that have no clear goal related to either the doer or to others. Actions that the human being does not perform with a motive, but rather due to a sense of conscientious duty, are moral actions. On the other hand, any action that includes some other factor, such as personal benefit or conditional altruism, is not a moral action.[131]

Muṭahharī believed there were disputes over this doctrine, since the individual does not perform an action that is of no benefit or interest to him. This is because the driving force towards a particular action is the perfection that one finds in it, regardless of whether this perfection is in the form of a certain materialistic benefit or as pleasure gained through benefiting others.[132] Pleasure is not limited to benefiting the doer or preventing personal harm, but attained likewise by benefiting others. What Kant said with reference to the possibility of an action being entirely without motive in order to be moral, is that this is impossible, since the individual does not perform an action that does not bring pleasure to oneself, irrespective of whether it is of benefit to oneself or to others.[133]

Darwin considered every creature to be naturally selfish. It strives for its survival, and thus there is a conflict which leads to natural selection by the survival of the fittest. This helps in the realisation of perfection. According to this philosophy, there is no room for moral action, because all actions are facilitated by the requirements of survival amidst a comprehensive and inevitable conflict. Some are of the opinion that this theory shakes the foundations of ethical cooperation amongst people, and suppose that the moral sense is not fundamental but rather an outcome of the principle of conflict. This is because the imperative that motivated the individual to cooperate was the desire to survive. Therefore, natural selection was unable to provide a basis for a moral philosophy.[134]

There is another theory by Russell in this context, which he referred to as the theory of individual mind, while Will Durant called it instinctive intelligence. It can be summed up by saying that ethics emanates neither from the conscience as in Kant's theory, nor out of love for the form – from the fact that the human being possesses reason and thought through which he recognises that his own benefit is contingent upon nourishing love for his counterparts. Russell stated:

> "I never steal my neighbour's cow, because I know that if I do this, then my neighbour will steal mine. Therefore, one does not perform any bad action, because he knows if he does, the negative results of his act will multiply. Therefore, common benefits necessitate ethics, and hence ethics emanates from intelligence."[135]

Consequently, Russell's theory is the theory of personal benefit and complete individualism. The individual seeks to realise his benefits through the best and the most reassuring means; when the individual's intelligence, he inclines towards the moral action, because he selects the least harmful, and predominantly chooses the relatively better means to secure his needs. This requires him to respect the rights of the others and abstain from harming them, since he knows that should he do otherwise, they will also counter him in a similar fashion.[136]

According to Muṭahharī, this theory shakes the foundations of ethics, it claims that ethics dictate only when there is an equality of capacities, such that I fear my counterpart as much as he fears me, and that I am safe from him as much as he is safe from me. However, when there is an imbalance of capacities, we find ourselves faced with the "weak" and the "strong," and the latter knows with certainty that the weaker one is unable to tackle him. In this situation, there is no cause for ethics, and whenever there is power, the moral conscience is extinguished. This is the essence of Russell's ethical theory, which in reality contests the idea of ethics, because there is nothing in it that prevents the exploitation of the weak, and the basis of this "ethic" is the individual reasoning intelligence.[137]

There exists a theory similar to this one, but replaces individual intelligence with the perception of beauty. It states that beauty is sensory and moral, and both these result from proportionality.[138] In a similar way that the perception of sensuous beauty causes a feeling of attachment, pleasure and attraction in the observer, moral beauty causes such a feeling of attraction. Therefore, proportionality is the basis of ethics or perception. Regulation and moderation between benign and malign actions results in proportionality, thus giving moral beauty to the action. Consequently, every beautiful action is moral, and it is beautiful due to its material or moral proportionality,[139] which is easily apprehended.

According to this theory, it is possible to connect the criterion of morality to the beauty of end-purposes, since there is a purpose and goal for the creation of the individual's abilities and energies. Hence, the individual's action that realises its end-purpose, into which one invests one's energies, is harmonious and beautiful, and consequently moral. Otherwise, it would either be excessive or inadequate, and consequently immoral. If the individual utilised all his abilities for the purpose they were intended, then all his actions would be beautiful and thus moral. Otherwise they would not be so.[140]

In arguing all these theories, Muṭahharī seemingly inclined towards Kant's viewpoint, albeit modifying some of his ideas. For instance, he replaces the concept of responsibility with the concept of moral conscience.[141] Muṭahharī thought that if an individual's action emanates from his feeling of love, his action is hence natural and defined as if it were inspired by instinct, whether his own or the collective instinct. The moral action on the other hand, is an action free from any motive that springs from a sense of responsibility and duty, disregarding any ulterior motive or benefit. As far as responsibility is concerned, it is a product of the conscience which Muṭahharī regards, similar to Kant, as an essential feature of the human being.[142] According to Muṭahharī, there is something in the inner depths of the human being that arouses a feeling of happiness when the individual rises above his nature, overcomes its imperatives, and acts according to his will, such that should his will prevail, he experiences satisfaction, whereas if his nature prevails, he feels defeated.

Despite Muṭahharī's positive disposition towards Kantian moral ethics, he emphasised that human morality cannot do without a religion that supports it and affirms. In his view, experience has proven that whenever religion is separated from ethics, the latter deteriorate and eventually disappear. Religion is the cornerstone of human morality, the guarantee of its efficacy and continuity.[143] Any moral action as such affirmed by religion is an act the individual performs disregarding personal motive or benefit. This is regardless of its performance being out love for his kind, for the beauty of it, or for preventing harm to others. When it is not a pragmatic action, then it is a moral one, for which it is unnecessary to choose any other theory to measure its degree of morality. According to Muṭahharī, the basis of every moral action is Allah, and thus the love of kindness, the sense of beauty, and the intelligence of the mind are heightened.[144]

2. The Relativity of Morality

There is yet another matter related to the subject of ethics, namely the relativity of morality. Irrespective of which theory we subscribe to concerning the nature of moral actions, one is confronted with the following question: Is morality relative or absolute? That is to say, is a particular quality or action always moral in all circumstances and for all people, or is it only moral according to specific circumstances?[145]

There is a theory that considers man the criterion for everything, and deems him the origin of truth, that is to say, reality is what man perceives it to be. This view originated in the realm of science and later moved on to ethics. Consequently, the standard for good and evil accorded with the perception of the individual.[146] Good ethics are those which the individual chooses to be so. Since individuals differ in what they choose at different times and in different circumstances, morality undergoes change as a result. Thus, a laudable action at one time may become worthy of contempt at another. According to the proponents of this theory, transformations in the choices we make are a result of the sequence of continuous perfection that humanity undergoes. Furthermore, different times have different principles, which thereby necessitate a change of values, attitudes and behaviour.

According to Muṭahharī, Hegel's theory of the essence of time and its perfection leads us in the same direction, because the essence of an integrated society causes it to take on a new form, that is, it constantly directs society, which in turn influences the ideas, beliefs, values and patterns of life that drive us to make choices[147] in a manner that is in harmony with the nature of the perfecting process. Hence, the social spirit and changes in time inspire good morals. Consequently, nothing remains constant; neither the generating social spirit nor its outcomes.[148]

But what is the reality of the essence of time? asks Muṭahharī. And what proves its flux and establishes that morality moves in accordance with the essence of time? Regardless of the answers to these two questions, this theory had a tremendous influence on European society and the world.

Muṭahharī unreservedly confirmed that human choices change with time and circumstances, but he did not believe that this results from a fundamental change in the essence of time, but rather from a change in mood.[149] The disposition of mankind is in either of two factors: equanimity or disruption; and these conditions describe the mood of society, and consequently influence the behaviour of both the individual and society. As such, when an individual's life is disturbed, and his disposition disrupted, his morals consequently deteriorate. Conversely, when his mood is in equilibrium and his life balanced, his morals are likewise nourished. The same applies to society as a whole, for it deteriorates and its moral standards decline when its disposition is disturbed, but prospers and preserves its morality when its mood is balanced. No other condition than these two dispositions can influence the individual or society, since the decline of morals is a sign of the deterioration of both the individual and society, whereas their increase is a sign of progress and prosperity. Society does not rise towards perfection without an elevation of morality and values.[150] Conversely, they decline when morality deteriorates, for there is no prosperous society that has no morality.

From Muṭahharī's point of view, Russell believed that a society develops involuntarily like plants do, and in order to reach the zenith of its perfection, its choices change in consonance with the nature of the stages of its perfection.[151] One who adopts this ideology necessarily believes in the relativity of morality, and that morals change in accordance with changes in the choices people make at a given level of their development. Consequently, a morality that is outside the scope of the individual's will and free choice is baseless, because any action or ethic he selects is good if compatible with the imperatives of his perfection. This choice invests action with value, making it general and universal. Hence, the criterion for the morality of a given action is the choice of the individual doer. Other European moral ideologies such as utilitarianism, romanticism and rationalism differentiated between moral principles and the moral action. They considered the former to be absolute, and the latter to be in a flux which accorded with the transformations of time.[152]

Those who consider love to be the criterion of morality believe that there are two other factors. Firstly, ethical values themselves are absolute and universal, and not relative. The second factor is the moral action, which changes from time to time, since the interest of the individual is considered to be the criterion of morals, and an action to be moral when its benefits reach others. Hence, they believe in the immutability of ethics which are adapted to the changes in times in a spontaneous sense, even if the latter is in flux, that is to say that the moral action is in harmony with the development and perfection of the person and consonant with the transformations of time.[153]

The same applies for those who perceive the criterion to be beauty, because beauty itself is an absolute quality which does not change, even when its manifestations change.[154] Regardless of the nature of the criterion for morals, Muṭahharī inclined towards this theory, because it is necessary to differentiate between absolute and changeless moral values and moral actions, which change in accordance with the changes of time and circumstances. This is because a given action may be moral in one situation and immoral in another. Therefore, moral guidelines differ according to considerations and circumstances. For example, withholding of the freedom of an individual is generally considered an immoral act. However, it becomes moral if it corrects the behaviour of an individual and protects others in the society from harm. Just as with the differentiation between morality and the moral action, Muṭahharī believes that there exists a similar idea in the Islamic shari'ah. The immutable primary law does not change with the flow of time and circumstance, whereas the secondary law, which applies to the diversity of considerations that surround it, adapt with the transformations of time as well as to the circumstances of an individual. Consequently, Muṭahharī upheld the immutability and universality of moral values, as well as the flexibility of moral action according to time and circumstances.

Notes

1. Alan Turin, *A Criticism of Modernity*, Ministry of Culture, Damascus; Jurgen Habermas, *The Philosophical Discourse of Modernity*, translated by Fatima al-Jiyousy, Ministry of Culture, Damascus; Jurgen Habermas, *The Political Discourse of Modernity,* Dār al-Nahār for Publishing, Beirut. Compare it with our book: *Ikhtibārāt al-Muqaddas* (*The Sacred Experiences*), Dār al-Amīr, Beirut, 2007, second part.

﴿يَا أَيُّهَا النَّاسُ إِنَّا خَلَقْنَاكُم مِّن ذَكَرٍ وَأُنثَىٰ وَجَعَلْنَاكُمْ شُعُوبًا وَقَبَائِلَ لِتَعَارَفُوا إِنَّ أَكْرَمَكُمْ عِندَ اللَّهِ أَتْقَاكُمْ﴾

﴿وَهُوَ الَّذِي خَلَقَ مِنَ الْمَاءِ بَشَرًا فَجَعَلَهُ نَسَبًا وَصِهْرًا﴾

﴿أَهُمْ يَقْسِمُونَ رَحْمَتَ رَبِّكَ نَحْنُ قَسَمْنَا بَيْنَهُم مَّعِيشَتَهُمْ فِي الْحَيَاةِ الدُّنْيَا وَرَفَعْنَا بَعْضَهُمْ فَوْقَ بَعْضٍ دَرَجَاتٍ لِّيَتَّخِذَ بَعْضُهُم بَعْضًا سُخْرِيًّا﴾

2. *Society and History*, p. 33.
3. Ibid.
4. Ibid., pp. 33-34.
5. Ibid., p. 34.
6. Ibid., pp. 34-35.
7. Ibid., p 35.

﴿وَلِكُلِّ أُمَّةٍ أَجَلٌ فَإِذَا جَاءَ أَجَلُهُمْ لَا يَسْتَأْخِرُونَ سَاعَةً وَلَا يَسْتَقْدِمُونَ﴾

﴿وَهَمَّتْ كُلُّ أُمَّةٍ بِرَسُولِهِمْ لِيَأْخُذُوهُ وَجَادَلُوا بِالْبَاطِلِ لِيُدْحِضُوا بِهِ الْحَقَّ فَأَخَذْتُهُمْ فَكَيْفَ كَانَ عِقَابِ﴾

8. Ibid., pp. 35-36.
9. Ibid., p 35.

﴿فَوَيْلٌ لِّلَّذِينَ يَكْتُبُونَ الْكِتَابَ بِأَيْدِيهِمْ ثُمَّ يَقُولُونَ هَٰذَا مِنْ عِندِ اللَّهِ لِيَشْتَرُوا بِهِ ثَمَنًا قَلِيلًا فَوَيْلٌ لَّهُم مِّمَّا كَتَبَتْ أَيْدِيهِمْ وَوَيْلٌ لَّهُم مِّمَّا يَكْسِبُونَ﴾

So woe to those who write the Book with their hands and then say, "This is from Allah," that they may sell it for a paltry gain. So woe to them for what their hands have written, and woe to them for what they earn!

﴿ضُرِبَتْ عَلَيْهِمُ الذِّلَّةُ أَيْنَ مَا ثُقِفُوا إِلَّا بِحَبْلٍ مِّنَ اللَّهِ وَحَبْلٍ مِّنَ النَّاسِ وَبَاءُوا بِغَضَبٍ مِّنَ اللَّهِ وَضُرِبَتْ عَلَيْهِمُ الْمَسْكَنَةُ ذَٰلِكَ بِأَنَّهُمْ كَانُوا يَكْفُرُونَ بِآيَاتِ اللَّهِ وَيَقْتُلُونَ الْأَنبِيَاءَ بِغَيْرِ حَقٍّ ذَٰلِكَ بِمَا عَصَوا وَّكَانُوا يَعْتَدُونَ﴾

Abasement has been stamped upon them wherever they are confronted, except for an asylum from Allah and an asylum from the people; and they earned the wrath of Allah, and poverty was stamped upon them. That, because they would defy the signs of Allah and kill the prophets unjustly. That, because they would disobey and used to commit transgression.

10. Muḥammad Husayn Ṭabāṭabā'i: *Al-Mizan fi Tafsir al-Qur'*an , Beirut, al- A'lami, part 4, pp. 105-106.

11. *Society and History*, pp. 37-38.

﴿وَقَضَيْنَا إِلَىٰ بَنِي إِسْرَائِيلَ فِي الْكِتَابِ لَتُفْسِدُنَّ فِي الْأَرْضِ مَرَّتَيْنِ وَلَتَعْلُنَّ عُلُوًّا كَبِيرًا * فَإِذَا جَاءَ وَعْدُ أُولَاهُمَا بَعَثْنَا عَلَيْكُمْ عِبَادًا لَّنَا أُولِي بَأْسٍ شَدِيدٍ فَجَاسُوا خِلَالَ الدِّيَارِ وَكَانَ وَعْدًا مَّفْعُولًا﴾

12. Ibid., pp. 42-43.

13. Ibid., pp. 43-44.

14. Ibid., pp. 44-45.

15. Ibid., pp. 46-47.

16. Ibid., pp. 48.

17. Ibid., pp. 48-49.

18. Ibid., p. 49.

19. Ibid., p. 49.

20. Ibid., p. 49.

21. Ibid., p. 53.

﴿شَرَعَ لَكُم مِّنَ الدِّينِ مَا وَصَّىٰ بِهِ نُوحًا وَالَّذِي أَوْحَيْنَا إِلَيْكَ وَمَا وَصَّيْنَا بِهِ إِبْرَاهِيمَ وَمُوسَىٰ وَعِيسَىٰ أَنْ أَقِيمُوا الدِّينَ وَلَا تَتَفَرَّقُوا فِيهِ﴾

22. Ibid., p. 53.

﴿يَا أَيُّهَا النَّاسُ إِنَّا خَلَقْنَاكُم مِّن ذَكَرٍ وَأُنثَىٰ وَجَعَلْنَاكُمْ شُعُوبًا وَقَبَائِلَ لِتَعَارَفُوا إِنَّ أَكْرَمَكُمْ عِندَ اللَّهِ أَتْقَاكُمْ﴾

23. Ibid., pp. 54-55.

24. Ibid., p. 55.

25. Ibid., p. 56.

26. Ibid., pp. 57-59.

27. Ibid., pp. 60-63.

28. Ibid., pp. 36 and 66-67.

29. Ibid., pp. 63-64.

30. Ibid., p. 64.

31. Ibid., p. 65.

32. Ibid., p. 70.

33. Ibid., p. 71.

34. Ibid., p. 72.

35. Ibid., p. 73.

36. Ibid., p. 72.

37. Ibid., pp. 75-77.

38. Ibid., p. 77.

39. Ibid., pp. 82-83.

40. Ibid., p. 88.

41. Ibid., p. 87.

42. Ibid., pp. 85 and 92-94.

43. Ibid., p. 99.

44. Ibid., pp. 102-104.

45. Ibid., pp. 104-107.

46. Ibid., pp. 114-115.

47. Ibid., pp. 116-117.

48. Muṭahharī read about Marxism in the Persian language through the writings of Arānī, one of the leading figures in Iranian Marxism, and some other translations. We suppose that this was enough for him to have a general collective perception of it especially because of the wide spread of Marxist thought in the Arab Muslim world allowed to view its principles through the efforts of its different currents and their statements and translations.

49. *Society and History*, pp. 121-122.

50. Ibid., p. 123.

51. Ibid., p. 124.

52. Ibid., p. 124.

53. Ibid., pp. 126-127.

54. Ibid., pp. 131-133.

55. Ibid., pp. 133-134.

56. Ibid., pp. 134-136.

57. Ibid., p. 141.

58. Ibid.

﴿وَمَا أَرْسَلْنَا فِي قَرْيَةٍ مِّن نَّذِيرٍ إِلَّا قَالَ مُتْرَفُوهَا إِنَّا بِمَا أُرْسِلْتُم بِهِ كَافِرُونَ﴾

﴿إِنَّ الْإِنسَانَ لَيَطْغَىٰ * أَن رَّآهُ اسْتَغْنَىٰ﴾

Indeed man becomes rebellious when he considers himself without need.

﴿إِنَّ قَارُونَ كَانَ مِن قَوْمِ مُوسَىٰ فَبَغَىٰ عَلَيْهِمْ وَآتَيْنَاهُ مِنَ الْكُنُوزِ مَا إِنَّ مَفَاتِحَهُ لَتَنُوءُ بِالْعُصْبَةِ أُولِي الْقُوَّةِ إِذْ قَالَ لَهُ قَوْمُهُ لَا تَفْرَحْ إِنَّ اللَّهَ لَا يُحِبُّ الْفَرِحِينَ﴾

Surely Qārūn (Korah) was one of Moses (Musa) people, but he bullied them. We had given him so much treasures that their keys indeed proved heavy for a band of stalwarts. When his people said to him, 'Do not exult! Indeed Allah does not like the exultant'.

59. Ibid., p. 141.

﴿هُوَ الَّذِي بَعَثَ فِي الْأُمِّيِّينَ رَسُولًا مِّنْهُمْ﴾:

It is He who sent to the unlettered [people] an apostle from among themselves.

60. Ibid., pp. 142-143.

61. Ibid., p. 144.

62. Ibid., pp. 145-148.

63. Ibid., pp. 149-150.

﴿فَلَأُقَطِّعَنَّ أَيْدِيَكُمْ وَأَرْجُلَكُم مِّنْ خِلَافٍ﴾

64. Ibid., p. 150.

65. Ibid., p. 150.

﴿اذْهَبْ إِلَىٰ فِرْعَوْنَ إِنَّهُ طَغَىٰ * فَقُلْ هَل لَّكَ إِلَىٰ أَن تَزَكَّىٰ * وَأَهْدِيَكَ إِلَىٰ رَبِّكَ فَتَخْشَىٰ﴾

66. Ibid., p. 155.

67. Ibid., p. 156.

68. Ibid., p. 156.

﴿وَعَدَ اللهُ الَّذِينَ آمَنُوا مِنكُمْ وَعَمِلُوا الصَّالِحَاتِ لَيَسْتَخْلِفَنَّهُمْ فِي الْأَرْضِ﴾

﴿وَالْعَاقِبَةُ لِلْمُتَّقِينَ﴾

﴿وَلَقَدْ كَتَبْنَا فِي الزَّبُورِ مِن بَعْدِ الذِّكْرِ أَنَّ الْأَرْضَ يَرِثُهَا عِبَادِيَ الصَّالِحُونَ﴾

69. Ibid., pp. 158-159.

70. Ibid., pp. 160-161.

71. Muṭahharī did not consider revolution in Islam as destructive, but as having a positive function. See: *Society and History*, p. 164.

72. Muṭahharī, *Motivations Toward Materialism* (*'Ilal Gerayesh be Madigari*), translated by Muḥammad 'Alī al-Taskhīrī, Beirut, Dār al-Ta'āruf, 1980, p. 17.

73. Ibid., p. 18.

﴿وَقَالُوا مَا هِيَ إِلَّا حَيَاتُنَا الدُّنْيَا نَمُوتُ وَنَحْيَا وَمَا يُهْلِكُنَا إِلَّا الدَّهْرُ﴾

74. Ibid., p. 20.

75. Ibid., pp. 23-24.

76. Ibid., pp. 28-30.

77. Ibid., pp. 34-36.

78. Ibid., pp. 39-40.

79. Ibid., pp. 46-49.

80. Ibid., pp. 50-54.

81. Ibid. For more details see pp. 62-63 and 66-67.

82. Ibid., p. 69.

83. Details of this controversy can be found in Muṭahharī's *Al-Tawhid*, pp. 333-381. However, it is noteworthy that Muṭahharī considers Darwin a believer in Allah, and that Lamarck developed a materialistic vision. Ibid., p. 341.

84. *Al-Tawhidd,* p. 360. Although Muṭahharī saw no contradiction between the theory of evolution and monotheism, he did not accept Darwin's theory of "the struggle to survive," "natural selection" and "survival of the fittest." Darwin himself admitted that there is an unknown factor that should be taken into consideration when we try to interpret living things and how they evolve. See p. 275.

85. Muṭahharī, *Motivations Toward Materialism*, p.71. Muṭahharī also discusses details of the theory of evolution according to Lamarck in *Al-Tawhid*, pp. 342-349.

86. Ibid., p. 72.

87. Ibid., p. 73

88. Muṭahharī, *Motivations Toward Materialism*, p.74; *Al-Tawhid,* p. 234

89. As also with the eye; how was it before, and what was its function? If the answer is the eye was found only in the environment which receives light, would

it be possible for a living organism without an eye to grow it just by moving to a similar environment? The eye might have reached its current state as a result of a long evolution, but not because of environmental circumstances or natural selection. It would be according to the formational guidance in nature which helped it to reach its current stage of integration. Ibid., p. 379

90. Muṭahharī, *Motivations Toward Materialism*, p. 75.

91. Ibid., p. 75.

92. *Al-Tawhid*, pp. 350 and 369. Darwin states: "they have objected by saying that I see the factor of natural selection as a metaphysical power ..."

93. Muṭahharī, *Motivations Toward Materialism*, p.77.

94. Ibid., p.78.

95. Ibid., p. 79.

96. Ibid., p. 84

97. *Al-Tawhid*, p. 380.

98. Muṭahharī, *Motivations Toward Materialism*, pp. 86-87.

99. Ibid., p. 90.

100. Ibid., p. 90.

101. Ibid., p. 91.

102. Ibid., p. 92.

103. Ibid., pp. 95-97.

104. Ibid., p 97.

105. Ibid., p. 98.

106. Ibid., pp. 105-107.

107. Ibid.

108. Ibid., pp. 109-111 and 112-115.

109. Muṭahharī, *Philosophy of Ethics*, translated by Muḥammad ʻAbd al-Munʻim al-Khāqānī, Tehran, Al Batha Organization. 1995, pp. 8, 21, 22, 26, 27, 23 and 33. See also: *Training and Education in Islam*, p 57.

110. *Training and Education in Islam*, pp. 59, 62, 66 and 67.

111. Ibid., pp 60-61. See also *The Philosophy of Ethics*, p. 29.

112. *Training and Education in Islam*, pp. 62-63. See also: *The Philosophy of Ethics*, p. 35. For more details about the analysis of the meaning of conscience in light of psychology, see the same reference, p. 37.

113. *The Philosophy of Ethics*, pp. 38-39, 41-43 and 45-50.

114. Ibid., p 64.

115. *Training and Education in Islam*, pp. 66-67.

116. Ibid., pp. 70-71.

117. Ibid., pp. 82-83.

118. Ibid., pp. 71-72.

119. Ibid., p. 72. See also: *The Philosophy of Ethics*, p. 57.

120. Ibid., pp. 72-73.

121. Ibid., p. 81.

122. *Monotheism*, p 193. He also supposes natural moral inspiration, based on the Qur'anic verse in which Allah says: ﴿فَأَلْهَمَهَا فُجُورَهَا وَتَقْوَاهَا﴾: *and inspired it with [discernment between] its virtues and vices*, (91:8). See also: *Training and Education in Islam*, pp. 195-196.

123. Ibid., p 69.

124. Ibid., pp. 74-75. See also his criticism of Marxist morality in *The Philosophy of Ethics*, p. 157.

125. *Training and Education in Islam*, pp. 85-88 and *The Philosophy of Ethics*, pp. 72, 106 and 109. His criticisms of Marx and Sartre are found on pp. 115-142.

126. *Training and Education in Islam*, p. 90.

127. Ibid., p. 90.

128. Ibid., p. 91.

129. Ibid., p. 92.

130. Ibid., p. 92.

131. Ibid., p. 93.

132. Ibid.

133. Ibid., p. 95.

134. Ibid., p. 96.

135. Ibid., p. 79.

CHAPTER 5

CONCLUSION

MUṬAHHARĪ, FOR HISTORY AND EXPERIENCE

A detailed summary of Muṭahharī's work may not fully reveal the lasting value it continues to have for contemporary issues. We will therefore refrain from attempting a comprehensive definition of his work in these concluding remarks. Discerning the actual value of Muṭahharī's thought for the present time, and what it may reveal in the future remains to be seen. However, we will briefly mention some of the important elements he considered necessary in all projects for reformation and revival in the modern Islamic world. Amongst these elements there is first of all the primary issue of monotheism or faith, at both the individual level of personal conscience and psychology, and in social identity. The second entails the legal infrastructure of Islam, and applying it in a practical and effective manner. Another element concerns the basis of a value system which would lead to prosperity, as expressed by Fahmi Jud'ān.[1] The final element is to do with the effect of modern Western intellectualism and epistemology on our culture.

As regards monotheism, Muṭahharī presented a vision that brought religion out from the realm of pure philosophy into the domain of psychological and social efficacy. He well understood how to do this, as well as the intellectual bases that would enable the principles of Islamic ideology to re-establish themselves in the minds of the people, restructure human relationships, and be a guiding principle in all the different spheres of life.

Muṭahharī was in agreement with those other Muslim reformist thinkers who deeply understood the widening rift that had gradually disconnected Islamic religious ideas from their broad application in the personal lives of Muslims. Consequently, they proceeded to recrystallise the dynamism of Islam so that it ceased to be simply an intellectual principle, and acquired a clear social and political function that would responsibly administer the affairs of civilisation.

If, in the Arab world, these endeavours had been limited to establishing a theoretical framework, in the case of Muṭahharī it was through practical experience that he strove to consolidate beneficial conditions for a vision of government. In essence, this vision translated into a theoretical framework that affirmed the teachings, laws and general outlook of Islam, and directed it in an open fashion to the contemporary world.

Muṭahharī was aware of the peculiarity of the political experience of the Islamic movements.[2] He knew only too well the danger of promoting Islam as a systematic way of life in a world that did not easily accept classical views, or readily submit to the internal moral guidance of faith. Such things seemed to exist only in the memory of bygone ages.

He was acutely conscious that the advances and fluctuations of the present reality were not conducive for the aspirations of humanity, which was heading towards a precipice. It was for that reason that he proceeded to delineate the core elements that would facilitate the success of a revolutionary experience, and make it stable and enduring. He went on to warn against being content with achievements made on the path to reform. He cautioned against a premature satisfaction that did not foresee unexpected consequences which might compromise the final goal, and which require a constant readiness to find new solutions. Prior to the Islamic Revolution, he clearly insisted on this in well-known articles on this matter. He suggested that each revolution or movement has its own peculiar characteristics, because of the idiosyncrasies of its environment, its proponents, and the reasons which brought it about.[3]

Within the context these key factors, Muṭahharī thoroughly analysed the aspirations for reform in Iran. He emphasised the need to thoroughly understand these factors in order for the process to be successful. To neglect any of them would lead to failure.[4] He outlined the framework of these factors as follows:

> An existing dictatorship that employs violence, brutality and the deprivation of freedom
>
> The prevalence of colonialism in politics, economics and culture
>
> The isolation of religion from everyday life politics

Efforts to revive ancient traditional cultures and rituals.

A distortion of Islamic culture

The dissemination of atheism and nihilism

Huge divisions between the social classes

Combating of the Arabic language and its related elements

Isolation from the wider Islamic world and its concerns[5]

According to Muṭahharī, these causes inflamed the minds of the masses and stimulated the will for reformation. These factors should be accurately assessed in order to achieve the desired aims. Muṭahharī considered that the actualisation of a revolution without a strong and prescient leadership, fully aware of enveloping crises, understanding the nature of the political and social movements, and well-versed in how to apply Islam and its laws to contemporary life, would not be possible.

Many of those with an inclination towards leadership explored the possibilities. They stirred the masses, raised the level of awareness, warned of the dangers, and drew up plans. Two major currents emerged, the first of which was to restore Islam to the lives of the people in order to guide them; the second was to construct a practical framework so that it was not just an aspiration lacking the necessary means for its actualisation.[6]

Since Muṭahharī advocated that revolutionary reform should project into the domain of political activity, he realised the danger in restricting it to defined areas, for it should be a "singular and radical source of legitimacy upon which the political apparatus and infrastructure is based." As a result, he believed it was necessary to lay the foundations for an intellectual and rational formulation for governance,[7] because socio-political struggle means – according to Fahmi Jud'ān – selecting the furthermost solution, life or death, and the risks in either case are enormous. Either success or failure would expose the whole endeavour to the risk of either sliding back or an extreme radicalism, and a political despotism of the most cruel form.

Muṭahharī believe that a liberal and visionary *ijtihād*, fully aware of the circumstances, would guarantee a rational formulation. He thought it necessary to have a wide knowledge of the practical horizons of the dimensions and objectives of the Islamic system.

Since life was too short to offer Muṭahharī the time to translate his convictions into a clearly defined project, we cannot say for sure what kind of position Muṭahharī would have taken regarding later developments and the trends that the state began to adopt after its establishment.

Nevertheless, we can acknowledge that Muṭahharī realised that any political experiment is an act of historical measure, and the legitimacy of any authority comes from its ability to answer the needs of the people. It should ensure the continuity of society within the context of a system that achieves its objectives in a just manner, and manages any conflict of interest between its members fairly.[8]

As for the value-based principles for renaissance postulated by Muṭahharī, they are exceptionally attractive in the way he presented them.

He staunchly believed in these principles as the mechanism for upholding one's life, for affirming one's identity in the face of loss and alienation. However, Muṭahharī did not reveal how these values can develop from an internal principle of piety and manifest as a fully operational practice which embodies the law. There remains a lingering question: To what extent is it possible to apply ethical values and religious piety as a basis of authority to the management of social-economic dealings, which are by nature purely materialistic ventures? [9]

In this context, Muṭahharī linked economic and social efficiency to the moral imperative, but he could not predict how things would translate into reality, without these pious internal values being transforming into an outward imperative clearly defined by an external law.

In the context of combating Western ideology, Muṭahharī's profound insight into the various hazardous consequences is noteworthy. He recognised what might result from imitating these trends. His perception reveals a profound awareness of the crisis affecting Western intellectual currents, which was already manifest during his lifetime as a complete renunciation of the soul and the total engrossment in materialism. He issued a forewarning of the dangers posed by these schools of thought, and underlined the necessity of instilling moral values as a safeguard from deviations that could lead to an unknown end.

Unfortunately, Muṭahharī did not live long enough to witness a time when Western civilisation and thought had found its way to corners of the globe, to such an extent that there is little alternative other than adopting its mores. In such a situation, Muṭahharī's call would appear to be more like attractive rhetoric than a viable prospect, which would protect people from total subordination to a powerful, hegemonic force, and their ultimate demise.

Since Muṭahharī's call was a product of his time, it should be understood in light of its context, in order to draw inspiration from it and develop a living paradigm – a vibrant worldview that would play an active role in shaping history and progress. This is a vision that focuses on realities rather than theories; an outlook whose influence can have tangible results rather than remaining no more than ideas. We must ask ourselves: Have those who are acquainted with his thought, and witnessed these things, striven with the required sense of duty; and have they realised the extent of this responsibility?

Notes

1. Fahmi Jud'ān, *Bases of Advancement according to Muslim Thinkers*, p. 551.
2. *Islamic Movements in the Last century*, introduction.
3. *Articles about the Revolution*, pp. 84-85.
4. Ibid., p. 86.
5. Ibid., pp. 87-88.
6. Ibid., pp. 90-108.
7. Ibid., pp. 30-34.
8. Ibid., pp. 78-95.
9. *The foundation of progress in view of the thinkers of Islam*, p. 553.

CHAPTER 6

BRIEF BIBLIOGRAPHY

INTRODUCTION

In reality, we do not know the entire corpus of publications authored by Shaykh Murtaḍa Muṭahharī in the Persian language. Similarly, we do not know whether all the works of this prolific thinker have ended up in publication. At the very least, however, we are able to ascertain, through reviewing the list of his publications (disseminated and verified by a committee tasked with supervision of his published works), that there are many articles, speeches and lectures, delivered by Muṭahharī over the course of more than twenty years, that still remain on tape recordings in their original form.

There are therefore only a few books that Muṭahharī initially intended for publication, and similarly few are the books he wrote after having compiled notes from his lectures.

As for Arabic translations of Muṭahharī's work, any researcher would encounter many difficulties; translations are hasty and full of mistakes, due to direct translation from the Persian without any formatting and organisation. For instance, the inspiration of the title of an article, lecture or a part of a book, as translated and published, is according to its content, and thus the reader is left confused about its nature and context. Also, the reader may come across several translations of the same text with different titles, leading him to believe that they are translations of completely different books. Because of this, we shall provide a comprehensive list of the books in Persian published as his collection. Moreover, we will briefly explore their contents, if necessary, and proceed to list their translations – if we have found them or know of them. Nevertheless, we acknowledge that the list will be incomplete and inadequate, and would require someone more familiar with this domain to complete this task, which is far from comprehensive. Our general intention is to shed some light on the volume and nature of Muṭahharī's works.

First: Books

1. *Akhlāq-e Jensī dar Islam,*[1] 8th ed., Tehran, Sadrā Publications Foundation, 1372 A.H.[2] This is a collection of articles published by Muṭahharī in Maktab-e Islām Journal, 1353 A.H.
2. *Ostād Muṭahharī va Roshanfekrān,*[3] 1st ed., published in 1372 A.H. This is a collection of various articles that outline Muṭahharī's position regarding western intellectuals.
3. *Islam and the Requirements of Time*, published in 2 volumes; the first in 1370 A.H, and the second in 1373 A.H. The first part contains twenty-six lectures delivered at Masjid Ittifaq, Tehran, in 1354 A.H. The second part is a collection of lectures delivered at the Muslims Students Union in 1351 A.H. The two volumes have been translated into Arabic by 'Alī Hāshim and published by Dār al-Amīr, Beirut, 1993.
4. *Knowing Islamic Sciences*, published in three volumes during 1368-1369 A.H, the first volume concerns logic and philosophy; the second is about theology, *'Irfān* (mysticism) and practical philosophy; and the final volume focuses on *fiqh* (Islamic jurisprudence) and *usul* (principles of jurisprudence). In general, this book is a brief course on these sciences. It has been translated into Arabic numerous times – either in parts or in one volume. Nour al-Mustafa Foundation in Beirut, 2007, published one of them. Salmān Tawhīdī and 'Alī Quli Qarā'i, Hekmat Publishers, Tehran, 2002, have also translated the book into English.
5. *Knowing the Holy Qur'an*, Published in eight volumes between 1369-1377 A.H. It is a partial exegesis of the Holy Qur'an, originally collected from lessons taught by Muṭahharī in Tehran at different times; vol. 3 covers the chapters *al-Anfāl* and *al-Tawbah*; vol. 4 covers the chapter *al-Nūr*; vol. 5 covers the chapters *al-Zukhruf*, *al-Dukhān*, *al-Jāthiyah*, *Al-Fatḥ* and *al-Qamar*; vol. 6 covers the chapters *al-Raḥmān*, *al-Wāqi'ah*, *al-Ḥadīd*, *al-Ḥashr* and *al-Mumtaḥanah*; vol. 7 covers the chapters *al-Ṣaff*, *al-Jum'ah* and *al-Taghābun*; and finally,

vol. 8 covers the chapters *al-Ṭalāq*, *al-Taḥrīm*, *al-Mulk* and *al-Qalam*. Parts of this book have been translated into Arabic.

6. *The Origins of Philosophy and Realism*, published in five volumes, 1372 A.H. This is regarded as a complete course in Islamic Philosophy. It is originally attributed to 'Allāmah Ṭabāṭabā'i an later Ayatullāh Muṭahharī revised and supplemented it with a commentary. The book compares subject matter in Islamic philosophy with that of modern Western philosophy using a new and unique methodology, as stated by Muṭahharī. The first volume was initially translated into Arabic by Ja'far Subḥanī without Muṭahharī's comments. Later, Muḥammad 'Abd al-Mun'im al-Khāqānī translated two other parts, published by Dār al-Ta'āruf, Beirut, 1988.
7. *Durūs al-Falsafīyah fī Sharḥ al-Manẓamah* (*Philosophical Lessons on the Commentary of al-Manẓamah*), published in two volumes, Hekmat Publishers, Tehran, 1360 A.H. Translated by Mālik Wahbī, and published under the same title by Shams al-Mashriq, Beirut, 1994. Also translated by 'Ammār Abū-Raghīf with the title *Muḥaḍarat fī Sharḥ al-Manẓamah*, in one volume, and published by Umm al-Qurā Institution, Tehran 1417 A.H. The book is a collection of lectures delivered by Muṭahharī to an audience of teachers and students at the Faculty of Theology at Tehran University.
8. *Sharḥ al-Mufassal li Manẓumah al-Hikmah* (*A detailed Commentary of Manẓamah al-Ḥikmah*).
9. *Al-Khilāfah wa al-Wilāyah* (*Caliphate and Leadership*): first ed., Ḥosseiniyeh Ershād, 1349 A.H.
10. *Al-Imāmat wa al-Qiyādah*, (*Imāmat and Leadership*), second edition published in 1364 A.H. This book is part of the series titled *An Introduction to the Islamic View of the Globe*. It covers six lectures delivered by Muṭahharī at the Union of Muslim Doctors in 1349 A.H. The initial publication was an introduction to *Al-Khilāfah wa al-Wilāyah* (*Caliphate and Leadership*). Originally, it was in the form of answers to some of the questions raised about the latter book, and later published separately.
11. *"Al- Imdādāt al-Ghaybiyah fī Hayāt al-Bashar"*, (*The Unseen Aids in the Life of Human Beings*) this was the first book of Ayatullāh Muṭahharī in 1354 A.H. In its first edition, it discussed four topics:

▪*Religion will never End* , a lecture Muṭahharī delivered at Abadan Oil Faculty in 1345 A.H. on the occasion of *al-Mab'ath* (the anniversary of the inauguration of the Prophet's Mission).

▪*The Metaphysical Supplies in the Lives of Human Beings* , a lecture Muṭahharī delivered at the Pahlavī College in Sha'ban 1346 A.H.

▪*Management and Leadership in Islam* .

▪*Al-Rushd al-Islami* (*Islamic Guidance*).

The following two topics added on to this edition:

▪An Interview with Behrouz Bushehri (journalist).

▪An Article on the film " *Al-Muhalill*".

Some of the above-mentioned topics such as: *al-Rushd al-Islami* (*Islamic Guidance*) and *al- Imdādāt al-Ghaybiah fi Hayāt al-Bashar* (*Metaphysical Supplies in the Lives of Human Beings*), have been translated into articles as enumerated later.

12. *Social Perfection of Man*, Tehran, Sadrā Publications Foundation. This book includes four articles:

▪"*The Goal of Human Life* " (covers five sessions on the same topic).

▪"*The inspirations of Shaykh al-Ṭā'ifah* "; a research article presented at the al–Shaykh al-Ṭusi conference hosted in Mashhad University in 1349 A.H. It was also published during Muṭahharī's lifetime as part of the book *Alfiyāt al-Shaykh al-Tusi*.

▪*The Merits and Services of Ayatullah Borūjerdī* . Muṭahharī wrote this after al-Borūjerdī's death, and it was published as part of the book *Religious Authority and Spirituality*, which has contributions from several authors.

▪*Social Perfection of Man* . This is taken from lectures delivered at Shiraz University. As far as we know, only the translation of one part into Arabic is available. It was published as *The Supreme Goal of Human Life*, by Dār al-Aḍwā', Beirut, 1989. According to Muṭahharī, this book is part of a series consisting of several discussions under the title *An Introduction to the Monotheistic View of the World and Social Integration*, published by the Organization of Islamic Media in Tehran.

13. *Al-Tawḥīd* (*Monotheism*), 12th ed., 1373 A.H. This book is a part of series consisting of 17 lectures on *Usul al-Din,* which he delivered at the Union of Muslim Doctors between 1346-1347 A.H. There are two Arabic translations of this book. Ibrahim al-Khazraji and Irfan Maḥmood are the translators, and the publishers are Dār al-Maḥajjah al-Bayḍā' and Dār al-Rasūl al-Akram, Beirut, 1989 and Dār al-Ḥawrā', Beirut, respectively. The book contains insightful views on the relationship between monotheism and knowledge.
14. *Polarization around the Character of Imam 'Alī*, published in 1368 A.H, translated into Arabic.
15. *Society and History*, 5th edition, 1372 A.H. It is a part of the book titled: *An Introduction to the Islamic View of the Globe.* It also has two translations: one by Dār al-Wafā', Beirut, 1983; and the other by Muḥammad 'Alī Ādharshab, published by al- Bi'tha Institution, Tehran 1403 A.H.
16. *Al-Jihād*, 7th Edition, 1373 A.H. The book includes a collection of lectures on Jihad, Martyrdom and Immigration. It has been translated into Arabic, and also published under the title *Jihād and Its Lawful Conditions in the Qur'an*, by the Organization of Islamic Media.
17. "*The Monotheistic View of the World*," 6th ed., 1372 A.H. This is a part of the book: *An Introduction to the Islamic View of the Globe.* There are two translations: *The Monotheistic Conception of the World*, Dār al-Tayyār al-Jadīd, Beirut, 1985; and *The Global Monotheistic View*, by Muḥammad 'Abd al-Mun'im al-Khāqānī, The Organization of Islamic Media, Tehran, 1403 A.H.
18. *Movement and time in Islamic philosophy*, 1st ed., in two volumes, published in 1371 A.H. This is a collection of lectures on power and change, from Mullā Sadrā Shirāzī's book *Asfār.*
19. *Truth and Falsehood* (*with the revival of thought in Islam*), 3rd ed., published in 1362 A.H.,translated by Muḥammad 'Alī Ādharshab under the title: *Between Truth and Falsehood*,al-Bi'tha Institution, Tehran, 1402 A.H. Ja'far Khalīl has also translated this book, and published it as a part of the book *Ijtihād in Islam*, Dār al-Rasūl al-Akram, Beirut.

20. *Al-Khātamiyya* (*The Finality of Prophethood with the Last Messenger*), 5th ed., published in 1370 A.H. It includes a collection of lectures on the finality of prophethood delivered in Ḥosseiniyeh Ershād in 1374 A.H. Muṭahharī paid special attention to these lectures and revised them himself. The first publication was called *Muḥammad, the last Messenger*. It was later published as a series of six articles, and finally in this edition.
21. *Wisdoms and Advice*, 23rd ed., published in 1373 A.H.
22. *Imām Ḥusayn's Revolution*, published in three volumes as 13th, 14th and 15th eds., between 1368-1371 A.H. consecutively. Translated into Arabic under the title *The Hussainian Epic*, and published by various publishers in Beirut, including Al-Dār al-Islamiyah, 1413 A.H. in three volumes.
23. *The Reciprocal Services between Islam and Iran* (*Khadamāt Mutaqābel Islam va Iran*), 12th ed., 1362 A.H. Translated into Arabic by Muḥammad Hādī al-Yūsufī under the title *Islam and Iran,* Dār al-Ta'āruf, Beirut. An English translation was published in 2004 by the International Centre for Islamic Sciences in Qom. Two other articles published in the 14th ed. of Muṭahharī's collection of publications under the titles *Islam's services for Iran* and *Iran's Services for Islam*.
24. *Stories of the Righteous* (*Dāstān Rāstān*), published in two parts, 10th ed., 1362 A.H. Translated into Arabic and published by al-A'lami Institute, Beirut.
25. *The Seal of the Prophethood* (*Khātamiyyat),* 26th ed., 1370 A.H. There are two translations: the first published in Ḍaka by 'Alī Okaz, and the second in English by Dār al-Hudā, Tehran, 1997.
26. *Lessons in the Spirituality of Healing,* two volumes, 1st and 2nd ed.s published by Hekmat Publishers, 1370 A.H.
27. *The Other or Eternal Life*, 28th ed., 1372 A.H. It is the sixth part of *An Introduction to the Islamic View of the Globe*, translated into Arabic and published by Dār al-Maḥajjah al-Bayḍā', Beirut, 2000.
28. *A Survey into the Lives of the infallible Imams,* 10th ed., 1373 A.H., and translated into Arabic as *A Journey into the Lives of the Pure Imams.*

29. *A Glance at the Life of the Prophet*, 6th ed., 1368 A.H., and translated by Ja'far Sādiq al-Khalīl as *A Glance at the Biography of the Prophet*, Islamic Media Organization, Tehran.
30. *A Glance at the Nahj al-Balāghah*, 2nd ed., 1354 A.H. Translated into Arabic by Muḥammad Hādī al-Yūsufī, Dār al-Ta'āruf, 1980 AD.
31. *Six Articles* (*Ghadir and Islamic Unity*), 24th ed., 1368 A.H and containing the following subjects.
    - Ghadir and Islamic Unity.
    - Islamic Unity.
    - Shaykh al-Amini.
    - What the others had from Ghadir
    - Conclusion.
32. *Six Articles* (*Divine and Materialistic Conception of the World*).
33. *Divine Justice*, 28th ed., 1372 A.H. Translated into Arabic by Muḥammad 'Abd al-Mun'im al-Khāqānī and published several times in Beirut, once by Dār al-Maḥajjah al-Bayḍā', 2004 AD.
34. *Motives towards Materialism*, 13th ed., 1372 A.H. Contains an introduction on materialism in Iran; translated by Muḥammad 'Alī al-Taskhīrī, Dār al-Ta'āruf, Beirut, 1980 AD. Majeed Karshanas, al-Hudā, Tehran, 1997 AD, have also translated it into French.
35. *The Primordial Nature*, 2nd ed., 1370 A.H. Research papers delivered by Muṭahharī between 1355 to 1356 A.H at the society of Muslim Physicians, as well as at Qom, Ḥawzah and in sessions with scholars and instructors.
36. *The Philosophy of Ethics*, 11th ed., 1372 A.H (collection of 12 sessions delivered in Arak mosque in Tehran, 1352 A.H). Translated into Arabic by Muḥammad 'Abd al-Mun'im al-Khāqānī, al-Bi'tha Organization, Tehran, 1995, a part of which was published by Dār al-Maḥajjah, Beirut, under the title *The Immutability of Ethics*, 1993 AD.
37. *The Philosophy of History*, two volumes: vol. 1 published in 1369 A.H, and vol. 2 published in 1377 A.H. It is a collection of lectures delivered between 1355 and 1357 A.H.

38. *The Mahdī's Revolution in Light of the Philosophy of History*, 13th ed., 1373 A.H., translated into Arabic, and published in Beirut.
39. *Moral Articles*, 14th ed., 1373 A.H. This is a collection of thirteen lectures on different topics.
40. *Lama'āt al-Shaykh al-Shahid.*
41. *A Martyr Talking about a Martyr*, The Grand Islamic Library, Tehran. This is a collection of speeches about 'Ashurā.
42. *The Question of Ḥijāb.* New Edition published in 1368 A.H. Translated into Arabic by Haidar al-Haidar, published by the Islamic Publishing House, Beirut, 1987 AD.
43. *Interest and Insurance*, 5th ed. This is a collection of lectures delivered by Muṭahharī at the Muslim Physicians Union in 1354 A.H. Translated by Mālik Wahbi, published by Dār al-Hādī, Beirut, 1993 AD.
44. *Mas'aleye Shenākht, 4* (*The Question of Knowledge*), 6th ed. This is a collection of ten lectures delivered in Muharram 1397 A.H at Maktab al-Tawhid, Tehran.
45. *Al-Ma'ād*, 1st ed., 1373 A.H. Ten lectures delivered at the Physicians Union in 1350 A.H. Translated into Arabic by Jawād 'Alī Kassār, published by Umm-ul-Qurā Organization, 1422 A.H. There are also other Arabic publications of this work.
46. *Philosophical Articles*, three volumes on various philosophical topics, most of which were translated into Arabic, including a specific translation of the section on the "History of Islamic philosophy" by 'Abd al-Jabbār al-Rifā'ī. Published by Dār al-Kitāb al-Islamī, Tehran, 1413 A.H. under the title: *Lectures in Islamic Philosophy*.
47. *Prophethood*, 1st ed., 1373 A.H. Part of the series on Principles of Religion (*Usul al-Din*); a collection of lectures delivered at the Muslim Physicians Union in 1348 A.H. Translated by Jawād 'Alī Kassār, published by Umm-ul-Qurā Organization in Beirut and Tehran.
48. *The System of Women's Rights in Islam*, 14th ed., 1369 A.H. Translated into Arabic by Abū Zahrā' al-Najafī and published by the Islamic Media Organization, Tehran, 1987. This work has numerous translations and publications.

49. *A Glance at the Islamic Economy*, 1st ed. in 1368 A.H. Translated into Arabic as Islamic Economy, and published by Dār al-Balāghah, Beirut, 1993 AD.
50. *A Critique of Marxism*, Sadrā Publications Foundation, Tehran.
51. *Knowledge in the Qur'an*, 1st ed., 1982 AD, 1363 A.H.
52. *Islamic Movements in the Last Century*, 12th ed., 1368 A.H. Translated into Arabic by Sādiq al-'Ibāadī and published by Dār al-Hādī, Beirut, 1982 AD.
53. *Revelation and Prophethood* (part of the Introduction to the Monotheistic View of the World), 6th ed., 1370 A.H. Translated into Arabic, and published by Dār al-Maḥajjah, Beirut, 2000 AD.
54. *Al-Walā' wa al-Wilāya* : 8th ed., 1370 A.H., also published as a part of the work *Al-Khilafa wa al-Wilāya*. Translated into Arabic and published by al-Bi'tha Organization, Tehran.
55. *The Human Being in the Qur'an*, 8th ed., 1383 A.H. Part of the introduction to The Islamic Conception of the World.
56. *The Perfect Human Being*, 11th ed., 1373 A.H. A collection of thirteen lectures delivered during the month of Ramadan at the Jawid Mosque in 1353 A.H. Translated into Arabic by Ja'far al-Khalīlī.
57. *The Human Being and Faith*, 8th ed., 1371 A.H. Translated into Arabic by Muḥammad 'Abd al-Mun'im al-Khāqānī, Published by the Islamic Media Organization, Tehran, 1403 A.H. It is a part of the series of the introduction on *The Islamic Conception of the World.*
58. *The Human Being, Fate and Destiny*. An introduction to the declining state of Muslims, translated by Muḥammad 'Alī al-Taskhīrī, al-Bi'tha Organization, Tehran.
59. *The Teacher's Answers to the Question of Ḥijāb*, 14th ed. of the new publication of the books authored by Muṭahharī. Translated into Arabic and published by Dār al-Hādī, Beirut, 1992 AD.
60. *The Unschooled Prophet*, 9th ed., 1373 A.H. Translated into Arabic and published by The Islamic Media Organization, Tehran.
61. *Regarding Islamic revolution*, 9th ed., 1372 A.H. See below.

62. *Regarding the Islamic Republic*, 24th ed., This and the above translated as Articles in Islamic Revolution by Muḥammad Jawād al-Mehry, Coordinating Council for Islamic Media, Tehran, and 1402 A.H. Muṭahharī wrote the first part of this book before the revolution and the second part after.
63. *Ta'līm wa Tarbiyat dar Islam*, 5 23rd ed., Two collections of lectures; Muṭahharī delivered the first collection to a group of religious teachers, and the second at the Muslim Physicians Union.
64. *The Imāmat.* A collection of lectures delivered by Ayatullāh Muṭahharī at the Muslim Physicians Union as part of series on Principles of Religion (*Usul al-Din*), translated into Arabic by Jawād 'Alī Kassār. Published by al-Thaqalayn Organization, Beirut, 1417 A.H.
65. *Commentary on the Book 'al-Tahsīl'*, by Bahmanyar bin Marzban, Dashgaah, Tehran.
66. *Twenty Articles.* Contains several articles on a variety of topics as follows:

- Justice according to Imām 'Alī (a).
- The Enjoining of Virtue and Prevention of Vice.
- The Basic Foundations for Islamic Rights.
- Rights are Important and the World is Despicable.
- Justice or Equality.
- God Provides Sustenance, Our Duty is to Strive and Struggle.
- Al-Imām al-Ṣadiq (a).
- Imām al-Kāzim (a).
- The Advantages of Calamities and Disasters.
- The Advantages and Effects of Faith.
- Life According to the Viewpoint of Religion.
- Science and Islam.
- Acts of Worship.
- Mind and Heart.

- What Spring Teaches us.
- Contemplation in the Qur'an.
- The Qur'an and Life.
- Supplication.
- Management System in Islam.
- Wrongful Denials.
- Two articles of which some have been translated: "Justice according to Imām 'Alī" and "Justice or Equality" under the title "Justice in Islam." Additionally, "Supplication" and "Qur'an and Life" in the collection *Monotheism and Perfection, and the Fundamentality of the Soul.*

67. *Ten Articles*, 5th ed., 1318 A.H. Contains a variety of articles and topics as follows:

- Piety in Islam.
- Effects of Piety.
- The Enjoining of Virtue and the Prevention of Vice.
- *Ijtihād* in Islam.
- The Revival of Religious Thought.
- Knowledge is Obligatory.
- Leading the Youth.
- Preaching and Public Speaking.
- Public Speaking and the Podium.
- The Fundamental Problem in the Religious Organisation.

One article amongst these, namely "*Ijtihād in Islam,*" was translated by Ja'far al-Khalīlī and published by Dār al-Rasūl al-Akram, Beirut. It is also published as "*Tajdid and Ijtihād in Islam*" by Dār al-Aḍwā', Beirut, 1999. The first of these three articles and the article entitled "*Knowledge is Obligatory*" were translated into Arabic and published in one collection of 111 pages.

68. *The Fundamentality of Soul*, translated by Khalīl al-Isāmī in a collection entitled *The Originality of Soul* and published by Dār al-

Maḥajjah and Dār al-Rasūl al-Akram, Beirut, 2004. It was also published in another collection containing "*The Qur'an and Life*" and "*Monotheism and Perfection*".

69. *God in the Life of the Human Being*, translated by Ja'far Hishmat Khah, Islamic Media Organization, Tehran, 1995. It appears to be a collection of lessons by Shaykh Muṭahharī about Allah, and was also recorded on tape as *The Concept of God in the Life of the Human Being*.

70. *The Truth about the Husaini Revolt*, translated by Sadiq al-Baqqāl, Al-Faqih Library, Kuwait, 1986. A lecture published in the book *The Husaini Epic*.

71. *Immigration and Jihad*. Consists of four tape recordings on this subject.

72. *Jihad and Martyrdom*. Consists of two tape recordings on this subject.

73. *The Human Being and Fate*. Lectures delivered by Muṭahharī at al-Mu'talifa Islamic Organization.

74. *Islamic Articles*. Contains a collection of articles published by Islamic Media Organization, Tehran, 2000. Includes the research paper "*Islamic Guidance*" which was initially published in "*The Unseen Facts in the Human Life*".

75. *The Values of Renaissance*, The Institute of Knowledge and Wisdom, 2007. Selected articles about development, justice and national independence.

76. *New Viewpoints in Islamic Thought*. Three volumes, Dār al-Jawādayn, Beirut. A selection of a large collection of his articles and lectures on revival.

Second: Articles

There is also a large collection of articles about which we are uncertain if they have been published or not. Some of these include:

1. Sexual Behaviour.

2. Iran and Islam. Published in the 14th volume of the new edition of Muṭahharī's works, 1420 A.H.

3. A Glance at Nahj al-Balāghah.
4. Women's Rights in Islam.
5. Islam and Iran.
6. Which Life does 'Alī Despise?
7. Is asceticism monasticism or spirituality?
8. Are the World and the Hereafter Opposites?
9. The Despised World.
10. Friendship of Blood.
11. The God of the World and the Scholar.
12. Monotheism and Perfection. Published in Arabic with a collection including "The Originality of the Soul" and "The Qur'an and Life".
13. Happiness.
14. Contradiction in the Islamic Philosophy.
15. The History of Philosophy in Islam.

Third: Multi-Session tapes

There is a huge collection of tape recordings of scholarly sessions about which we are unsure about how much of it has been published or not.

1. The Qualities of the Perfect School. (10 sessions)
2. The Islamic Liberation Movement. (3 sessions)
3. The Human Being: Between Islam and Marxism. (2 sessions)
4. History and Philosophy. (3 sessions)
5. The Philosophy of *Ḥijāb*. (2 sessions)
6. Monotheism. (6 sessions)
7. Worship and Supplication. (3 sessions)
8. Intercession. (1 sessions)
9. Contradiction in Islamic Philosophy. (2 sessions)

10. Spirituality of Hafiz, *Tamāshākah Rāz* (5 sessions).

Fourth: One-Session tapes

1. The Era of al-Sadiq (a).
2. Freedom of Religion.
3. Collective Justice.
4. Al-Taqlid.
5. Moral Freedom.
6. Islam and the Needs of the Present World.
7. The Objectives of Religious Scholars in Islamic Movements.
8. Renewing Intellectual Life in Islam.
9. Women's Rights in Islam.
10. Enjoining of Virtue.
11. Slogans of 'Ashurā'.
12. Freedom and Progress.
13. The Burning of Books in Alexandria.
14. Al-Roqia and the Greatness of the Soul.
15. Will.
16. The Perfect Human Being and Examples of Human Beings.
17. Imām 'Alī (a).
18. Al-Fiqh al-Ja'farī.
19. Principles of Research in Fiqh.

Notes

1. English translation with the title *Sexual Ethics in Islam and in the Western World*, Islamic Centre of England, May 17, 2011.The title of the Arabic translation is *Al-Ḍawābit al-Akhlāqiyyah li al-Sulūk al-Jinsī*, published by Dār al-Rasūl al-Akram, Beirut, 1988. [Trans.]

2. Any book with no mention of place of publication should be assumed to be published by Sadra Publications.

3. Muṭahharī and the Enlightened Thinkers. There is no information regarding an English translation. [Trans.]

4. The English translation is called *The Theory of Knowledge*, translated by Mansoor Limba, Institute for Humanities and Cultural Studies, published by ICAS press London, 2011, ISBN: 978-1-904063-45-2. [Trans.]

5. The English translation is called *Training and Education in Islam*, translated by: Mansoor Limba, Institute for Humanities and Cultural Studies, published by ICAS press London, 2011, ISBN: 978-1-904063-45-2. The title of the Arabic translation is al-*Tarbiyah wa al-Ta'līm fi al-Islam*, translated into Arabic by 'Alī Hāshim Published in Dār al-Hādī, Beirut, 1993. [Trans.]

THE LIST OF SOURCES AND REFERENCES

A. Muṭahharī's Books

A Critique of Marxism, Sadrā Publications Foundation, Tehran.

Al-Ḍawābit al-Akhlāqiyyah li al-Sulūk al-Jinsī, published by Dār al-Rasūl al-Akram, Beirut, 1988.

Allah in the Life of the Human Being, translated by Ja'far Hishmat Khah, Islamic Media Organization, Tehran, 1985.

Al-Ma'ād (The Hereafter), translated by Jawād Kassār, Umm-ul-Qurā, Tehran, 1420 A.H.

Al-Tarbiyah wa al-Ta'līm fi al-Islam, translated into Arabic by 'Alī Hāshim Published in Dār al-Hādī, Beirut, 1993.

Articles on the Islamic Revolution, translated by Muḥammad Jawād al-Muhrī, The Revolution Media Centre, Tehran, 1402 A.H.

Education and Pedagogy in Islam, translated by al-Huda Committee, Beirut, Dār al-Hādī, 1993.

Education in Islam.

Freedom of Faith or Freedom of Thought: Jihad and its Legitimacy in Islam, Arabic translation.

God and Man, translated by Ja'far Hishmat Khāh, Tehran, Islamic Media Organization, 1985.

Ijtihād in Islam, translated by Ja'far al-Khalīlī, al-Bi'tha Organization, Tehran.

Ikhtibārāt al-Muqaddas (The Sacred Experiences), Dār al-Amīr, Beirut, 2007.

Islam and Iran, translated by Muḥammad Hādī al-Yūsufī, Dār al-Ta'āruf, Beirut.

Islam and the Demands of the Era, translated by 'Alī Hāshim, Beirut, Dār al-Amīr, 1992.

Islam and the Requirements of Time, translated by 'Alī Hāshim, Dār al-Amīr, Beirut, 1992.

Islamic Guidance within "Islamic Articles", Islamic Media Organization, Tehran, 2000.

Judgment Day, translated by Jawād 'Alī Kassār, Tehran, Umm-ul-Qurā, 1420 AH.

Lectures on Islamic Philosophy, translated by 'Abd al-Jabbār al-Rifā'ī, Dār al-Kitāb al-Islamī, Tehran, 1415 A.H.

Man and his Faith, translated by Muḥammad al-Khafani, Tehran, Islamic Media Organization, 1403 AH.

Man and Predestination, translated by Muḥammad 'Alī al-Taskhīrī, Tehran: National Library of the Islamic Republic of Iran, no date.

Monotheism, translated by 'Irfān Maḥmūd, Dār al-Hawrā', Dār al-Hawrā', Beirut, 1424 A.H.

Monotheism, translated by Ibrahim al-Khazraji, Dār al-Rasūl al-Akram and Dār al-Maḥajjah, Beirut, 1998.

Monotheistic View of the World and Man and Faith.

Motives towards Materialism (*'Ilal Gerayesh be Madigari*), translated by Muḥammad 'Alī al-Taskhīrī, Dār al-Ta'āruf, Beirut, 1980.

Muṭahharī and Enlightened Thinkers, Tehran, Sadrā Publications Foundation, 1372 A.H.

Piramun Inqilab Islami, Tehran, Sadra Publications.

Prophecy, translated by Jawād Kassār, Umm-ul-Qurā, Tehran, 1420 A.H.

Prophethood, translated by Jawād 'Alī Kassār, Tehran, Um al-Qurā Company, 1420 AH.

Regarding the Islamic Revolution, Sadrā Publications Foundation, Tehran, 1372 A.H.

Sexual Ethics in Islam and in the Western World, (arabic translation with title *Al-Ḍawābit al-Akhlāqiyyah li al-Sulūk al-Jinsī*), Beirut, Dār al-Rasūl al-Akram, 1988.

Sexual Ethics in Islam and in the Western World, Islamic Centre of England, May 17, 2011.

Society and History, al-Wafa' Organization, Beirut, 1983.

Society and History, translated by Muḥammad 'Alī Adharshab, al-Bi'tha Organization, Tehran, 1402 A.H.

The Basics of Philosophy, translated by Muḥammad 'Abd al-Mun'im al-Khāqānī, Beirut, Dār al-Ta'āruf.

The Goal of Life, Beirut, Dār al-Aḍwā', 1989.

The Human Being and Faith, translated by Muḥammad 'Abd al-Mun'im al-Khāqānī, Islamic Media Organization, Tehran, 1403 A.H.

The Human Being, Fate and Destiny, translated by Muḥammad 'Alī al-Taskhīrī, al-Maktabah al-Islamiyyah al-Kubrā, Tehran.

The Imāmat, translated by Jawād Kassār, ath-Thaqalayn, Beirut, 1418 A.H.

The Islamic Movements of the Last Century, translated by Sādiq al-'Ibādī, Dār al-Hādī, Dār al-Hādī, Beirut, 1982.

The Issue of the Veil, translated by Haidar al-Haidar, Beirut, al-Dar Islamiyah, 1987.

The Legitimate Purpose of Jihad in Islam, Islamic Media Organization, Tehran.

The Monotheistic Conception of the World, Dār al-Tayyār al-Jadīd, Beirut, 1985.

The Monotheistic Outlook of the World, (*Muqaddame-yi bar Jahānbīnī Islami*, section of *Jahanbini Tawhidi*) translated by Muḥammad 'Abd al-Mun'im al-Khāqānī, Islamic Media Organization, Tehran, 1403 A.H.

The Moral Standards of Sexual Behaviour, Dār al-Rasūl al-Akram, Beirut, 1988.

The Philosophy of Ethics, translated by Muḥammad 'Abd al-Mun'im al-Khāqānī, al-Bi'tha Organization, Tehran, Beirut, 1995.

The Principle of Ijtihād in Islam, translated by Ja'far al-Khalīlī, Dār al-Rasūl al-Akram and Dār al-Ta'āruf. (With *Right and Truth*.)

The Question of the Ḥijāb, translated by Haidar al-Haidar, al-Darul Islamiah, Beirut, 1987.

The Revival of Thought in Islam, translated by Muḥammad 'Alī Adharshab, al-Ba'thah Organization, Tehran, 1402 A.H.

The Supreme Objective of Human Life, Dār al-Aḍwā', Beirut, 1989.

The System of Woman's Rights in Islam, translated by Abū Zahrā' al-Najafī, Tehran, Islamic Media Organization, 1987.

The System of Woman's Rights in Islam.

The Theory of Knowledge, translated by Mansoor Limba, Institute for Humanities and Cultural Studies, published by ICAS press London, 2011.

The Turban for the Crown.

Training and Education in Islam, translated by 'Alī Hāshim, Dār al-Hādī, Beirut, 1993; also translated by: Mansoor Limba, Institute for Humanities and Cultural Studies, published by ICAS press London, 2011.

Women's Rights in Islam, translated by Abū Zahrā' al-Najafī, Islamic Media Organization, Tehran, 1987.

B. General References

'Abd al-Hādī al-Ḥā'irī: *Shi'ism and Constitutionalism in Iran* (*Tashayyu' wa Mashrutiyyat Dar Iran*), Tehran, 1975 (in Persian), Tehran. 1985.

'Abd al-Jabbār al-Rifā'ī: Muḥammad 'Abduh and Muḥammad Iqbāl, *Al-Tasamoh Magazine*, Issue No. 15, Summer 2006.

'Abd al-Karīm Surūsh: *Sunnat wa Secularism* (*Tradition and Secularism*), Farhang Serat Organization, Tehran, 1382 A.H. (in Persian)

'Alī Akbar Hāshemī Rafsanjānī: *Muṭahharī Whom I Knew* (*Muṭahharī Kama 'Araftoh*), in *Journey in the Life of Martyr Muṭahharī.*

'Alī al-Wardī: *Social Glimpses of the Modern History of Iraq* (*Lamahat Ijtima'iyyah min Tarikh al-Iraq al-Hadith*), Dār al-Amīr, Qom, 1991.

'Alī Davānī: *A Journey in the Life of Martyr Muṭahharī.*

'Alī Davānī: *Memories with the Martyr Muṭahharī*, translated by Khaled Tawfiq, Umm-ul-Qurā Organization, Tehran, 1417 A.H.

'Alī Sharī'atī: *A Group of Effects*, Ilham, Tehran, 1988 (in Persian).

'Alī Sharī'atī: *Islam Shenasi* (*Islamic Studies*), Ḥosseiniyeh Ershād, Tehran (in Persian).

'Alī Sharī'atī: *A Set of Relics* (*Majmu'eh Athār*), Tehran, Ilham, 1988.

'Alī Sharī'atī: *Criticism and Perspective Magazine*, Qom, Iran, Vols. 3 and 4.

'Alī Sharī'atī: *Dialogue Alone* (*Goftoguhā-ye Tanhay'i*), Vol. 2.

'Alī Sharī'atī: *Mi'ad Ba Ibrahim*.

'Alī Sharī'atī: *Nation and Leadership*, (*Al-Ummah wa al-Imāmah*).

'Alī Sharī'atī: *Talked in this Way* (*Hakadha Takallama 'Alī Sharī'*atī).

'Alī Sharī'atī: *What We Should do?* (*Cheh Bayad Kard*).

A group of researchers: *Muṭahharī and Intellectuals*, Tehran, Sadra.

A group of researchers: *A Glance at the Life of the Martyr Muṭahharī* (*Jawlatun Fi Hayat al-Shahid Muṭahharī*), Dār al-Hādī, Beirut, 1997.

A group of researchers: *A Journey in the Life of Shaykh Muṭahharī*, Dār al-Hādī, Beirut, 1992.

A group of researchers: *Muṭahharī: The Genius and Visionary* (*al-Muṭahharī al-'Abqari al-Resaly*), Iranian Cultural Chancellery, Damascus, 1991.

Abbās Khāmah-Yār: *Iran and the Muslim Brotherhood* (*Iran wa al-Ikhwan al-Muslemon*), translated by 'Abd al-Amīr al-Sā'idī, Centre of Strategic Studies, Beirut, 1997.

Alan Turin: *A Criticism of Modernity*, Ministry of Culture, Damascus.

Al-Faḍl Shalaq: *Ijtihād Magazine*, V.5, 1989.

Al-Maududī: *Renewal and Revival of Religion*.

Amal al-Sobki: *'Alam al-Ma'rifah*, 1999.

Amal al-Sobki: *The Political History of Iran between the Two Revolutions* (*Tarīkh Iran al-Islami Bayna Thawratain*), 'Alam al-Ma'rifah, Kuwait, 1999.

Dorothea Kravolski: *The Arabs and Iran* (*al-'Arab wa Iran*), Dār al-Muntakhab al-'Arabī, Beirut, 1993.

Durant: *The Pleasures of Philosophy*.

Fādel Rasul: *'Alī Sharī'atī Talked in this Way* (*Hakadha Takalama 'Alī Sharī'atī*), Dār al-Kalimah, Beirut, 1987.

Fahmi Jud'ān: *The Foundations of Progress According to Islamic Intellectuals*, Amman, Dar al-Shuruq, 1988.

Fardin Quraishy: *Renewal of Religious Thought in Iran (Tajdid al-Fikr al-Dini fi Iran)*, translated by 'Alī al-Mūsawī, Markaz al-Hadara, Beirut, 2008.

Fat'hī Malkāwī: *Islamic Instillation of the Concept of Values: Journal of Islamic knowledge (Al-Ta'sīl al-Islamī Li Mafhūm al-Qiyām: Islamiyat al-Ma'rifah Magazine)*, The International Institute for Islamic Thought, Washington, Year 14, Issue no. 54, Autumn 2008.

Fu'ād Ibrāhīm: *The Faqih and the State (Al-Faqīh wa al-Dawlah)*, Dār al-Kunūz al-Adabiyyah, Beirut, 1998.

George Sarton: *Six Wings*, Persian Translation.

Hādi KhosroShāhi: *Islam Commandos, History of Action and Thinking (Fadā'iyān-e Islam, Tarikh 'Amalkerd wa Andisheh)*, Ittilā'āt, Tehran, 1995.

Hamid Enayat: *The Current Islamic Political Thought (Al-Fikr al-Siyasi al-Islami al-Mu'asir)*, translated by Ibrahim al-Dasouqy Shata, Madbuly, Cairo, 1988.

Hosseiniyeh Ershād: *Understanding Islam, Muḥammad the Final Prophet.*

Ḥasan Ḥifnī: *Philosophical Studies in Current Islamic Thought*, Dār al-Tanwīr, Beirut, 1995.

Ibrahim al-'Ayāḍi: *Ijtihād and Renewal (Ijtihād wa Tajdid)*, "*Current Islamic Issues*", 3rd issue, The Philosophy of Religion Centre in Baghdad, published by Dār al-Hādī, Beirut.

Ikhtibārāt al-Muqaddas, Beirut, Dār al-Amīr, 2007.

Imām Khomeinī: *Analects*, Vol. 1

Imām Khomeinī: *A Letter to the Constitution's Guardian Council*, 29-12-1988.

Imām Khomeinī: *Integrity and Stability*, Imām Khomeinī Cultural Centre, Beirut.

Imām Khomeinī: *Islamic Government (Al-Hukumat al-Islamiyah)* 1st ed., The Publishing and Organization of the Imam's Heritage, Tehran, 1996.

Imām Khomeinī: *Revolution Newspaper*, Ministry of Culture and Islamic Guidance, Tehran.

Imām Khomeinī: *Selections*, Beirut.

Imām Khomeinī: *Statement to Scientific Seminaries and References*, Ragab 1404 AH / 1989 AD.

Ishāq al-Naqqāsh: *The Shi'ites in Iraq* (*Shi'at al-Iraq*), Damascus, 1987.

Jalāl Āl-e-Ahmad: *al-Mustanīrūn*, arabic translation by Haydar Najaf, Beirut, Dār al-Hādī, 2000

Jalāl Āl-e-Ahmad: *Enlighteners* (*Roshanfekran*) which is translated into Arabic as *al-Mustanīrūn*, translated by Haydar Najaf, Dār al-Hādī, Beirut, 2000.

Jalāl Āl-e-Ahmad: *Khasi dar Miqat,* translated into Arabic as *Qashah Fi al-Miqat*, translated by Haydar Najaf, Current Islamic Issues, Dār al-Hādī, Beirut, 2003.

Jalāl Āl-e-Ahmad: *The Trend of Westernization*, translated by Haydar Najaf, Current Islamic Issues, Dār al-Hādī, Beirut, 2000.

Jalāl Āl-e-Ahmad: *Weststruckness* (*Gharb Zadegi*), Rawaq, Tehran, 1964. (in Persian)

Jamāl-al-Dīn al-Afghānī, *Theology of Predestination* (part of the full work).

Jamāl-al-Dīn al-Afghānī: "*Al-Rad 'Alā al-Dahriyyīn,*" in *The Complete Works*, by Muḥammad 'Imārah.

Jamāl-al-Dīn al-Afghānī: "*Risalat al-Qaḍā' wa al-Qadar,*" in The Complete Works.

Jamal-al-Din al-Afghani: *Responding to Atheists*, part of his work translated by Muḥammad Amara, Cairo, General Authority for Books.

Jurgen Habermas: *The Philosophical Discourse of Modernity*, translated by Fatima al-Jiyousy, Ministry of Culture, Damascus.

Jurgen Habermas: *The Political Discourse of Modernity*, Dār al-Nahar for Publishing, Beirut.

Kāmil al-Hāshimī: *Manifestations of Political Policy in Imām Khomeinī's Thought* (*Ishrāqāt al-Falsafa al-Seyāsiya fe Fikr al-Imām Khomeinī*), *Islamic Contemporary Issues*, Vol. 1, Centre of Religion Philosophy Studies in Baghdad.

Kāmil al-Hāshimī: *Reflections of Islamic Philosophy in the Thought of Muṭahharī*, "*Current Islamic Issues*" book, 1st ed., The Philosophy of Religion Centre in Baghdad, published by Dār al-Hādī, Beirut.

Khalīl Haydar: *Turban and Mace: Shi'ite Reference in Iran and Iraq* (*Al-Ammamāh wal Sawlajan, al-Marja'iyyah al-Shi'iyyah fi Iran wa al-Irāq*), Dār Qirtās, Kuwait, 1997.

Khanjar Hamiyyah: *Ikhtibārāt al-Muqaddas*, Dār al-Amīr, Beirut, 2007.

Mahdī Bāzargān: *A Lesson in Piousness.*

Mahdī Bāzargān: *Behind Inference*, Tehran, Inteshar.

Mahdī Bāzargān: *The Infinite Entity.*

Mahdī Bāzargān: *The Mission and Ideology*, Mashhad, Dar Tolu'.

Mahdī Bāzargān: *The Traversed Road.*

Mahdī Bāzargān: *The Young Islam.*

Mahdī Bāzargān: *Afāq Tawḥīd* (*Horizons of Monotheism*), published by al-Thaqafa al-Islamiah, Tehran (in Persian).

Mahdī Bāzargān: *Bi'that wa Ideology* (*Prophecy and Ideology*), Tolu', Tehran/Mashhad (in Persian).

Mahdī Bāzargān: *Intezār Az Din* (*What is Expected from Religion*), Intisar, Tehran (in Persian).

Mahdī Bāzargān: *Kār Dar Islam* (*Work in Islam*), published by al-Thaqafa al-Islamiah, Tehran (in Persian).

Mahdī Bāzargān: *Marz-e Miyan Din va Siyāsat* (*Boundaries between Religion and Politics*), Intisar, Tehran (in Persian).

Mahdī Bāzargān: *Mazhab Dar Europa* (*The Ideology of Europe*), published by al-Thaqafa al-Islamiah, Tehran (in Persian).

Mahdī Bāzargān: *Rah Tay Shodeh* (*The passed Way*), Intisar, Tehran. (in Persian).

Mālik Ibn-Nabī: *The Destination of the Muslim World*, translated by 'Abd al-Sabūr Shāhīn, Cairo, 1995.

Mehrzad Borūjerdī: *Roshanfikrān Iran wa Gharb* (*Iranian and Western Intellectuals*) translated by Jamshid Shirazi, Farzan, Tehran, 1998 (in Persian).

Mohsen Kadivar: *The Theories of State in the Shi'ite Jurisprudence*, (in Farsi: *Nazareyye-hāye Dowlat Dar Feqh-e Shī'i*), Ney Publication, Tehran, 1988 (in Persian).

Muḥammad 'Abduh: *Islam and Christianity in Relation to Science and Civilization* (*Al-Islam wa al-Nasrāniyyah bayn al-'Ilm wa al-Madaniyyah*), Cairo, 1902.

Muḥammad 'Abduh: *Theology of Unity* (*Risālat al-Tawḥīd*), Dār al-Ma'arif, Cairo, 1971.

Muḥammad 'Imāra: *Islam between Enlightenment and Malpractice* (*Al-Islam bayn al-Tanwir wa al-Tazwir*), Dār al-Shurooq, Beirut, 1995.

Muḥammad al-Bāhi: *Contemporary Islamic Thinking.*

Muḥammad al-Bāhi: *Modern Islamic Thought and its relation with the Western Colonialism*, Dār al-Fikr, Beirut, 1991.

Muḥammad Bāqir al-Ṣadr: *Al-Sunan al-Tarīkhiyyah fi al-Qur'an al-Karīm*, Dār al-Ta'āruf, Beirut, 1989.

Muḥammad Bāqir al-Sadr: *Our Economy*, Beirut, Dār al-Ta'āruf.

Muḥammad Iqbāl: *Renewing Religious Thought*, translated by 'Abbās Maḥmūd, Cairo, 1995.

Muḥammad Ḥossein al-Amin: *Modernity and Heritage*, Al-Haya al-Tebya Magazine, Issue no. 5, Winter 2001.

Muḥammad Ḥossein Fadlullah: "*Ijtihād and Renewal Capacities*, (*Al-Ijtihād wa Imkānyat al-Tajdid*)," part of Zainab Shorba: *Towards a Modern Understanding of Ijtihād*, Dār al-Hādī, Beirut, 2004.

Muḥammad Ḥossein Fadlullah: *Authenticity and Renewal* (*Al-Asāla wa al-Tajdid*), Al-Minhaj Organization, Issue no. 2, Sayf, Beirut, Summer 1996.

Muḥammad Ḥossein Ṭabāṭabā'i: *Al-Mizan fi Tafsir al-Qur'an*, Beirut, al-A'lami, part 4.

Muḥammad Ḥossein Ṭabāṭabā'i: *Al-Mizan, al-A'lamī*, Beirut.

Muḥammad Mahdī Shams al-Dīn: *Ijtihād and Renewal* (*Al-Ijtihād wa al-Tajdid*), The International Organization for Studies and Publishing, Beirut, 1996.

Muḥammad Riḍā Wasfi: *The History of the Current Islamic Thought in Iran* (*Al-Fikr al-Islami al-Mu'asir fi Iran*), Dār al-Jadid, Beirut, 2000.

Naqd wa Nazar Magazine, issues 3 and 4, 1998, "*Sunnat gerayan*" ("*Traditionalists*") (in persian).

Omar Farrukh: *Tajdid in Muslims not in Islam*, Dār al-Kitāb al-' Arabī, Beirut, 1986.

Rashid Riḍā: *Tafsir al-Manar*, Cairo.

Riḍwān al-Sayyid: "*Terminology and Trends in the Current Islamic Thought*," *Current Islamic Issues Magazine*, 2004.

Riḍwān al-Sayyid: *The Politics of the Contemporary Islam* (*Sīyāsāt al-Islam al-Mu'asir*), Dār al-Kitāb al-'Arabī, Beirut, 1997.

Roger Garaudy: *Islam*, Beirut.

Russell, *Marriage and Morals*, Persian translation.

Russell, *The Universal Vision of Science.*

Sayed Qutb: *In the Light of Qur'an* (*Fi Zilāl al-Qur'an*), Dār al-Shurūq, Cairo, 1986.

Sayyed Hossein Nasr: *Islamic Studies*, al-Darul Muttahida, Beirut, 1975.

Sayyed Hossein Nasr: *Sufism between Past and Present* (*Al-Sufeyah Bayena al-Ams Wa al-Youm*), al-Darul Muttahida, Beirut, 1975.

Ṭāhā Jābir al-'Ilwānī: *Reforming the Islamic Thought*, Al-A'raf Organization, Tehran.

Talal Majzoub: *Iran from the Constitutional Revolution to the Islamic Revolution* (*Iran min al-Thawrah al-Dustūrīyyah illā al-Thawrah al-Islamīyyah*), Dār Ibn-Rushd, Beirut, 1980.

Thomas W. Lippman: *Islam, Politics and Religion in the Muslim World*, Arabic translation with title of: *Jamā'at al-Islam al-Siyāsī* (*Political Islam Groups*), translated by Rif'at al-Sayyid Ahmad, Yafa for Studies and Publishing, Cairo, 1989.

William James: *Religion and the Soul.*

Yahyā Muḥammad: *Polemics of Rhetoric and Reality*, Beirut, Arab Diffusion Company, 2002.

Yahyā Muḥammad: *The Dialectic of Discourse and Reality*, Al-Intisār al-'Arabī Organization, Beirut, 2002.

Yūsuf al-Qaraḍāwī: *Ijtihād in Islam*, translated by Ja'far Khalīl, Tehran, al-Bi'tha Foundation, no date.

Yūsuf al-Qaraḍāwī: *Ijtihād in the Islamic Shari'ah*, Dār al-Qalam, Kuwait, 1996.

Zaki al-Milād: *Islam and Revival*, Arab Cultural Centre, Beirut, 2008.

Ziad Khaleel al-Deghamen: "*Building the Universe in the light of the Texts*", *Journal of Islamic Knowledge* ("*I'mar al-Kawn fi Daw' Nusus al-Wahy*"), Islamiyat al-Ma'rifah, 54, 2008.

INDEX

A

'Abbās Khāmah-Yār 51, 279
'Abbasids 163
'Abbās Maḥmūd 179, 283
'Abd al-Amīr al-Sā'idī 51, 279
'Abd al-Hādī al-Ḥā'irī 49, 278
'Abd al-Jabbār al-Rifā'ī 173, 174, 180, 266, 276
'Abd al-Karīm Surūsh 174, 278
'Abd al-Qādir al-Jazāirī's Movement....47
'Abd al-Qadir al-Maghribī 130
'Abd al-Sabūr Shāhīn 179, 282
'Abduh 129, 130, 174,
see also Muḥammad 'Abduh
'Alī Akbar Hāshemī Rafsanjānī.....81, 278
'Alī al-Mūsawī 50, 280
'Alī al-Wardī 50, 278
'Alī Davānī 60, 81, 83, 184, 278
'Alī Hāshim..... 82, 260, 273, 275, 276, 278
'Alī Sharī'atī....26, 27, 28, 30, 31, 34, 35, 36, 37, 50, 52, 53, 60, 63, 64, 78, 79, 83, 278, 279
see also Sharī'atī
'Alī Quli Qarā'i 260
Abomination 45
Abraham 201
Abū Zahrā' al-Najafī 82, 266, 278
Abul Alā Maudūdī 87, 172, 279
Activist 27, 28
Adam 134, 226
Advocates .... VIII, 25, 222
African 34
Afterlife 77
see also Hereafter
Age of Enlightenment 11
Agha Khān 38
Akhbāri 95
al-Afghānī 174
see also Jamāl-al-Dīn al-Afghānī
Alan Turin 241, 279
Albert Einstein 140
see also Einstein
Al-Dīn al-Qayyim 152
Āl-e-Ahmad 17, 50
see also Jalāl Āl-e-Ahmad
Al-Faḍl Shalaq 52, 279
Algeria 30
Al-Hāshimi 54
Al-Ḥayy 152
Al-Jabr wa al-Ikhtiyār 230
Al-Jawād Mosque 83
Al-kutub al-qayyimah 152
Allied Forces 14
Al-Mahdī 23, 47
Al-Majālis al-Ḥosseiniyah 13
Al-ṣirāṭ al-mustaqīm 152
Al-Qayyūm 152
Al-Qiyāma 149, 150, 151
Al-Quds 21
Al–Shaykh al-Ṭusi conference 262
Altruism 95, 136, 235
Amal al-Subky 49, 50, 279
America 16, 29, 38, 213
America's Central Intelligence Agency 16
American 7, 16, 139
American influence 7
American University 38
Ammār Abū-Raghīf 261
Ancient 18, 37, 95, 166, 167, 223, 253
Animal 103, 115, 116, 117, 121, 226
Animalistic 155, 169
Animality 134
Anjoman-e Hojjatiyeh 23
Anthropocentric outlook 11
Anthropomorphic 140

Aqwam.......182
Arab... 14, 15, 21, 22, 34, 173, 174, 222, 230, 243
Arab renaissance.......91
Arab world..... 14, 15, 21, 23, 26, 27, 34, 91, 130, 166, 252
Arabic.......3, 65, 185, 260, 264
Arabic grammar.......65
Arabic language.......57, 65, 253
Arabic literature.......57, 65
Arabic philosophical.......66
Arabic translations.......259
Arabic word.......152
Arak mosque.......265
Arānī.......58, 243
Aristotelian.......41
Armed activity.......29, 34
Armed militia.......30
Armed movements.......28
Armed struggle.......28, 29, 30
Arrogance.......45, 46, 157, 215
Art......11, 141, 190, 200, 207, 212, 214, 233
Artist.......37
Artistic.......18, 24, 155, 213
Asceticism.......77, 94, 132, 137
Ash'ari.......95
Aspiration.. 3, 8, 9, 18, 27, 46, 63, 139, 165, 230, 232, 253
Assassination.......29, 64, 78
Atā'-Allah Shehāb.......26
Ataturk.......18
Atheism.......3, 40, 253
Atheistic.......64
Atheistic doctrines.......129
Attitudes.......75, 106, 169, 231, 238
Attributes 68, 91, 92, 105, 112, 113, 114, 115, 118, 120, 121, 122, 124, 126, 134, 146, 152, 219, 232
Auguste Comte.......223
see also Comte
Authorities.......23, 28, 31, 93, 185, 190
Authority .. 8, 10, 13, 21, 22, 23, 62, 87, 92, 107, 120, 122, 127, 130, 159, 160, 161, 163, 164, 189, 190, 229, 230, 232, 254
Averroes.......179
Avicenna.......38, 77
Avicennian philosophy.......59
Awareness..VII, 3, 17, 18, 28, 34, 35, 37, 43, 45, 46, 59, 63, 75, 92, 93, 94, 95, 98, 113, 114, 115, 116, 127, 129, 137, 138, 141, 154, 156, 160, 162, 164, 165, 166, 190, 191, 209, 210, 253, 254
Awqāf.......13
Azerbaijan.......14

B

Baha'ism.......23
Bāhonar.......63, 83
Bay'ah.......32
Bāzargān.. 27, 28, 29, 30, 32, 33, 34, 36, 52, 60, 63, 144, 145, 146, 147, 148, 151, 181, 182
see also Mahdī Bāzargān
Beauty. 65, 135, 138, 156, 158, 236, 237, 238, 240
Behaviour. 35, 36, 68, 73, 77, 101, 104, 105, 106, 124, 151, 152, 153, 155, 190, 191, 196, 197, 198, 199, 201, 219, 238, 239, 240
Beheshti.......25, 63
Behrouz Bushehri.......262
Beirut 38, 183, 245, 264, 265, 269, 273, 281
Belief (s)... 12, 15, 20, 24, 30, 33, 36, 37, 40, 48, 57, 61, 68, 77, 105, 106, 110, 115, 116, 118, 121, 123, 125, 129, 132, 133, 138, 150, 151, 152, 191, 193, 198, 199, 200, 205, 206, 208, 214, 215, 216, 218, 219, 221, 222, 224, 225, 228, 229, 230, 234, 238
Believers.......78, 113, 130, 215, 217, 219
Benefit.... 9, 11, 63, 66, 67, 69, 92, 100, 105, 107, 111, 116, 135, 139, 143, 169, 179, 191, 219, 234, 235, 236, 237
Bertrand Russell.......111
see also Russell
Biblical.......134
Biography.......VII, 3
Biologist.......225
Book of Genesis.......134
Borūjerdī.......21, 22, 58, 81, 262
Boundaries.......2, 11, 35, 49, 116, 170, 171
Brutal.......16, 28, 31
Brutality.......252

C

Capabilities.....17, 33, 62, 79, 119, 124, 125, 133, 135, 158, 162, 165, 168, 228
Carlyle.......181
Cartesian rationalism.......38, 41

Change 7, 8, 9, 13, 14, 15, 16, 19, 20, 37, 40, 41, 42, 47, 48, 49, 58, 60, 62, 63, 72, 88, 92, 97, 104, 105, 106, 107, 113, 116, 120, 124, 136, 146, 154, 160, 165, 190, 191, 194, 199, 200, 206, 208, 209, 210, 211, 212, 213, 214, 215, 216, 218, 219, 225, 228, 232, 233, 238, 239, 240
Character of religion....36
Characterised 8, 9, 17, 24, 27, 47, 105, 110, 112, 121, 124, 135, 140, 141
Characteristic (s).... 2, 3, 9, 12, 72, 88, 106, 115, 135, 146, 151, 193, 194, 195, 202, 209, 226, 252
Chinese....211, 212
Chinese revolution....211
Christian.... 40, 101, 141
Christian legacy.... 40
Christian nations....134
Christianity....39, 102, 140, 223
Church (es)....223, 231, 223
Civilisation (s). 9, 10, 17, 18, 35, 41, 45, 47, 71, 73, 74, 75, 76, 96, 97, 106, 108, 128, 129, 132, 133, 137, 153, 155, 156, 167, 189, 191, 201, 233, 252
Class......16, 23, 47, 149, 209, 210, 211, 212, 213, 214, 215, 216, 217, 218, 219, 220
Class distinctions....23, 211
Class tension....16
Classical ethics....39
Clergy.......14, 22, 23, 25, 26, 35, 46, 63, 165
Clergymen....13, 26, 50, 78
Coalition Committee....64
College of Theology....59
Colonialism....45, 74, 252
Colonisation....161, 163
Combatant Clergy Association.... 81
Common law.... 13
Communism....16
Communist (s)....30, 79, 149
Comte....223, 224
see also Auguste Comte
Concept (s)..7, 11, 15, 23, 26, 32, 35, 36, 74, 75, 76, 77, 79, 88, 90, 91, 92, 93, 94, 95, 108, 109, 117, 125, 126, 131, 132, 141, 143, 151, 152, 158, 166, 167, 195, 199, 214, 215, 222, 223, 224, 229, 237
Conflict (s)..... 10, 11, 16, 37, 43, 44, 45, 87, 102, 209, 212, 217, 219, 226, 227, 229, 235, 254
Conscience.. 58, 103, 113, 121, 123, 129, 131, 137, 153, 155, 195, 235, 236, 237, 251
Conservatism....35, 61
Constitutional.... 48
Constitutional Movement....15, 47
Constitutional Revolution.... 9, 30
Contemporary. VII, VIII, 9, 12, 14, 24, 25, 26, 37, 38, 40, 46, 47, 48, 49, 60, 65, 66, 76, 92, 99, 101, 111, 149, 151, 161, 163, 181, 251, 252
Contemporary life....253
Contemporary problems....VII, 63
Contemporary society....99
Controversy....78, 79, 127
Conviction (s).... 22, 30, 31, 32, 42, 48, 63, 67, 68, 98, 108, 111, 112, 125, 149, 157, 254
Corrupt....105, 106, 169, 199
Corruption....42, 45, 51, 88, 102, 104, 105, 134, 140, 165, 171, 197, 231
Creation ...108, 118, 123, 124, 125, 127, 129, 138, 143, 145, 150, 168, 189, 223, 225, 226, 227, 228, 237
Creativity.... 92, 102, 114, 157, 163, 184, 223
Critical evaluation....2
Critical period.... 64
Criticism 17, 47, 68, 129, 151, 157, 166, 205, 210, 213
Critique.... 17, 204
Cruel....104
Cuba....15, 30
Cultural. 8, 10, 13, 14, 17, 18, 21, 36, 37, 43, 44, 45, 46, 47, 49, 69, 74, 75, 87, 92, 125, 128, 161, 164, 165, 189, 202, 213, 214
Cultural activity....69
Cultural assets....36
Cultural deterioration....10
Cultural dilemmas....43, 45
Cultural disintegration....75
Cultural dynamism....8
Cultural élite (s)....43, 46
Cultural heritage....37
Cultural imperialism....37
Cultural independence....46, 75
Cultural Invasion....165
Cultural renaissance....49
Cultural values....192
Cultural westernisation....166

Culture (s) 1, 28, 40, 45, 46, 47, 70, 75, 78, 98, 128, 132, 190, 197, 198, 199, 201, 202, 203, 208, 211, 212, 213, 222, 251, 252, 253
Customs 98, 101, 106, 157, 166, 167, 170, 193, 197, 198, 199, 200, 208, 213, 233

D

Dār al-Tablīgh 81
Darwin 143, 225, 227, 228, 235, 245, 246
Darwin's theory 143
Day of Judgment 125, 130, 131, 149
Day of Reckoning 129, 149
Day of Resurrection 149, 151, 152
Death 11, 20, 29, 36, 90, 100, 121, 134, 144, 148, 253, 262
Decadence 39, 88
Decay 103, 147, 148
Deception 68, 137
Decline 9, 22, 31, 36, 57, 104, 105, 106, 130, 158, 160, 167, 184, 190, 196, 197, 204, 205, 239
Defeatism 46, 94
Definition 2, 32, 42, 47, 49, 75, 116, 251
Definitive transition 8
Demise 39, 255
Democracy 8, 18, 26, 27, 30, 32
Democratic movement 8
Deprivation 46, 219, 252
Desire (s) 11, 13, 14, 15, 18, 19, 27, 44, 57, 59, 94, 95, 101, 102, 108, 118, 124, 129, 137, 139, 153, 155, 158, 159, 169, 170, 171, 172, 184, 192, 194, 198, 223, 229, 230, 236
Destiny 11, 77, 93, 110, 114, 115, 117, 118, 119, 123, 125, 128, 129, 131, 143, 152, 153, 155, 159, 195, 196, 197, 201, 202, 227, 229
Destroyed 10, 79, 161, 165, 167
Destruction 10, 11, 137
Destructive 11, 39, 95, 104, 129, 130, 136, 137, 163, 164, 227
Deterioration 16, 24, 70, 72, 74, 239
Determinism 205, 206, 230
Develop 23, 25, 75, 91, 97, 99, 103, 107, 141, 153, 155, 162, 171, 208, 211, 214, 254, 255
Development (s) ..... VII, 2, 9, 11, 12, 17, 19, 25, 26, 27, 28, 35, 40, 43, 44, 47, 48, 49, 57, 66, 73, 91, 96, 99, 101, 102, 103, 104, 107, 109, 126, 133, 135, 136, 138, 154, 155, 156, 159, 161, 162, 190, 204, 205, 207, 208, 209, 211, 212, 213, 214, 222, 223, 228, 239, 240, 254
Deviate 153, 200, 201
Deviation 45, 92, 93, 94, 107, 152, 196, 222, 231
Dewey 80
Dialectic 126, 131, 208
Dialectical arguments 127, 128
Dialectical influence 131
Dialectical nature 127
Dictatorship 14, 20, 214, 252
Differences .. 8, 14, 30, 39, 60, 89, 126, 130, 146, 168, 194, 203, 227
Dignity 63, 106, 129, 139, 155, 158, 169, 218, 220, 226
Dilemmas ... 15, 19, 24, 25, 42, 47, 192, 225
Discovery 102, 121, 135, 138, 142
Disposition 13, 237, 239
Disputes 7, 60, 235
Dissemination 17, 253
Distinguished 9, 91, 168
Distortion 7, 80, 129, 168, 205, 253
Diversity 3, 8, 109, 110, 146, 201, 240
Divine VIII, 32, 33, 38, 39, 40, 42, 118, 154, 179, 201, 226, 227, 228, 229, 230
Divine action 127
Divine attributes 125
Divine authority 125
Divine beauty 39
Divine efficiency 127
Divine essence 39
Divine guidance 39
Divine idea 164
Divine institution 163
Divine justice .... VIII, 125, 230
Divine law (s) 32, 33, 40, 45
Divine occurrences 141
Divine origin 38
Divine presence 39, 133
Divine Will 33, 40, 127, 229
Divinity 143, 150, 228
Doctrine (s). 64, 80, 132, 137, 149, 151, 155, 179, 199, 216, 222, 233, 235
Domains 12, 156, 164
Domination 44, 45, 163, 169
Dominion 11, 46, 217, 229

Dorothea Kravolski........................ 50, 279
Downfall 15, 25, 48, 104, 192
Dowry.......................................79, 100, 168
Dr. Arrani 149
Dr. Sahābī 26, 60
Durkheim..199
Dynamic (s) 31, 96, 102, 123, 159, 210
Dynamism 8, 12, 15, 31, 252

E

Earth 36, 51, 120, 150, 153, 197, 219
Eastern 39, 62, 70, 77
Eastern civilisations 39
Eastern philosophy 109
Economic.... 7, 10, 13, 17, 24, 161, 164, 165, 168, 190, 208, 210, 211, 212, 213, 214, 215, 216, 217, 219, 234, 254
Economic development.................... 15, 27
Economic factor 207, 208, 214
Economic structure..............................190
Economical influence 166
Economics 12, 16, 25, 34, 166, 190, 212, 252
Economy 166, 208, 215, 216
Education..... 1, 8, 13, 23, 28, 31, 44, 46, 57, 65, 66, 151, 153, 154, 159, 160, 198, 199, 209
Educational . 7, 13, 17, 18, 46, 128, 154, 155, 164, 184, 234
Educational curricula 7, 13, 18
Educational institutions 165
Educator (s) 24, 64, 169
Einstein 140, 141, 181, 222
see also Albert Einstein
Elements....1, 2, 3, 26, 93, 110, 111, 114, 123, 124, 125, 133, 136, 144, 145, 146, 148, 150, 168, 194, 200, 202, 211, 251, 252, 253
Energy..... 8, 98, 107, 113, 129, 144, 145, 148
Engels...212
Enslavement 11, 39, 104
Enthusiasm....................... 99, 135, 160, 161
Entropy 147, 148
Environment. 9, 61, 116, 156, 168, 191, 198, 202, 206, 227, 231, 252
Environmental factors......................... 202
Epistemological 2, 4, 9, 60, 221, 222
Epistemology...... 2, 12, 25, 45, 110, 111, 251
Equality 13, 15, 45, 71, 77, 168, 169, 216, 236
Era VII, 2, 7, 8, 9, 10, 13, 14, 24, 26, 44, 61, 73, 87, 91, 95, 100, 132, 133, 134, 139, 140, 160, 161, 166, 184, 189
Esoteric knowledge................................. 40
Essence... 2, 4, 32, 35, 36, 39, 41, 44, 66, 94, 104, 105, 117, 121, 135, 136, 145, 146, 150, 196, 197, 200, 201, 212, 223, 225, 236, 238, 239, 252
Establishment.... 14, 19, 21, 23, 25, 46, 162, 209, 254
Eternal truth.................................. 40, 103
Eternal wisdom 38
Ethical.... 61, 65, 76, 127, 154, 172, 231, 233, 234, 235, 236, 240
Ethical issues 171
Ethical outlook 61
Ethical principles.................................. 105
Ethical values............................87, 233, 254
Ethics 3, 25, 27, 33, 66, 68, 73, 80, 103, 117, 169, 170, 172, 191, 192, 207, 213, 233, 236, 237, 238, 240
Europe 10, 11, 12, 34, 101
European.......................12, 13, 40, 191, 239
European nationalist 13
European origin......................................12
European philosophical........................ 40
European society...................................191
Evidence ... 112, 126, 138, 139, 140, 141, 142, 143, 145, 146, 147, 149, 150, 211, 215, 216, 218, 225, 226
Evil 93, 103, 116, 134, 169, 238
Evolution37, 143, 204, 225, 226, 227, 228, 246
Exile 28, 48, 60, 64
Existence..8, 9, 11, 12, 35, 36, 39, 58, 63, 66, 70, 103, 105, 108, 109, 110, 111, 112, 114, 115, 117, 118, 119, 120, 122, 123, 124, 125, 126, 128, 135, 138, 139, 140, 141, 142, 143, 145, 146, 148, 149, 151, 154, 162, 185, 195, 196, 197, 198, 199, 202, 204, 206, 213, 221, 223, 224, 226, 227, 228, 229
Experience (es)... 2, 8, 9, 12, 14, 15, 28, 39, 62, 69, 70, 74, 78, 79, 90, 92, 103, 106, 107, 114, 116, 117, 119, 121, 124, 128, 130, 131, 136, 139, 155, 156, 158, 159, 160, 162,

163, 192, 196, 197, 203, 204, 210, 211, 212, 214, 217, 223, 225, 232, 237, 252
Experiment.........VIII, 2, 13, 18, 19, 69, 135
Experimentation.....110, 111, 135, 189, 204, 214, 222, 223
Exploitation......8, 10, 17, 45, 80, 102, 138, 209, 214, 236
External. 17, 88, 135, 136, 160, 161, 193, 195, 205, 254
Extinction..196, 197
Extreme............................8, 18, 71, 169, 253
Extreme nationalist..................................23
Extremist...60

F

Factor......15, 18, 37, 78, 148, 195, 202, 206, 207, 208, 211, 212, 213, 214, 215, 216, 217, 219, 226, 228, 230, 235, 240
Factors....VII, 2, 8, 9, 19, 31, 34, 37, 45, 62, 71, 72, 74, 76, 78, 79, 96, 140, 148, 155, 160, 189, 190, 191, 193, 198, 199, 201, 202, 206, 207, 208, 210, 212, 213, 214, 223, 228, 239, 240, 252, 253
Fadā'iyān-e-Islam Movement... 20, 21, 22, 29
Fādel Rasul.......................................50, 279
Fahmi Jud'ān...........179, 251, 253, 255, 280
Faith... 27, 33, 35, 37, 67, 73, 77, 82, 83, 92, 93, 96, 113, 114, 115, 117, 118, 121, 122, 126, 127, 128, 131, 132, 133, 134, 135, 136, 137, 138, 151, 1890, 219, 222, 223, 225, 230, 251, 252
Fakhr al-Dīn al-Razī..............................143
Family................................168, 169, 171, 185
Family system..168
Family ties...171
Family unit..169
Family values...168
Faqih...22, 33
Farah Antun...130
Fardin Quraishy............................50, 280
Farīmān...57
Fascism...13, 192
Fat'hī Malkāwī.......................................280
Fatima al-Jiyousy...........................241, 281
Fatwā...21
Faydiyya Massacre...................................63
Fear.................. 21, 24, 37, 87, 140, 218, 236
Feudalism..212
Fight...20, 25, 165
Financial...7, 10
Financial independence..........................25
Fiqh.................... 25, 33, 47, 66, 91, 151, 260
Fir'awn..218
see also Pharaoh
First Cause............................223, 224, 225
Forbidden..75, 134
Foreign.............14, 18, 71, 161, 163, 165, 191
Foreign domination..................................49
Foreign forces...20
Foreign ideas...61
Foreign intellectual...................................77
Foreign intervention........................14, 20
Foreign material..80
Foreign policy..48
Foreign support...14
formation. 7, 16, 19, 25, 26, 38, 63, 79, 118, 126, 143, 148, 168, 198, 202, 226
Fouad Ibrahim...51
Foundation 2, 58, 60, 77, 97, 109, 110, 130, 131, 135, 140, 154, 171, 191, 225
Foundations ..1, 9, 10, 26, 69, 96, 102, 110, 111, 112, 114, 126, 133, 153, 161, 163, 222, 233, 235, 236, 253
France...60
Frankfurt School.......................................17
Frantz Fanon...34
Free will..104, 116, 155, 199, 200, 205, 206, 230, 232
Freedom... 3, 9, 11, 13, 15, 26, 27, 30, 31, 32, 33, 37, 44, 45, 46, 62, 63, 68, 71, 77, 103, 116, 118, 119, 121, 128, 129, 132, 157, 161, 163, 164, 165, 167, 168, 169, 170, 171, 185, 190, 198, 199, 200, 205, 206, 207, 208, 209, 220, 223, 229, 232, 240, 252
Freedom of choice...........................32, 33
French..225
Friends...68
Fu'ād Ibrāhīm...280
Fndamental 1, 9, 19, 20, 36, 44, 48, 62, 74, 76, 77, 91, 93, 97, 103, 107, 111, 113, 118, 149, 195, 210, 212, 220, 224, 225, 235, 239
Fundamental nature...............................106
Furqān..60
Furqān Group..78

Future 11, 20, 37, 45, 49, 61, 62, 75, 76, 87, 97, 100, 102, 108, 116, 123, 133, 157, 159, 161, 164, 171, 197, 203, 211, 223, 251

G

Gender (s) 44, 168, 202
Generation 3, 26, 31, 38, 58, 62, 93, 159, 165, 172, 206
George Sarton 138, 181, 280
George Washington University 38
Gharbzadegi 17
Global 8, 14, 16, 18, 80, 201
Global system 43
Governance 21, 47, 126, 164, 197, 253
Government. 7, 16, 19, 21, 63, 166, 190, 252
Greed 122, 134, 137, 231
Greek heritage 179
Greek philosophers 150, 222
Greek philosophy 38
Groups. 8, 19, 22, 26, 28, 64, 126, 226, 230
Guardianship of the Jurisprudent 48
Guidance. 19, 32, 33, 34, 39, 44, 60, 64, 97, 125, 138, 141, 143, 153, 154, 163, 246, 252
Guide. 28, 33, 47, 59, 60, 64, 100, 104, 119, 124, 132, 136, 153, 154, 157, 164, 202, 253
Gustave Le Bon 102

H

Hādi KhosroShāhi 51, 280
Hadith literature 65
Ḥafiz 65
Haidar al-Haidar 186, 266, 277, 278
Hamid Enāyat 51, 280
Hanoteau 130
Harām 75
Harmonious 45, 103, 110, 122, 124, 237
Harmony33, 40, 48, 101, 105, 109, 113, 122, 123, 131, 136, 152, 153, 158, 170, 227, 234, 238, 240
Ḥasan al-Bannā 21
Ḥasan al-Qommi 81
Ḥasan Ḥanafī 34, 174
Ḥasan Ḥifnī 280
Hasan Mudarris 13, 15, 50
Haydar Najaf 50, 281
Ḥawzahs 22, 25, 57, 58, 80
Heaven 41, 134
Hegel 223, 224, 225, 238
Hegemony 11, 43, 78, 232
Heidegger's 17
Hellenistic philosophy 126
Hereafter 125, 151
see also Afterlife
Heresies 92, 126
Heritage 3, 27, 39, 59, 66, 97, 105, 166, 167, 179, 189, 192
Ḥijāb .... VIII, 13, 100
Hijra 199
Hijrī calendar 13
Historical .....VI, 2, 9, 11, 12, 18, 35, 65, 73, 80, 93, 117, 125, 203, 204, 205, 207, 209, 210, 211, 212, 213, 214, 216, 217, 218, 219, 223
Historical awareness 35
Historical causes 206
Historical conditions 201
Historical determinism 205, 206
Historical events 204
Historical formation 66
Historical materialism .. 26, 208, 210, 211, 217
Historical measure 254
Historical narrations 205
Historical record (s) 143, 205
Historical research 48, 204
History... 3, 11, 12, 17, 33, 35, 36, 37, 39, 40, 42, 45, 46, 67, 70, 74, 77, 79, 95, 103, 104, 105, 106, 107, 109, 114, 115, 151, 153, 155, 159, 161, 162, 166, 191, 192, 198, 201, 202, 203, 204, 205, 206, 207, 208, 209, 210, 211, 212, 213, 216, 217, 218, 223, 255
Homogenous system 36
Hospitals 14
Ḥossein al-Jisr 130
Hossein Hujjat 58
Ḥosseiniyeh Ershād 31, 34, 52, 60, 83, 261, 264, 279, 280
Hossein Nasr, Sayyed 38, 39, 40, 41, 42, 53, 284
see also Nasr
Human 9, 11, 12, 15, 24, 33, 36, 70, 93, 107, 113, 117, 119, 138, 171, 185, 198, 199, 203, 205, 208, 209, 214, 217, 218, 219, 220, 221, 222, 225, 226, 229, 231, 234, 235, 236, 237, 239

Human achievement ... 109
Human action (s) ... 15, 93, 119, 206, 234
Human activity ... 75, 102, 190
Human aspirations ... 33
Human behaviour ... 151, 153
Human being 11, 37, 44, 193, 194, 195, 198, 199, 200, 202, 203, 206, 207, 208, 226, 229, 234, 235, 236, 237
Human choice ... 205
Human considerations ... 42
Human culture ... 202
Human diversity ... 201
Human endeavour ... 38
Human essence ... 202, 217
Human freedom ... 205, 229
Human interaction ... 34
Human knowledge ... 41, 162
Human life ... 31, 106, 204
Human mind ... 33, 111, 112
Human motivation ... 117
Human nature ... 34, 168, 200, 201, 203, 206, 208, 231
Human needs ... 103
Human perfection ... 119
Human problems ... 99
Human procreation ... 203
Human relationships ... 129, 251
Human resources ... 76, 77
Human rights ... 9, 44, 71, 185
Human societies ... 200, 201
Human society 109, 194, 195, 196, 197, 198, 200, 201, 207
Human soul ... 108, 123
Human values ... 11, 12, 36
Human virtue ... 39
Human will ... 33, 205
Humanity ... 11, 24, 32, 33, 35, 39, 109, 122, 127, 130, 134, 171, 200, 202, 208, 223, 229, 231, 238, 252
Humankind ... 105, 106, 148, 168
Hume ... 80
Hypothesis ... 110, 207, 211, 212, 213, 225

I

Ibn-Badīs ... 47
Ibrahim al-'Ayāḍi ... 54, 280
Ibrahim al-Dasouqy Shata ... 280
Ibrahim al-Khazraji ... 263, 276
Idea .. 14, 20, 30, 40, 43, 59, 74, 93, 114, 115, 121, 134, 143, 148, 159, 169, 170, 190, 220, 225, 236, 240
Ideas ... VII, 1, 2, 8, 10, 11, 12, 13, 23, 25, 26, 30, 37, 42, 47, 60, 64, 67, 68, 69, 70, 71, 72, 73, 75, 77, 78, 79, 80, 87, 88, 90, 93, 95, 97, 99, 101, 104, 116, 125, 126, 128, 130, 132, 140, 144, 151, 152, 158, 166, 167, 185, 189, 190, 191, 193, 207, 210, 214, 225, 230, 237, 238, 255
Identity 10, 11, 12, 18, 35, 37, 46, 62, 75, 80, 155, 161, 165, 166, 174, 194, 195, 197, 199, 201, 202, 216, 234, 254
Ideological. 7, 8, 9, 16, 24, 30, 66, 160, 161, 191, 210, 213, 216, 219
Ideological outlook ... 16
Ideologies ... 8, 10, 15, 71, 239
Ideology V, 9, 15, 22, 23, 27, 28, 30, 31, 32, 34, 35, 39, 64, 70, 74, 108, 109, 113, 201, 209, 211, 212, 214, 221, 239
Iftā' ... 25
Ignorance ... 37, 40, 91, 102, 134, 163, 228, 231
Ijtihād ... 25, 48, 49, 70, 77, 88, 91, 97, 98, 99, 100, 101, 102, 107, 108, 109, 157, 160, 162, 174, 253, 263
Imam ... 47, 48, 49, 60, 64
Imitate ... 11, 67, 118, 166
Imitation ... 9, 17, 75, 96, 98, 121, 156, 165, 192, 234
Imperial Iranian Academy of Philosophy ... 38
Imperialism ... 19, 232
Imprisoned ... 29, 30, 32
Imprisonment ... 34, 64
Inception ... 3, 8, 73, 110
Independence . 15, 30, 45, 46, 130, 159, 161, 165, 166, 219
Individual (s) .. VII, 9, 25, 31, 32, 33, 36, 37, 45, 75, 76, 95, 116, 117, 123, 126, 151, 170, 171, 194, 195, 196, 197, 198, 199, 200, 201, 202, 205, 206, 207, 208, 210, 214, 221, 229, 230, 231, 235, 236, 237, 238, 239, 240, 251
Individual action ... 63
Individual awareness ... 95
Individual thought ... 41
Individualistic ... 136

Individualistic goals 136
Individuality 16
Industrial 101, 108, 211, 212, 213
Industry 10, 104, 190
Inferior 44, 124, 129, 218
Influence ... 12, 13, 16, 18, 20, 23, 26, 35, 36, 38, 43, 46, 58, 76, 79, 94, 95, 128, 154, 156, 164, 165, 166, 167, 169, 189, 190, 191, 200, 206, 207, 212, 213, 214, 216, 234, 239, 255
Infrastructure 10, 19, 117, 231, 253
Injustice 45, 134, 219, 232
Innovation ... 74, 92, 105, 108, 137, 157, 233
Insight ... 41, 45, 49, 59, 71, 97, 98, 108, 254
Inspiration ... 9, 18, 22, 26, 31, 87, 109, 133, 154, 164, 179, 192, 199, 255, 259
Instinct 103, 116, 136, 138, 140, 169, 170, 193, 198, 199, 218, 231, 237
Instincts 136, 140, 169, 198, 218, 231
Institutions .. 7, 11, 18, 46, 47, 62, 164, 167, 184, 196, 207
Integrity ... 17, 47, 48, 97, 122, 125, 153, 170, 198
Intellect 104, 114, 131
IntellectualVII, 1, 2, 3, 4, 7, 8, 9, 12, 14, 15, 19, 26, 27, 28, 31, 34, 36, 37, 41, 42, 44, 58, 59, 60, 61, 62, 64, 66, 68, 69, 70, 71, 73, 74, 75, 88, 95, 108, 126, 139, 144, 151, 155, 161, 162, 164, 165, 166, 172, 179, 189, 190, 231, 234, 251, 252, 253
Intellectual activities 140
Intellectual background 110
Intellectual challenges 69
Intellectual confrontation 64
Intellectual decline 74
Intellectual dispersion 74
Intellectual efforts 73
Intellectual environment 191
Intellectual movements 160
Intellectual personality 58
Intellectual perspective 98
Intellectual position 113
Intellectual relationship 121
Intellectual resources 74
Intellectual revival 71
Intellectual stagnation 70
Intellectual traditions 70
Intellectual trends 70, 98
Intellectually 12, 88
Intellectuals 26, 67, 78, 80, 91, 128, 144
Intelligentsia 3, 14, 17, 25, 46
Interests 10, 11, 18, 34, 35, 44, 47, 49, 67, 95, 103, 104, 106, 156, 165, 167, 170, 171, 184, 193, 194, 210, 219, 232, 234
Internal 7, 14, 17, 19, 20, 29, 88, 135, 136, 160, 161, 202, 211, 214, 218, 252, 254
Interpretation .. 2, 21, 30, 31, 33, 66, 91, 96, 100, 108, 110, 132, 189, 190, 204, 209, 210, 223, 227
Intizār 23
Intolerance 91, 92, 105, 157, 166
Intolerant 67, 91, 105, 136
Intuition 38, 120, 142, 153, 194
Iran ..... V, VIII, 3, 7, 8, 9, 12, 13, 14, 17, 18, 19, 20, 23, 25, 26, 29, 31, 32, 34, 42, 43, 44, 49, 50, 51, 53, 58, 59, 60, 64, 79, 80, 82, 161, 164, 167, 252
Iranian 8, 9, 19, 167, 185, 243
Iranian Communist Party 16
Iranian community 38
Iranian culture 14, 79
Iranian history 60
Iranian intellectuals 172
Iranian intelligentsia 17, 25
Iranian Islamic Revolution 26
Iranian National Intelligence and Security Organisation 29
Iranian people 17, 172
Iranian political life 8, 15
Iranian politics 20
Iranian Revolution 9, 28
Iranian society 9, 14, 17, 24, 26, 59, 89
Iranian thinkers 16
Iraq 14, 19, 20, 48
Irfān 39, 260
Irfān Maḥmūd 263, 276
Isfahan 58
Ishāq al-Naqqāsh 50, 281
IslamV, 8, 15, 20, 21, 22, 23, 24, 25, 26, 28, 29, 30, 32, 34, 35, 36, 38, 39, 40, 41, 42, 45, 47, 48, 49, 51, 52, 53, 59, 60, 61, 62, 63, 64, 66, 68, 70, 71, 72, 73, 74, 76, 77, 78, 79, 80, 82, 83, 87, 88, 90, 91, 92, 93, 96, 97, 98, 100, 101, 102, 103, 105, 106, 107, 108, 109, 110, 112, 117, 122, 125, 126, 128, 130, 132, 134, 144, 151, 153, 154, 155, 156, 157, 158, 159, 160, 161, 162, 163, 166, 167, 168, 169, 171, 172, 183, 184,

196, 200, 201, 202, 210, 214, 215, 216, 220, 229, 230, 231, 232, 234, 251, 252, 253
Islamic 1, 3, V, VI, VII, VIII, 1, 2, 3, 7, 8, 9, 12, 13, 14, 15, 16, 19, 20, 21, 22, 23, 24, 25, 26, 27, 28, 29, 30, 32, 34, 35, 37, 38, 39, 41, 42, 43, 44, 45, 46, 47, 48, 49, 50, 51, 52, 53, 54, 59, 60, 61, 62, 63, 64, 65, 66, 70, 71, 72, 73, 74, 76, 77, 79, 80, 82, 83, 87, 88, 89, 91, 92, 93, 94, 96, 97, 98, 99, 100, 105, 169, 174, 179, 183, 203, 225, 240, 251
Islamic Arabia 169
Islamic belief (s) 98, 126, 129, 130, 132
Islamic civilisation 44, 74, 79, 102, 192
Islamic Coalition 28
Islamic Coalition Association 63
Islamic Coalition Authorities 28
Islamic community 20
Islamic concepts 21, 32, 46, 62, 79, 93, 94, 100
Islamic Conference 21
Islamic countries 160
Islamic culture 35, 39, 65, 94, 167, 219, 253
Islamic democracy 41
Islamic doctrines 179
Islamic epistemology 73
Islamic equivalent 41
Islamic façade 41
Islamic government 15, 23, 29, 32
Islamic groups 24
Islamic guise 79
Islamic heritage 7, 77, 96, 102, 109, 151
Islamic history 7, 134, 160
Islamic ideological 32
Islamic ideology 27, 32, 34, 44, 251
Islamic intellectual 30, 39, 66
Islamic issues 38
Islamic jurisprudence 99, 103, 167
Islamic law 14, 46, 48, 164, 168
Islamic legacy 14
Islamic legislation 48, 103
Islamic legislative 109
Islamic life 87
Islamic literature 119
Islamic Marxist revolutionary movements 79
Islamic mindset 37
Islamic movement (s) ... 15, 20, 72, 76, 252
Islamic nations 12, 190
Islamic opposition 13
Islamic outlook 77
Islamic Peoples' Party 28, 29
Islamic perspective 42, 61, 76, 169, 202
Islamic philosophical 59
Islamic philosophy 59, 66, 76, 179
Islamic pillars 151
Islamic political 47
Islamic precepts 25
Islamic principl (es)27, 44, 48, 74, 75, 101
Islamic projects 47
Islamic rationalism 41
Islamic reform movements 8, 19, 24
Islamic reformist movements 16
Islamic response 108
Islamic revival 96
Islamic Revolution .... VIII, 29, 60, 252
Islamic revolutionary 64
Islamic sciences .. 23, 65, 66, 70, 91, 97, 98, 99
Islamic social movements VIII
Islamic socialism 41
Islamic society 3, 22, 39, 43, 92, 94, 126
Islamic standpoint 110
Islamic state (s) 20, 21, 25
Islamic Studies 38
Islamic system 88, 109, 133, 253
Islamic teachings 62
Islamic theology 126
Islamic theory 88
Islamic thought .... VIII, 87, 129
Islamic traditions 167
Islamic ummah 59
Islamic unity 20
Islamic values 48, 153, 154
Islamic view 168
Islamic vision 62, 109, 114, 125, 151
Islamic world .... VII, 2, 3, 9, 12, 20, 22, 41, 43, 44, 45, 70, 71, 72, 80, 89, 165, 179, 191, 251, 253
Isolation 2, 17, 21, 35, 36, 46, 61, 70, 77, 94, 96, 162, 163, 166, 214, 223, 252

J

Ja'far al-Khalīlī 267, 269, 275, 277
Ja'far Hishmat Khāh 177, 270, 275
Ja'far Sādiq al-Khalīl 174, 263, 265, 284

Ja'far Subḥanī 261
Jalāl al-Dīn al-Rūmī 65
Jalāl al-Dīn Ashtiyānī 26
Jalāl Āl-e-Ahmad 16, 17, 50, 281
see also Āl-e-Ahmad
Jamāl-al-Dīn al-Afghānī. 47, 129, 132, 179, 281
see also al-Afghānī
Jāmi'a-ye Ruhāniyyat Mubārez 81
Jamshid Shirazi, Farzan 53, 282
Japan 213
Jawād 'Alī Kassār ...175, 180, 181, 266, 268, 275, 276, 277
Jawid Mosque 267
Jāwidān kherad 38
Jerusalem 21
Jesus 201
Jihad 21, 71, 83, 159, 263
Judaism 140
Judgment Day 125, 126, 181
Judicial 29, 208
Judicial immunity 29
Jürgen Habermas 17, 241, 281
Jurisprudence 25, 51, 58, 59, 61, 99, 100, 184
Jurisprudent 22, 33, 48, 58
Jurisprudential council 162
Jurist (s) 33, 48, 98, 99, 101
Justice. 8, 9, 11, 13, 15, 18, 31, 32, 44, 45, 62, 71, 77, 122, 124, 125, 127, 129, 130, 149, 216, 217, 219

K

Kalām 126, 127, 128, 130, 131, 132
Kāmil al-Hāshimī 54, 281
Kant 235, 236, 237
Kantian 237
Karg 81
Kāshāni 18, 20, 21
Kāshāni Movement 20, 22
Kasravi 20
Khadijah 217
Khalīl al-Isāmī 269
Khalīl Haydar 49, 51, 282
Khaled Tawfiq 278
Khāmeneī 66
Khān al-Kirmānī 13
Khanjar Hamiyyah 3, 4, 282
Khārijite 95
Khomeinī V, 27, 28, 44, 45, 46, 47, 48, 54, 58, 59, 60, 61, 63, 64, 81, 280, 281
KhosroShāhi 51
Khurāsān 57, 59
Knowledge 38, 47, 58, 61, 65, 66, 70, 76, 98, 102, 108, 109, 111, 112, 114, 116, 118, 121, 125, 127, 128, 130, 131, 132, 134, 136, 141, 143, 156, 157, 162, 163, 166, 167, 179, 182, 190, 202, 203, 205, 206, 207, 208, 213, 214, 219, 222, 223, 228, 231, 253
Korah 216, 244

L

Labour 168, 208, 209, 210, 213
Lamarck 225, 245
Language..... 12, 33, 44, 65, 68, 80, 139, 163, 243
Latin America 15
Lavoisier 143
Law 4, 13, 33, 40, 50, 63, 77, 91, 98, 103, 118, 125, 142, 147, 148, 194, 195, 199, 205, 207, 209, 218, 240, 254
Law of Probability 142, 147, 148
Laws....7, 13, 24, 35, 47, 90, 96, 97, 98, 103, 110, 111, 114, 116, 117, 118, 119, 122, 123, 133, 143, 148, 152, 156, 166, 167, 189, 194, 197, 203, 204, 205, 206, 207, 208, 209, 211, 214, 221, 223, 233, 252, 253
Laws of evolution 204
Leaders. 15, 22, 29, 30, 31, 46, 64, 160, 210, 216, 219
Leadership 15, 32, 44, 253
Lectures...... 1, 4, 28, 62, 71, 72, 77, 79, 110, 132, 144, 167, 259
Leftist 16, 19, 64
Leftist Islamists 26
Leftist philosophy 27
Legacy 3, 15, 18, 39, 99
Legal 21, 48, 66, 97, 185
Legal applications 100
Legal infrastructure 251
Legal principles 48
Legal ruling 21
Legal system 70
Legislation (s) ... 7, 13, 14, 46, 48, 61, 64,71, 87, 88, 90, 92, 98, 116, 124, 152, 154, 155

Legislative........................... 33, 97, 162, 164
Legislative methods.............................. 162
Legislative system................................. 102
Legitimacy.... 41, 95, 98, 126, 164, 190, 230, 253, 254
Legitimate 91, 105, 107, 165
Lenin 212
Leninist-Marxist......................................30
Liberal........................... 2, 7, 8, 60, 61, 253
Liberalism 12, 13
Liberation .. 13, 25, 47, 49, 78, 95, 121, 160, 166, 168, 232
Liberation Movement...........26, 29, 30, 31
Liberty..8
Light.... VII, 1, 2, 3, 9, 24, 33, 35, 36, 38, 39, 40, 41, 48, 62, 66, 67, 71, 74, 76, 88, 91, 92, 104, 109, 110, 128, 134, 137, 138, 139, 141, 142, 144, 145, 153, 183, 192, 198, 208, 219, 223, 255, 260
Limitations 111, 121, 225, 228
Literary 1, 2, 24, 213
Literature.....38, 57, 137, 191, 207, 212, 214, 233
Logic .. 1, 9, 57, 58, 67, 68, 79, 116, 126, 131, 134, 137, 138, 149, 160, 166, 167, 170, 179, 216, 217, 218, 219
Logical 2, 3, 67, 71, 97, 113, 126, 131, 147, 157, 158, 179
Logical method 138

M

Madian 217
Mahdī Ashtīanī.......................................66
Mahdī Bāzargān.... 25, 26, 31, 60, 144, 282
see also Bāzargān
Mahdī Iraqi...28
Mahmūd Shehābī 26
Mahmūd Taleqāni............................25, 26
Majeed Karshanas................................265
Maktab-e Islām 81
Mālik Bin-Nabī.....................128, 179, 282
Mālik Wahbī 261, 266
Malkom Khān.. 13
Manifest7, 16, 24, 37, 39, 116, 121, 122, 195, 203, 223, 254
Mankind...36, 104, 106, 107, 120, 124, 128, 129, 130, 131, 133, 137, 138, 141, 148, 149, 153, 155, 156, 162, 169, 170, 185, 201, 203, 218, 239
Mansoor Limba........................... 273, 278
Mansour Qader....................................... 29
Mao Tse-Tung..212
Maoist 15, 30
Maoist China.. 15
Markus..17
Martyrdom....................................... 13, 263
Martyrs 215
Marwy School..59
Marx..............................210, 212, 213, 247
Marxism 8, 12, 15, 30, 58, 64, 80, 192, 205, 207, 208, 209, 211, 212, 214, 243, 267
Marxist (s) 15, 16, 17, 60, 66, 172, 192, 205, 206, 211, 212, 213, 215, 243, 247
Marxist movements...............................23
Marxist views 16
Mashhad........................20, 52, 57, 65, 262
Masjid Ittifaq... 260
Massacre of Faydiyya 81
Material 1, 11, 38, 39, 45, 46, 58, 62, 98, 108, 110, 113, 114, 117, 135, 137, 145, 191, 206, 207, 208, 212, 213, 216, 219, 221, 237
Material evidence 150
Material gain...45
Material hegemony................................45
Material progress 11, 46
Material wealth..................................... 105
Material world..39
Materialism.....3, 43, 44, 61, 109, 207, 210, 211, 212, 213, 214, 216, 217, 218, 219, 221, 222, 223, 226, 229, 230, 231, 232, 254
Materialist arguments 80
Materialistic......38, 40, 43, 64, 66, 80, 117, 136, 139, 154, 172, 189, 218, 221, 223, 235
Materialistic civilisation........................38
Materialistic doctrine............................. 80
Materialistic framework 116
Materialistic philosophy 59
Materialistic problems...........................87
Materialistic society.............................. 137
Materialistic tendencies 93
Materialistic trends 192
Materialistic ventures..........................254
Materialists 149, 221, 228, 232

Materials..........................10, 146, 202, 204
Matter 13, 72, 73, 88, 106, 108, 111, 112, 117, 132, 139, 141, 143, 144, 145, 146, 147, 148, 160, 194, 199, 206, 207, 225, 228, 234, 238, 252
Max Horkheimer....................................17
Meaning....3, 40, 49, 71, 73, 75, 78, 79, 91, 92, 94, 97, 100, 102, 104, 106, 111, 112, 113, 114, 115, 116, 117, 118, 123, 124, 127, 129, 131, 132, 135, 137, 140, 145, 146, 152, 157, 159, 185, 189, 204, 216, 219, 229
Mechanism (s)....9, 11, 45, 48, 49, 123, 156, 163, 193, 211 254
Mehrzad Borūjerdī..........................53, 282
Mental........................10, 137, 154, 155, 224
Message..............21, 37, 60, 81, 88, 201, 219
Metaphysical.. 37, 38, 41, 42, 108, 143, 189, 223, 227
Metaphysical reality...............................37
Metaphysical schools............................131
Metaphysics.....................................77, 126
Method................ 67, 72, 97, 109, 147, 204
Methodological.......................... 1, 108, 131
Methodological approach........................1
Methodological concept.......................189
Methodology.1, 2, 3, 21, 24, 37, 39, 63, 77, 80, 96, 100, 108, 109, 110, 124, 139, 142, 143, 159, 160, 215, 222, 227
Methods..... 9, 22, 67, 70, 72, 97, 103, 107, 108, 126, 133, 135, 136, 137, 138, 142, 144, 145, 156, 163, 171, 172, 184, 211, 213
Militant..20
Militant activism...................................28
Militant movements..............................28
Militant opposition...............................29
Militant revivalist..................................26
Military...7, 16, 45
Military camps.......................................64
Military service......................................63
Mind.....38, 39, 40, 59, 67, 68, 75, 107, 112, 115, 116, 129, 131, 135, 152, 154, 156, 157, 163, 164, 165, 171, 179, 197, 204, 223, 224, 236, 238
Mirzā 'Alī al-Shīrāzī...............................58
Mirzā Kochek Khān's Movement..14, 30

Moderation....... 105, 125, 152, 153, 159, 237
Modern world 27, 39, 40, 41, 42, 101, 102, 105
Modernisation..........................43, 132, 191
Modernism.......................... 12, 15, 40, 105
Modernity 27, 31, 38, 40, 42, 102, 108, 128, 154, 173, 189, 190, 233
Muhammad Rezā Wasfy........................50
Mohsen Kadivar.............................51, 282
Monotheism. 26, 33, 36, 37, 39, 40, 48, 52, 77, 78, 114, 115, 117, 118, 119, 120, 121, 122, 125, 126, 127, 128, 129, 130, 131, 133, 138, 142, 149, 203, 222, 251
Monotheism attributes........................130
Monotheist (s)............................... 142, 215
Monotheistic 30, 76, 114, 115, 117, 118, 120, 121, 123
Monotheistic principles......................129
Monotheistic system..............................30
Monotheistic understanding.............. 114
Monotheistic vision. 76, 115, 118, 120, 121, 125
Montazeri...81
Moral (s)...57, 62, 63, 94, 106, 114, 115, 117, 118, 123, 135, 140, 152, 154, 155, 161, 179, 192, 207, 212, 215, 218, 221, 234, 235, 236, 237, 238, 239, 240, 252
Moral actions............................... 235, 240
Moral concepts.....................................154
Moral imperative.................................254
Moral values................................240, 254
Moses......................201, 217, 218, 219, 244
Musaddiq....7, 15, 16, 18, 19, 20, 21, 22, 24, 34
see also Muhammad Musaddiq
Musaddiq's government........16, 18, 19, 21
Motivation.... VII, 3, 9, 19, 75, 94, 113, 114, 121, 123, 128, 140, 151, 152, 210, 222, 230
Movement. 3, 15, 18, 19, 20, 22, 26, 28, 29, 30, 31, 34, 46, 63, 64, 117, 118, 120, 143, 146, 150, 162, 174, 196, 203, 206, 207, 208, 210, 211, 212, 213, 215, 217, 228, 252
Movement for Social Humanism.........73
Movements 9, 12, 14, 15, 16, 18, 23, 24, 27, 42, 46, 47, 60, 63, 95, 103, 109, 116, 136, 138, 146, 156, 160, 161, 191
Mu'tazilah...129
Muhammad Musaddiq..........................18
see also Musaddiq

Muḥammad 'Abd al-Mun'im al-Khāqānī 246, 261, 263, 265, 267, 277
Muḥammad 'Abduh 47, 129, 130, 132, 173, 174, 179, 278, 283
see also 'Abduh
Muḥammad 'Alī al-Taskhīrī 82, 245, 265, 267, 276, 277
Muḥammad 'Alī Adharshab...... 263, 277, 278
Muḥammad 'Imāra 281, 283
Muḥammad al-Bāhi 91, 173, 175, 283
Muḥammad al-Khāqāni 176, 177, 276
Muḥammad Amara 173, 175, 179, 281
Muḥammad Ādharshab 172
Muḥammad Bāqir al-Ṣadr..... 88, 142, 175, 283
Muḥammad Hādī al-Yūsufī 185, 264, 265, 276
Muḥammad Iqbāl....88, 128, 173, 174, 179, 278, 283
Muḥammad Ḥossein al-Amin 173, 283
Muḥammad Ḥossein Fadlullah... 173, 283
Muḥammad Ḥossein Muṭahharī 57
Muḥammad Ḥossein Ṭabāṭabā'i ..25, 27, 31, 59, 66, 242, 283, 261
Muḥammad Jamāl-al-Dīn Qasimī...... 130
Muḥammad Jawād al-Muhrī 82, 268, 275
Muḥammad Kāzem Bojnourdi.............29
Muḥammad Khaiabani's Democratic Radical Movement 14
Muḥammad Mahdī Shams al-Dīn..... 173, 283
Muḥammad Muhaqqiq 58
Muḥammad Rezā 7, 14, 16, 38
Muḥammad Riḍā Wasfi 283
Muḥammad Sharī'atī 63
Muḥammad Taqi Sharī'atī 26, 60
Muntaẓerī 58
Musa 244
see also Moses
Musawi Zanjāni 25
Muslim 9, 20, 22, 31, 47, 51, 66, 75, 87, 94, 101, 126, 131, 134, 153, 219, 224, 225, 229, 230, 233, 234, 251
Muslim Brotherhood 22, 47
Muslim character 87
Muslim community 20
Muslim culture 66
Muslim identity 75
Muslim nations 191
Muslim Physicians Union 266, 268
Muslim scholars 141
Muslim society 9, 31, 190
Muslim thinkers 66, 87
Muslim world 47, 191
Muslims....18, 22, 35, 41, 49, 71, 72, 73, 74, 76, 88, 92, 93, 94, 102, 105, 125, 127, 128, 130, 133, 154, 159, 160, 163, 190, 191, 231, 232, 233, 252
Muslims Students Union 260
Mustaqīm 182
Mutakallimīn 144
Mutakallimūn 127, 149
Mysticism 38, 39, 53, 58, 137, 179

N

Nahj al-Balāghah 31, 58, 65
Najaf 14, 20, 29, 50
Nascent Communism 30
Nasr 31, 38, 39, 40, 41
see also Hossein Nasr
Nation...7, 8, 18, 76, 80, 87, 88, 90, 92, 93, 95, 161, 196, 201, 202, 203
National 7, 15, 17, 19, 75, 167, 202, 203
National consciousness 19
National Democratic 15
National diversity 202
National economy 17
National Front 8, 19, 21, 22, 24, 34
National government 7
National Resistance Movement 34
National security 15
National superiority 202
Nationalisation 20, 21
Nationalisation of Oil 9, 21, 30
Nationalism 12
Nationalist 8, 15, 18, 60
Nationalist currents 64
Nationalist liberation movements 15
Nationalist movement 8, 18
Nationalist orientation 15
Nationalistic 13, 18, 19, 20, 30, 167
Nationalistic trends 167
Nations.. 10, 11, 12, 43, 44, 45, 70, 97, 104, 105, 132, 155, 163, 165, 196, 202, 203
Natural balance 38
Natural disposition 116

Natural instincts 218
Natural intrinsic 168
Natural law (s) 33, 103, 208
Natural methods 169
Natural phenomenon .. 24, 135, , 202, 223
Natural purpose 194
Natural reactions 227
Natural reflection 207
Natural sciences 66, 149, 204
Natural selection 227, 235, 245, 246
Natural system 34
Natural world 32, 139, 142, 145, 189
Nature.... 3, 9, 33, 37, 39, 48, 62, 74, 77, 81, 88, 93, 100, 101, 103, 104, 106, 108, 111, 112, 115, 116, 117, 119, 123, 124, 125, 131, 133, 134, 135, 136, 140, 142, 143, 144, 146, 151, 153, 154, 155, 156, 158, 168, 193, 195, 198, 200, 202, 208, 210, 218, 220, 222, 223, 224, 228, 230, 233, 234, 237, 238, 239, 240, 246, 253, 254, 259
Nature of things 39
Navvāb Safavi 15, 20, 21
Nazism 13, 18, 167
Nihilism. 3, 24, 123, 137, 159, 221, 229, 253
Nihilist 64
Nihilistic 172
Nikba 14

O

Objectives...VII, 8, 9, 12, 18, 36, 60, 63, 69, 201, 202, 205, 231, 253, 254
Observation 99, 108, 110, 111, 142, 225, 232
Obstacles 3, 31, 61, 70, 79, 93, 107, 123, 160, 161, 163, 165 167, 170
Omar Farrukh 173, 175, 284
Opposition 7, 15, 16, 19, 30, 63, 78, 215
Opposition groups 14, 62
Oppression 13, 15, 123, 137, 216, 232
Organisation.. 4, 14, 22, 26, 32, 63, 75, 259
Orientalism 179
Origin 17, 39, 74, 128, 141, 146, 163, 238
Original 3, 4, 41, 80, 92, 102, 108, 259
Originality VII, 37, 39
Ottoman Empire 15

P

Pahlavī College 262
Pahlavī dynasty 48
Palestine 30
Palestinian 14, 20
Parliament 14, 19, 20, 21, 26
People.....8, 9, 10, 12, 13, 20, 22, 25, 32, 40, 44, 46, 48, 58, 59, 61, 62, 63, 66, 77, 78, 79, 80, 87, 90, 92, 93, 94, 95, 97, 101, 102, 105, 109, 117, 121, 122, 130, 131, 132, 134, 137, 138, 140, 149, 153, 155, 159, 160, 161, 162, 163, 164, 165, 166, 167, 169, 170, 190, 191, 193, 194, 200, 203, 205, 208, 214, 215, 216, 217, 218, 219, 222, 223, 229, 230, 232, 233, 235, 238, 239, 251, 253, 254, 255
People's Combatants 28
People's Fadā'iyān 30
People's Mujahedin 28, 29, 30, 64, 79
People's Party 19
Persian 3, 167, 222, 243, 259, 279
Persian civilisation 79
Persian culture 167
Persian heritage 18
Persian language 65, 259
Persian literature 65
Persian nationalism 13
Persian translations 67, 80
Personalities 20, 21, 26, 37
Personality ... VII, 4, 19, 38, 58, 68, 88, 121, 122, 153, 221, 231
Perspective.....3, 9, 19, 21, 33, 35, 36, 39, 42, 76, 80, 87, 88, 97, 116, 129, 133, 147, 195, 196, 199, 201
Peykār group 79
Pharaoh 217, 218
see also Fir'awn
Pharaoh's wife 217
Phenomena 108, 110, 111, 116, 135, 152, 197, 207, 225
Phenomenon 17, 35, 36, 135, 147, 169
Philosopher (s) 139, 144, 146, 222, 224, 225, 228, 229
Philosophical.... 1, 3, 12, 36, 48, 69, 70, 73, 77, 80, 109, 110, 111, 112, 113, 126, 129, 131, 133, 139, 141, 143, 172, 179, 192, 202, 214, 223, 224, 225, 233, 234
Philosophical attitude 133
Philosophical ideas 129
Philosophical knowledge 126
Philosophical methodology 131
Philosophical position 110, 111, 112

Philosophical schema 48
Philosophical themes.... 126
Philosophical thought....113
Philosophical view.... 70
Philosophical vision 112
Philosophies 39, 42, 128, 214
Philosophy...VII, 25, 26, 27, 38, 39, 41, 57, 58, 59, 66, 74, 108, 110, 112, 151, 168, 179, 191, 204, 207, 211, 214, 221, 222, 223, 224, 225, 227, 235, 251
Physical..10, 110, 112, 119, 154, 155, 164, 195
Physical bodies....149
Physical composites 195
Physical dimension 154
Piety ...123, 139, 140, 151, 156, 215, 217, 230, 254
Pious ... 57, 139, 152, 193, 202, 215, 219, 254
Poincaré....181
Political .. V, 2, 7, 8, 9, 12, 13, 14, 15, 16, 17, 18, 19, 20, 21, 22, 24, 27, 28, 34, 36, 48, 49, 51, 54, 60, 61, 62, 63, 126, 127, 161, 163, 164, 165, 189, 190, 208, 210, 212, 213, 214, 229, 230, 233, 234, 253
Political abstention 23
Political action....8, 28
Political activity....16, 21, 32, 50, 59, 253
Political alliances....14
Political apparatus.... 253
Political arena....23
Political authorities....23, 63, 165
Political authority 78, 93, 161, 163
Political change.... 101
Political control....161
Political despotism....43, 230, 253
Political development....76
Political diversity....14
Political élite....163, 164, 166
Political experience....252
Political experiment 15, 254
Political framework.... 19
Political function 252
Political groups....16, 28
Political history.... 31
Political Islam 27
Political leadership....37
Political life 14, 19
Political movements.... 7, 15
Political opposition 28
Political oppression 15
Political outlooks 66
Political participation.... 165
Political practices....190
Political reform.... 7, 19, 20, 32
Political renaissance 26
Political scene....16, 29
Political system 34, 128, 213
Political tyranny 62, 74, 163
Political upheaval....14
Politician....20, 33
Politics 12, 15, 16, 20, 22, 23, 25, 33, 34, 37, 42, 46, 48, 49, 66, 166, 190, 252
Polygamy.... 79, 100
Polytheism 33, 36, 37, 40, 42
Polytheists.... 215
Popularity 17, 19, 20, 23, 25, 26
Poverty....8, 31, 43, 62, 163, 215, 219, 225
Power....11, 14, 16, 18, 20, 21, 32, 35, 45, 62, 63, 67, 78, 79, 87, 92, 102, 114, 115, 117, 118, 119, 121, 124, 128, 129, 132, 133, 137, 140, 142, 143, 144, 145, 146, 147, 159, 160, 163, 164, 165, 166, 167, 169, 212, 220, 223, 226, 227, 230, 236
Practical....2, 18, 22, 23, 26, 29, 48, 69, 70, 76, 87, 88, 95, 100, 111, 112, 114, 125, 161, 251, 252, 253
Practical display....87
Practical fashion 111
Practical framework....253
Practical legislation 119
Practical monotheism....118
Practice 48, 49, 68, 88, 97, 99, 100, 103, 109, 126, 128, 131, 135, 154, 160, 192, 199, 219, 234, 254
Predestination 73, 125, 126, 129, 132
Principle of Causality 224
Principles of belief.... 139
Production....135, 184, 207, 208, 209, 210, 211, 212, 213, 214
Progress.. 7, 9, 11, 12, 17, 24, 43, 46, 47, 69, 71, 74, 92, 96, 102, 103, 105, 106, 107, 108, 128, 129, 137, 159, 160, 161, 164, 167, 170, 191, 192, 197, 204, 233, 239, 255
Prohibited 19, 36
Proletariat.... 210, 211, 212
Prophet....74, 125
Prophet's mission....88
Prophethood....77, 125, 126, 130, 149

Prophets ..32, 34, 39, 87, 119, 148, 201, 215, 216, 218
Prosperity. 24, 43, 44, 47, 74, 78, 106, 132, 133, 134, 159, 160, 164, 167, 190, 191, 192, 197, 198, 204, 233, 239, 251
Psalms ... 219
Psychological ... 24, 80, 109, 110, 113, 121, 124, 125, 127, 131, 136, 154, 155, 171, 207, 251
Psychological attitude ... 45
Psychological consistency ... 122
Psychological dimension ... 155
Psychological effects ... 127
Psychological efficiency ... 125, 128, 165
Psychological factors ... 40
Psychological framework ... 121
Psychological impact ... 123
Psychological implications ... 205
Psychological influence ... 122
Psychological makeup ... 131
Psychological position ... 113
Psychological unity ... 122
Psychologist ... 139
Psychology ... 66, 137, 143, 251
Public campaigned ... 8
Public interest ... 19
Public life ... 191
Public opposition ... 14
Punishment ... 196, 199

Q

Qajar Dynasty ... 15
Qajarite ... 13, 20
Qārūn ... 244
Qayyim ... 182
Qiwām ... 152, 182
Qiyam ... 152, 182
Qom ... 14, 50, 57, 58, 59, 61, 62, 65, 66, 278
Qur'an 23, 30, 31, 35, 45, 57, 59, 65, 66, 68, 76, 92, 93, 94, 97, 98, 105, 120, 134, 139, 141, 143, 144, 145, 149, 150, 151, 152, 182, 193, 196, 197, 199, 201, 215, 216, 217, 218, 219, 222, 226, 229, 232
Qur'anic .. 41, 59, 66, 92, 93, 145, 199, 200, 203, 210, 215, 217, 218, 247
Qur'anic concepts ... 41
Qur'anic exegesis ... 59
Qur'anic studies ... 66
Qutb ... 91

R

Racial ... 13, 18, 203
Racial discrimination ... 202
Racism ... 38
Radical ... 11, 15, 19, 22, 23, 24, 88, 129, 212, 233, 253
Rashīd Riḍa ... 21, 51, 284
Rational 33, 41, 57, 59, 71, 88, 119, 125, 129, 143, 190, 197, 198, 199, 204
Rational formulation ... 253
Rational method ... 41
Rational organisation ... 33
Rational practice ... 130
Rational presentation ... 41
Rational sciences ... 57
Rational thinking ... 41
Rational wisdom ... 41
Rationalism ... 41, 239
Rationality .. 32, 38, 110, 129, 152, 190, 200
Realities ... 3, 22, 36, 206, 255
Reality ... 21, 35, 40, 41, 45, 61, 62, 70, 91, 92, 93, 100, 108, 110, 111, 117, 120, 147, 163, 165, 166, 195, 197, 198, 202, 203, 221, 224, 225, 232, 236, 238, 252, 254, 259
Reason16, 20, 27, 35, 36, 37, 38, 46, 47, 68, 69, 71, 78, 88, 96, 100, 103, 104, 106, 111, 113, 114, 119, 121, 124, 126, 128, 129, 131, 133, 134, 155, 156, 162, 165, 170, 190, 199, 204, 209, 210, 219, 222, 223, 231, 235, 236, 252
Reconstruct ... 10, 141, 189
Reflection ... 12, 41, 45, 197, 210, 216
Reform.VIII, 8, 9, 15, 16, 18, 19, 20, 21, 22, 24, 25, 26, 27, 28, 30, 32, 34, 35, 43, 44, 46, 47, 48, 59, 60, 61, 63, 69, 70, 74, 76, 95, 99, 144, 164, 169, 179, 184, 218, 252
Reform experiment ... 89
Reform figures ... 60
Reform movement (s) ... 15, 19, 20, 22, 28, 59, 63, 69, 106, 107
Reform project ... 70
Reformation .VII, 1, 4, 9, 11, 19, 22, 24, 31, 32, 42, 49, 88, 218, 251, 253
Reformation Ideology ... 31

Reformative 15
Reformatory legislation..........................59
Reformer (s) VIII, 44, 67, 88, 106, 216, 218
Reformist 16, 60, 71, 87, 88, 91, 251
Reformist clergy.......................................63
Reformist cultural 64
Regime..... 7, 10, 15, 23, 29, 48, 64, 213, 215
Regression71, 72, 74, 88, 127, 130, 131, 134, 140, 160, 164
Reign....................... 7, 12, 13, 16, 20, 38, 57
Rejuvenation 76, 77, 91
Religion....12, 22, 23, 24, 27, 32, 33, 34, 35, 36, 37, 38, 39, 40, 42, 44, 47, 48, 54, 61, 73, 75, 90, 91, 92, 97, 100, 102, 103, 110, 113, 128, 130, 133, 134, 138, 140, 141, 144, 151, 152, 160, 163, 166, 179, 200, 201, 203, 207, 208, 209, 212, 213, 218, 222, 223, 228, 230, 231, 232, 237, 251, 252, 280, 281
Religious ..VIII, 1, 13, 14, 18, 19, 20, 23, 33, 37, 43, 58, 93, 98, 108, 126, 137, 140, 155, 161, 162, 163, 167, 184, 208, 222, 223, 230
Religious affiliation 78
Religious aristocracy 33
Religious authorities......................... 14, 21
Religious awareness 64
Religious belief...................................... 128
Religious concept (s)....... 70, 100, 101, 165
Religious Courts 13
Religious currents...................................63
Religious doctrine 132
Religious endowments.......................... 13
Religious establishment 21, 22, 23, 25, 46, 57, 61, 77, 82, 161, 162, 166
Religious expression 13
Religious faith.................. 33, 123, 133, 144
Religious garb... 40
Religious group...................................... 60
Religious ideas 251
Religious identity 21
Religious institution........... 19, 25, 59, 162
Religious interpretation 100
Religious knowledge 162
Religious legislation...............................78
Religious life.. 139
Religious men 141
Religious message 141
Religious mindset...................................95
Religious people.....................................28
Religious piety.......................................254
Religious position 112
Religious practice 100
Religious precepts..................................32
Religious principle 93, 138
Religious quality....................................113
Religious revival........................74, 75, 109
Religious scholars 13, 23
Religious seminary 22, 25, 59
Religious sense 141, 155
Religious sensibility 141
Religious tendency 140
Religious texts 97
Religious thought 1
Religious traditions........................ 40, 102
Religious values....................... 154, 161, 164
Religious visions 139
Renaissance... VI, 12, 15, 23, 39, 43, 49, 70, 72, 74, 79, 87, 89, 96, 102, 161, 154, 159, 160, 161, 162, 163, 164, 174, 189, 254
Renaissance movement.................. 79, 161
Renaissance project 79
Renewal 4, 11, 23, 70, 71, 74, 75, 78, 87, 90, 100, 105, 125, 148, 157, 164, 173
Renewal of Islamic Thought.................32
Research. VII, 1, 58, 59, 72, 73, 101, 111, 131, 140, 146, 147, 150, 157
Resources.....10, 11, 14, 65, 66, 165, 190, 191
Resuscitation 36, 37
Retrogression..................................47, 197
Revelation 33, 34, 36, 37, 112, 125, 126
Revival 1, 3, 9, 18, 35, 36, 38, 39, 46, 62, 74, 77, 78, 79, 87, 88, 90, 91, 92, 96, 97, 109, 125, 154, 160, 162, 251
Revival movement 23, 79
Revolt................................41, 217, 223, 232
Revolution VIII, 28, 30, 34, 38, 47, 48, 49, 54, 58, 60, 64, 78, 135, 137, 167, 185, 209, 211, 212, 213, 218, 220, 232, 252, 253
Revolution, 1920 .... 9, 14, 20
Revolution Command Council........... 64
Revolutionary. 15, 16, 21, 23, 31, 34, 58, 64, 79, 87, 88, 209, 212, 213, 214, 216, 217, 219, 252
Revolutionary character 15
Revolutionary reform 253
Revolutionary struggle...........................87

Rezā Khān 12, 13, 57
Rezā Shāh 14, 15, 16, 20, 24
Rhetoric 57, 65, 255
Riḍwān al-Sayyid 49, 50, 51, 174, 284
Rif'at al-Sayyid Ahmad 51, 284
Roger Garaudy 53, 284
Roman law 40
Roshanfekran 50, 53
Ruin 46, 105, 204
Russell....80, 138, 176, 180, 222, 231, 236, 239, 284
Russia 212, 213

S

Sa'dī 65
Sabzwari 77
Sadiq 'Abidi 83
Sadiq Amāni 28
Sādiq al-'Ibādī 267, 277
Sadiq al-Baqqāl 270
Sadrā Shirāzī 38, 263
Safavi 21
Salafi 23, 73, 91, 174
Salmān Tawhīdī 260
Sartre 80, 224, 225, 229, 247
Satan 94, 134, 231
SAVAK 29, 34
Sayyid Quṭb 21, 51, 91, 284
Schism 29, 30, 43
Scholar (s) ...VII, 12, 16, 20, 27, 28, 37, 46, 57, 58, 59, 63, 66, 67, 127, 139, 151, 172, 184
Schools 14, 22, 57, 191, 254
Science (s) 12, 13, 24, 25, 27, 37, 38, 39, 42, 43, 50, 57, 59, 65, 66, 68, 90, 99, 105, 108, 110, 111, 112, 114, 117, 126, 130, 131, 132, 133, 134, 135, 136, 137, 138, 139, 141, 142, 143, 144, 145, 154, 167, 189, 190, 203, 204, 205, 222, 225, 226, 238
Scientific ..V, 24, 25, 38, 54, 67, 73, 76, 80, 101, 108, 109, 110, 133, 138, 139, 140, 141, 172, 189, 192, 209, 213, 222, 233
Scientific achievements 108
Scientific activity 38, 213
Scientific advances 25
Scientific developments 163
Scientific discovery 141, 137, 139
Scientific evidence 141, 144
Scientific explanation 108
Scientific history 204
Scientific investigation 73
Scientific knowledge 24, 132, 138, 222
Scientific method 111
Scientific methodology 135
Scientific outlook 110
Scientific research 111
Scientific view 108, 113
Scientist (s).... 37, 78, 93, 110, 111, 130, 140, 149, 172, 181
Second National Front 26
Second World War 14, 20
Secular 13, 14, 20, 24
Secularism 12, 39, 40
Secure 10, 11, 18, 44, 46, 194, 236
Security 7, 45, 129, 136, 137, 171, 232
Sexual behaviour 169
Sexual desire 169
Sexual energy 171
Sexual ethics 170
Sexual freedom 170
Sexual impulses 172
Sexual intimacy 169, 172
Sexual liberation 171
Sexual lusts 171
Sexual pleasure 231
Sexual relationships 169
Sexuality 169
Shafā'ah 23
Shāh 7, 14, 16, 22, 24, 29, 63, 64, 81
Shahada 77
Shakīb Arsalān 130
Shari'ah....14, 21, 22, 26, 32, 40, 41, 42, 57, 77, 97, 98, 101, 107, 109, 127, 132, 151, 167, 240
Sheikh Gūdarzi 83
Shi'ite 25, 62, 109
Shiraz University 262
Slavery 31, 45, 100
Social activities 75
Social affairs 46, 49
Social breakdown 63
Social category 24
Social change 35, 87
Social classes 253
Social conscience 127
Social degradation 62
Social deterioration 74

Social development 14, 46, 76
Social dynamics 33
Social efficiency 254
Social entity 195, 200
Social environment 116
Social essence 197, 201
Social experiment 8, 69
Social factors 198, 208
Social framework 193
Social humanism 77
Social identity 251
Social ills 37
Social interaction 7
Social justice .... VIII, 23, 26, 27, 45
Social level 130
Social life 25, 122, 125, 194, 204
Social movements 253
Social opportunists 47
Social philosophy 101
Social plane 33
Social position 199
Social practice 35
Social problems 45
Social proclivities 78
Social reality 218
Social relationships 171, 208
Social responsibility 37
Social spirit 195, 238
Social standards 12
Social status 163, 220
Social structure 34, 207
Social system 66, 198
Social trends 109
Socialism 12, 14, 212
Socialist 13, 26, 210, 211, 212, 213
Societies 101, 104, 133, 166, 167, 191, 196, 197, 200, 204, 209, 213, 221, 222, 230
Sociological 33, 36, 73, 110
Sociology 1, 12, 27, 37, 66, 191
Socio-political 3, 253
Socrates 222
Soroush 52
Soul (s) 38, 40, 44, 68, 74, 90, 91, 92, 93, 96, 100, 113, 114, 115, 116, 122, 123, 124, 125, 128, 129, 131, 132, 134, 137, 143, 148, 149, 150, 151, 152, 153, 154, 156, 157, 171, 179, 207, 222, 254
South-East Asia 15
Spencer 224
Spirit . 35, 40, 46, 75, 91, 100, 109, 156, 195, 201, 207, 238
Spiritual 38, 40, 57, 63, 68, 76, 88, 116, 119, 121, 125, 129, 135, 137, 154, 155, 164, 179, 231
Spiritual concepts 116
Spiritual dimension 38
Spiritual disorders 137
Spiritual ineffectiveness 63
Spiritual makeup 125
Spiritual meaning 68
Spiritual perfection 129
Spiritual suicide 40
Spirituality 17, 38, 87
Stagnation 35, 45, 46, 70, 75, 91, 92, 96, 131, 191
State ... VII, 10, 11, 13, 14, 18, 20, 22, 28, 32, 39, 44, 48, 60, 62, 63, 72, 74, 75, 88, 91, 93, 102, 105, 110, 120, 134, 139, 140, 143, 146, 153, 157, 163, 194, 202, 212, 214, 216, 219, 222, 225, 231, 236, 246, 254
Strategy 22, 29, 30, 63
Structure 8, 9, 16, 20, 22, 23, 25, 34, 35, 36, 58, 64, 65, 66, 131, 167, 171, 189, 208, 210
Struggle 11, 21, 30, 34, 44, 46, 47, 58, 60, 63, 64, 69, 87, 93, 210, 219, 227, 253
Students 24, 68
Submission 8, 10, 13, 36, 37, 40, 232
Sudan 47
Sufi, sufism 37, 38, 41, 65, 66, 179
Suhrawardī 38, 179
Sunnah 35, 66, 97, 134
Sunni 109
Superficial 9, 23, 78, 80, 223
Superiority 38, 48, 102, 116, 121, 163
Surrender 11, 33, 96, 132
Surveillance 34, 64
Symptomatic 12, 106
System .. 4, 11, 22, 32, 37, 41, 47, 48, 77, 87, 103, 106, 107, 108, 110, 111, 116, 118, 123, 124, 125, 126, 133, 146, 151, 152, 153, 155, 156, 160, 163, 164, 165, 190, 191, 193, 201, 208, 209, 210, 211, 213, 214, 226, 227, 231, 234, 254
System of governance 47
System of rule 48
Systematic 16, 31, 40, 43, 44, 49, 64, 78, 92, 190, 210, 252

Systematic degradation........................... 40
Systematic framework........................ 49, 64
Systematic plunder.................................. 43
Systematic suppression........................... 31

T

Ṭabāṭabā'i................. 25, 27, 31, 59, 66, 261
Ṭanṭāwī Jawharī...................................... 130
Tablīgh-e Islamī.. 26
Tahir bin 'Āshūr.. 26
Talal Majzoub.......................... 49, 50, 284
Tāleqāni.. 18, 30, 31
Taqiyyah 23
Taqwīm... 152, 182
Tawḥīd................................ 78, 117, 121, 203
Technology ... 10, 13, 17, 24, 39, 42, 43, 74, 104, 105, 137, 154, 190
Tehran 24, 53, 59, 60, 62, 176, 275, 282
Terminology............................ 68, 131, 150
Theologians 225, 226
Theological ... 33, 36, 77, 126, 138, 143, 189, 223
Theological institution......................... 163
Theology..... 25, 26, 27, 58, 66, 98, 126, 225
Theoretical..... 2, 31, 100, 103, 108, 111, 118, 126, 208, 212, 252
Theoretical dialectic.............................. 127
Theoretical framework................... 47, 252
Theoretical ideas.................................... 128
Theoretical methodology....................... 126
Theoretical vision............................ 45, 112
Theories..... 2, 31, 97, 99, 110, 143, 191, 194, 196, 202, 234, 237, 255
Theory..... 26, 33, 36, 38, 47, 48, 49, 69, 70, 88, 110, 112, 135, 143, 145, 149, 150, 192, 194, 195, 196, 197, 202, 207, 209, 211, 214, 223, 225, 226, 227, 234, 235, 236, 237, 238, 239, 240
Theosophical texts.................................. 65
Theosophy 38, 66
Thermodynamic 145, 147
Thinker (s) ....VII, 2, 18, 26, 31, 32, 34, 42, 41, 44, 130, 166, 172, 210, 219, 233, 235, 251, 259
Third World 31
Thomas W. Lippman...................... 51, 284
Throne 7, 13
Torah 134
Tradition..... 12, 27, 29, 31, 42, 97, 99, 166, 168, 193
Traditional. 9, 11, 12, 15, 22, 24, 25, 27, 36, 108, 128, 132, 149, 154, 162, 164, 167, 189, 191, 211, 223, 253
Traditional concept....................... 24, 109
Traditional dialectical.......................... 129
Traditional knowledge............................ 38
Traditional perspectives 12
Traditional revivalist.............................. 15
Traditional values..................................... 9
Traditional wisdom................................. 41
Traditions 9, 10, 17, 28, 46, 79, 98, 123, 163, 166, 167, 170, 189, 190, 193, 197, 198, 199, 200, 201, 208, 209, 213, 233
Transcendent 39, 91, 111, 112
Transformation.. 14, 35, 36, 37, 42, 44, 48, 104, 109, 142, 144, 146, 174, 204, 221, 227, 238, 239, 240
Treachery.. 129, 134
Trust.................................... 36, 77, 94, 204
Truth 40, 44, 73, 79, 99, 114, 120, 127, 134, 138, 140, 145, 157, 194, 196, 205, 218, 219, 220, 229, 230, 232, 238
Tudeh Party 16, 58
Turkey.. 14
Tyrannical.......................... 62, 127, 161, 167
Tyrannical authority............................. 127
Tyranny .. 15, 45, 63, 163, 164, 197, 218, 232
Tyrants... 217, 218

U

Umayyids 163
Ummah 20, 36, 44
Union of Muslim Doctors........... 261, 263
United Nations 185
Unity......37, 66, 92, 118, 122, 123, 124, 129, 153, 158, 201
Universal 1, 15, 32, 100, 111, 112, 114, 119, 124, 125, 151, 203, 239, 240
Universal conception........................... 204
Universal guidelines............................. 107
Universal harmony................................ 141
Universal ideology.................................. 35
Universal implication............................. 97
Universal interests 170
Universal laws.......................... 70, 102, 205

Universal monotheistic 77, 113
Universal norms 201
Universal organiser 142
Universal phenomenon 110
Universal precepts 203
Universal principle 98, 154
Universal purpose 124, 154
Universal questions 109
Universal rules 204
Universal traditions 197
Universal vision . 70, 109, 110, 111, 112, 113, 115, 117, 123, 125, 137, 153, 154, 159
Universe 24, 33, 36, 37, 88, 108, 110, 111, 115, 116, 123, 125, 133, 139, 141, 143, 145, 152, 203, 204, 226, 233
University 31, 34, 164
University of Tehran 60
Urbanisation 12, 105, 191, 193, 194, 233
Usul al-Din 263

V

Value .... VIII, 44, 87, 99, 104, 108, 110, 111, 112, 114, 123, 130, 135, 152, 159, 169, 214, 218, 231, 239, 251, 254
Value system 44, 108, 251
Values 3, 7, 12, 15, 33, 36, 46, 47, 60, 62, 74, 75, 102, 106, 113, 116, 123, 129, 151, 152, 153, 154, 161, 162, 164, 166, 169, 170, 190, 193, 196, 213, 214, 219, 230, 233, 234, 238, 239, 240, 254
Veil .... VIII, 13, 101, 172
Vice 25, 231
Violence 38, 159, 223, 252
Virtue 25, 130, 131, 153, 190, 230
Vision 8, 9, 24, 31, 32, 36, 38, 44, 45, 48, 62, 63, 67, 68, 69, 70, 71, 72, 74, 75, 77, 89, 96, 97, 108, 109, 110, 111, 112, 113, 114, 115, 116, 117, 120, 123, 124, 125, 129, 145, 151, 154, 155, 160, 161, 162, 164, 165, 172, 192, 197, 211, 251, 252, 255
Vital .... VIII, 35, 45, 62, 165, 191, 228, 231
Vitality 36, 46, 77, 105

W

Wahhābism 95
Wars 10, 190
Weak 19, 41, 78, 209, 230, 236
Weakness 17, 31, 46, 71, 92, 94, 102, 161, 227, 230, 232
Wealth 10, 14, 31, 38, 43, 104, 215, 216, 217, 218, 219, 231
Weber 30
Welfare 18, 43, 122, 124, 235
West 7, 12, 17, 18, 39, 43, 44, 45, 74, 102, 137, 164, 166, 169, 190, 191, 192, 223, 227, 229, 230
Western 3, 7, 8, 12, 13, 14, 17, 18, 20, 24, 37, 39, 40, 41, 42, 44, 45, 46, 62, 66, 70, 77, 80, 109, 172, 189, 224, 225, 229, 233, 234
Western civilisation 3, 13, 44, 164, 165, 166, 189, 190, 233, 234, 254
Western concepts 169
Western culture 17, 153, 166
Western epistemological 24
Western experiences 168
Western hegemony 20
Western history 134
Western ideals 18
Western ideas 80
Western ideology 254
Western industrial 17
Western influence 17, 164
Western intellectual 12, 37, 41, 254
Western intellectual schools 3
Western intellectualism 24, 251
Western languages 67
Western modernisation 24, 78
Western modernity 42
Western monopoly 44
Western nationalistic 167
Western nihilism 24
Western origin 39
Western outlook 45
Western philosophical 116
Western philosophy 39, 66, 228
Western political 8, 166
Western predisposition 7
Western presence 14
Western pressure 40
Western revolutionary ideologies 64
Western society 189, 192, 223
Western teachings 191
Western techniques 13
Western technology 108
Western thinkers 80, 169

Western thinking..............................41, 154
Western thought...3
Western values................ 7, 18, 46, 191, 234
Western world...108
Westernernised intellectual..................221
Westernisation ..13, 17, 18, 38, 64, 106, 167
Westernised...233
Westernised academics 46
Westernised civilisation...........78, 105, 137
Westernised cultural 166
Westernised thinkers.............................. 40
Westoxification...17
Wilāyat al-faqīh.......................................48
Will Durant.................................... 137, 236
William James..................139, 155, 181, 284
Wisdom................38, 41, 117, 137, 160, 230
Woman..................... 168, 169, 171, 172, 217
Women........................79, 153, 168, 169, 171
Workers.................................... 24, 209, 213
World Wars 10, 11
Worship....35, 37, 68, 77, 121, 122, 124, 151, 153, 156, 157, 158, 231
Writers 18, 20, 66
Writings...1, 2, 3, 36, 65, 66, 67, 68, 69, 78, 79, 87, 130, 132, 133
Wrongdoers 215

Y

Yahyā Muḥammad.........................173, 284
Yūsuf al-Qaraḍāwī 174, 284
Yūsuf Khān..13

Z

Zabūr 219
Zahedī..22
Zainab Shorba 173, 283
Zaki al-Milād.................................. 173, 285
Zionist 14
Ziyād Khalīl al-Dgamin................ 183, 285

www.ingramcontent.com/pod-product-compliance
Lightning Source LLC
Chambersburg PA
CBHW021429080526
44588CB00009B/469